HAZARD

HAZARD

A

A SISTER'S FLIGHT FROM FAMILY AND A BROKEN BOY

MARGARET COMBS

Skyhorse Publishing

Skyhorse Publishing books may be purchased in bulk at special discounts for sales promotion, corporate gifts, fund-raising, or educational purposes. Special editions can also be created to specifications. For details, contact the Special Sales Department, Skyhorse Publishing, 307 West 36th Street, 11th Floor, New York, NY 10018 or info@skyhorsepublishing.com.

Skyhorse® and Skyhorse Publishing® are registered trademarks of Skyhorse Publishing, Inc.®, a Delaware corporation.

Visit our website at www.skyhorsepublishing.com.
10 9 8 7 6 5 4 3 2 1

Library of Congress Cataloging-in-Publication Data is available on file.

Cover design by Rain Saukas, with Jesse Aronson

Print ISBN: 978-1-5107-1531-8
Ebook ISBN: 978-1-5107-1532-5

Printed in the United States of America

for my family

Contents

Prologue ix

Part I: Family

Chapter 1. All Fall Down 3

Chapter 2. Great Expectations 8

Chapter 3. Back Seat 18

Chapter 4. Home to Hazard 22

Chapter 5. Jesus Is Calling 30

Chapter 6. Monkey Bird 44

Chapter 7. Among the Dead 51

Chapter 8. Put 'em Up, Boys 58

Chapter 9. Aileron 66

Chapter 10. Split Levels 75

Chapter 11. Mercy 83

Chapter 12. Laundromat 96

Chapter 13. All God's Children 101

Chapter 14. Pieces 112

Chapter 15. Guns in the Family 119

Part II: Flight

Chapter 16. Wings 129

Chapter 17. Cracker Jacks 135

Chapter 18. Tears 144

Chapter 19. Trapeze 150

Chapter 20. Chant from Another World 156

Chapter 21. Dive   162
Chapter 22. Falling   175

Part III: Fortuity

Chapter 23. Coppertone   185
Chapter 24. Sebastian   197
Chapter 25. Apparition   202
Chapter 26. Implosion   219
Chapter 27. Dave's Diner   225
Chapter 28. Losing It   234
Chapter 29. Lift Off   241
Chapter 30. Batman   252
Chapter 31. Valentine   258
Chapter 32. Little Wing   265

Epilogue   269
Acknowledgments   275

Prologue

I imagined myself the child of a perfect family when my brother arrived. It was April 15, 1956, a time on the calendar that spoke of Easter and spring. But in the dry stretches of Wichita, Kansas, the date meant little more than a dearth of color in our backyard. We lived near the airport, where nothing blossomed, much less the dogwood and crocus I'd come to love years later in New England. Still, I didn't mind; dirt was fine with me. Already a tomboy at three, I thrilled to the wonders of a grassless backyard: potato slugs nuzzling in the dust, the miracle of dark mud spreading beneath the spigot, and the pitch of my swing set, its iron-red posts steepled to the sky. In my flitting and leaping about the yard, always in concert with my big sister, Barbara Ann, I loved my world; it was timeless and it was mine.

My grandmother's call that one morning in April pulled me from the swing set and into the kitchen. I sensed something vastly changeable had come into my life, nestled inside the bundle of blue folds in the doorway. My mother, twenty-six years old and a heartbreaking beauty, stood holding and parting the blankets. It was a boy, a real boy, completing our family in a way I never could as a girl, a second daughter. He was a fuzzy-haired, rosy baby, whose dimply smile and sweet wail brought joy into our little home in the middle of nowhere. I sensed a specialness, a surge of pleasure, like a sweet had just been placed on my tongue, unexpectedly—the way joy can arrive randomly, without warning or reason.

The lightheartedness extended at least a while longer as my family packed up and moved out of flat, barren Wichita, and trundled west across the prairie to much greener and craggier Colorado. My father, rapidly moving up in the world as an aeronautical engineer, had captured a promising job with Martin Marietta, uplifting us to Denver and the Rocky Mountains. This is where the deeper root of my memory begins.

To anyone parting the curtains the afternoon of our arrival on Jewell Avenue, we appeared blessed. A lean and agile father, tall and dark-haired, unfolding from the driver's side, hefting boxes and suitcases from the car; a petite and fine-figured mother with a glamorous, garnet smile; two bright and lively girls, one brunette and the other blonde, each a different ribbon of the family; and finally, the baby boy, a happy and robust kicker, who would carry on the family name. I couldn't have known what was coming. None of us knew.

As I bounded out of the car, giggling with my sister, and flailed onto the grass, and as my mother, her arms bundled with my chubby brother, clucked at my father to hasten with the high chair, fate was already with us. Soon, it would turn our translucent skins inside out, so that our most delicate parts glared out to the world, showing what we were made of: bravery, cowardice, substance, *rubbery-ness*—our characters forever blanched and outlined in deepest black. Soon, our hearts would flay open, and we would, in many ways, remain veined and naked for the rest of our lives.

Part I

Family

Chapter 1

All Fall Down

One afternoon, deep into the month of September 1957, I burst from a bush and skittered along the back fence, making my way back to my porch and family. Shadows smeared across the grass and light riffled up walls in magical ways. I was five years old, and I relished being alive. My neighborhood was a tiny one on the outskirts of Denver—little more than a huddle of duplexes in an open field—but to me it was a glorious frontier, marked by grassy unfenced yards and a single thatch of spindly bushes thick enough to hide me from evil bandits, or even the Devil if it came down to it. I did not fear Satan; Jesus was on my side, and besides, I could outrun any beast or brute in the neighborhood.

Yanking open our screen door, I landed inside my living room, the door whapping behind me. Ahead of me lay the promise of something special: the taste of my mother's puffy biscuits and hot, crispy chicken, and, especially, my father's homecoming. Within minutes, I'd hear the gravelly crunch of his tires on the driveway.

If I had known my life was about to change—that it was already crumbling and in another moment would ash apart—I wonder what I might have done. Rewound my steps out the door to the farthermost corner of my neighborhood and hunkered in the bushes until darkness yawned and swallowed me?

I stood on the threshold and breathed. All was tidy and well. *Ladies' Home Journal*s and *Aviation Week*s sat neatly stacked on the coffee table; the floor was damp-mopped and the throw rug vacuumed as always at this time of day; and the fold-top desk, where Mama answered letters in clean, pretty handwriting, was cleared of clutter and folded away. Still, a ping of worry sparkled up my spine. The house was thick with quiet and the supper table empty of plates and silverware. I lifted my nose but couldn't smell anything close to the tang of hot oil, or hear the sounds of chicken parts flipping through flour and meeting the bright hissing heat of a skillet.

"Where's Mama?" I asked, breathily.

My older sister, Barbara Ann, sat a few feet away on our green, knobbly couch, her school dress and shoes still on, a book open in her lap. At seven years old, she was my safety. Her dark hair touched her shoulders like Mama's, and she knew things, like how to tie shoes and how to last nap-less through an afternoon.

"Shush!" she hissed, wrinkling up her face. She looked like an old biscuit, and I started to giggle. But she didn't smile or look at me. She darted her eyes down the hallway. "Mama's resting."

I stared at her, folding my brow in a way that would, over time, dig trenches into my forehead. She had never shushed me this way, and Mama, for her part, had never napped in the afternoon.

Blowing out my lips, I flounced over to the playpen where my little brother, Roddy, sat like a baby blob. Scooping up a squishy ball, I beeped it on his nose and a warble of giggly noises came from his throat. He was a smiley, lazy boy, so big I could hardly pick him up anymore. At his last checkup I'd held him on my lap, my legs falling asleep from his weight as Mama looked down at her pocketbook and Dr. Gibbs tapped on her pillbox hat. *Thump thump thump. If you don't stop babying your boy, he'll never bother to stand up and walk.*

But it was hard not to gather up Roddy like a fat puppy and carry him around. He was a roly-poly and I wanted to lift him up now, even though it was against our new family rules. I was supposed to leave him alone so he'd stand up by himself and get on with it. In a few minutes, Daddy would come in and lift Roddy out of the playpen, prop him up against the couch, squat down on the far side of the rug with arms outstretched, coat bunched around his shoulders, and call out, grinning, "Come on, Buddy, come on."

Every night before we sat to supper, Barbara Ann and I planted ourselves like stepping stones across the "rug pond," slapping our thighs and cheering for Roddy as he plunged from the couch to me, from me to Barbara Ann, from Barbara Ann to Daddy's arms. Mama would leave her cooking and pause in the kitchen doorway, wiping her hands on her apron and giving us a smile.

Suddenly, the screen door screaked on its hinge.

"Daddy!" I sputtered, springing up.

I adored my father. I was his girl, though he never said as much or offered me kisses or hugs. I didn't expect these things; we came from a long line of Appalachian mountain people who didn't waste effort on emotion. Instead, my father reached me in other ways: teasing me after supper, taking my hands and stomping around the room with each of my sneakered feet riding on top of his big, wing-tipped shoes. "S'margic, Pargie, puddin' and pie," he'd chant above my giggles, "kissed the boys and made them cry." Or he'd settle at the kitchen table with me and my litter of dinosaur bones, well past lamplight, as if there were nothing else to do. He'd trim and hand me plastic parts, showing me how to bead the glue and press delicately on two knobs of vertebrae until the glue took hold.

Now, my father stepped through the door, his dark hair and black suit filling up the doorframe. He didn't look at me, not even a glance, touching off another pop of alarm in my chest. In the next instant, my mother appeared from nowhere, moving past me like a footless shadow. Her arms reached out, and she clutched Daddy's lapels, pressing her face close to his ear. I saw her tremble. Her voice quivered as she whispered, her words spilling in a rush. Suddenly, she collapsed, her legs crumpling and her body melting to the floor as if she'd lost her bones. I stood in the middle of the room, mute and speechless. I had never seen my mother this way. There she was in a blue heap, sprinkled with white daisies and rickrack, bunched in a mess.

Without a sound, I retreated, tucking my body back into a kitchen chair. As long as I had been alive, my mother had been the keeper of "lady-ness" and manners in my family. Seeing her fall, her limbs bouncing off the floor, I knew I was seeing what I wasn't meant to see, ever—a kind of cracking inside her. My chest felt cottony. Barbara Ann slid off the couch a few feet from me and stood still, her mouth hidden beneath her hands.

There were so many things I didn't know. My mother had felt little flints of worry before that moment in our living room: her baby boy's first words had vanished, the brown pools of his eyes rarely settled on hers, and he had never crawled on all fours. Dr. Gibbs had said, "Boys are different; he'll catch up soon enough." Still, something had haunted her—the way Roddy had started fiddling with his hands, twining his fingers; the way he rocked in his crib, banging his head against the bars, not seeming to mind the pain, not crying as she hurried to him. An ember of anxiety in her chest had driven her to call a special doctor, and that morning while my sister and I were in school, she had taken Roddy to a faraway clinic. Much later in life I would learn my mother had hardly been able to drive home.

Neither she nor any of us would know for years what to call my brother's affliction, but she had heard enough that day to know her baby boy was damaged and would never lead a normal life.

Across the room, my father lowered his briefcase to the floor. Stooping, he shoveled his hands beneath the pile of my mother. When he lifted, her limp weight fell against his chest. He was an achingly young man, lean and long-limbed, with a straight nose and thick shock of black hair he'd inherited from his father—features that had made him the catch of his hometown of Hazard, Kentucky. Unlike his Pappy before him, my father had turned away from dirt farming and plumbing repairs in the back woods of Appalachia, and headed instead toward aeronautics and the dream of flight. He'd wanted to find out what makes a four-hundred-ton, winged machine lift and float on a gust of air as if it were a silver feather.

And he'd taken with him the girl who'd won his heart, my mother, who sang like a meadowlark and was so clever she'd gone to college at sixteen.

But right then, in my living room, I knew my mother wasn't a songbird or a beauty queen. She was someone whose legs were dangling, and whose high heel was falling to the floor. And my father was someone who had forgotten I was there. He moved down the hallway, his black-coated shoulders slung backward, swaying heavily, side to side.

I slid from my chair and padded to my sister's side. My insides felt slippery and cold.

"What's wrong with Mama?" Barbara Ann whispered, hardly loud enough to hear. She didn't ask the real question, and neither did I, the one that would stay buried for years, inside a time and a household that didn't speak of such things: *What's wrong with our family?*

My father didn't answer. He sidestepped down the narrow hallway, carefully, at an angle, so my mother wouldn't bump her head. Then, at the far end, he turned, maneuvering her, feet-first, around the corner and into the bedroom, the soft cloud of her hair vanishing last.

Chapter 2

Great Expectations

For a time, I thought I might have dreamed my mother's fall. Barbara Ann didn't speak of it, nor did either of my parents. If there was a name for what I had seen, I sensed it was better left alone, like the darkening mound I once came upon in my grandfather's chicken coop, deep inside an empty nest, a matted thing I hadn't touched.

Instead, I turned to my family's rhythms. My father's stories, for one, spun a fabric that held my five-year-old world together. Woven in with baths and bedtimes, his tales took me to another world. Not long after my mother's fall, he spun a story that swept me far away from our duplex on Jewell Avenue.

"A long time ago in the Great Smoky Mountains, two little girls went messin' around," he began, propping himself in my bedroom doorway, the long reeds of his arms folded across his chest.

"By themselves?" my voice twanged in the air.

I was a child who couldn't imagine being alone. Nestled in the dark, the soft pelt of my bed covers pulled to my chin, I listened, wide-eyed and riveted on his backlit head and shoulders. Shadows ruffled about the room and bright stars of hall light scattered across the foot of my bed.

"Yessiree," he went on, shaking a finger in the air. "No sooner had they jumped the crick but a twig crackled behind them, and there came big old grizzly bear."

I gasped, cupping my mouth.

"Oh, for pity's sake," groaned Barbara Ann. I felt her eyes rolling at me through the darkness. Inches away in her own twin bed, she sat tucked up against the opposite wall. I couldn't see her face, only the mounds of her knees, still as moles beneath the dark covers. "Calm down," she admonished with the full authority of a seven-year-old.

But I couldn't. I was desperate for Daddy's rollicking stories. They caught me up and flung me about so thoroughly that I let go of where I was, never guessing how improbable it was for him, a man of physics, to be there in our doorway, crafting scenes and garnished plots. It seemed an utterly natural and easy thing for him, this art of story-telling, as if he were born to it.

My life felt restored. My father's stories ferried me to sleep, and come morning, my mother's household devotions carried me through the day: the ironing of clothes, the stacking of towels, the doing of dishes. After her brief collapse, she had rallied again, and each eve-ning we gathered around a table spread with hot Southern dishes: pork chops and white peppery gravy, smoky shucky beans, and a bowl of steaming biscuits whipped up by hand, drizzled with sweetly sour sorghum. Often, she pulled from the oven her blessedly tart rhubarb pie, with its elegant fluted edges and velvety crust, my father's favorite. Though she'd followed my father from Kentucky to the wild prairies of the West, my mother never took to rolling tortillas or rustling up chili; we ate as if we were in the Appalachians, tethered to our roots.

These rituals steadied me so thoroughly that whole months passed without me thinking of my mother's collapse. Not until one solitary Saturday in January did my memory stir again. That morning, the first big snow of the Colorado winter began, and by noon, icy snow pecked on our kitchen window like tiny beaks.

I looked up from where I was: at the kitchen table, its Formica surface littered with plastic bones. In one hand, I held the skull of a pterosaur, and in the other, a dainty spine. Lost in the debris of dinosaurs, I'd ignored my mother's voice a few moments before and only now missed the soft *wuffing* of her iron and the clicking of drawers. The room yawned with quiet. Neither my father nor sister was home.

Softly, I laid down the skeleton and slid off my chair, peering down the hallway. My head, woozy from glue, made me totter and grip the table.

"Mama?" I called.

The image of her crumbling body slid down inside me like a snake, slithering around in my belly. Cautiously, my feet moved. Padding down the hallway, I paused at the nursery, peeking into where Roddy was snoozing beneath a hill of baby blankets. Onward to my parents' bedroom, I let go a puff of air and peered around the door. Inside, the bed was neatly made, its spread white and smooth as icing. The pillows were just as they should have been, crisply plumped and unflustered. Still, standing there in the quiet, I felt my heart slip backward. How long after my father had carried my mother to this bedroom had she lain on the mattress, unable to rise? What had buckled her so? I couldn't remember supper that evening or whether I'd fallen asleep without my father's story.

My eyes slid from the pillows to the bedside table where my grandparents from both sides of the family gazed from metal frames. Their portraits soothed me. None of their faces wore smiles—they were mountain-raised and empty of nonsense—but I knew their kindness, which drew me now into the room and up the near side of the bed. I reached for the faces of my mother's parents, Marguerite and Benjamin Franklin Lutes—"Annie" and "Grandpa" to me. Their frame was hinged at the center and I closed it like a book, pressing it to my chest as I circled the bed and gathered all the other family portraits. Shinnying up and under the blankets, my head sinking into my mother's pillow, I spread my family around me: Annie and Grandpa Lutes, Grandma and Grandpa Combs, Mama, looking pretty in high school, Daddy, handsome in his Air Force cap, and, lastly, a trio of soft-lit images framed in a row. This last was my favorite, with Barbara Ann wearing dark curls and a pretty six-year-old smile, Roddy giggling at the camera, dimpled and toothless, as if someone was tickling his belly, and me, in the center, crowned with sunny pin curls and a shy smile, trying my best to hold still. The creamy-white mat ovaled my face the same way my mother might cup and lift my chin with her hand.

I don't know how long I lingered there—it wouldn't be the only or the last time—lifting the frames like delicate plates, sliding my fingers around the silky curves of the wood. I must have startled when I heard the quick, distant sound of the back door and my mother coming into the house, her voice calling that she was back with that cup of sugar for the batter. Slipping out from under the covers, I set the portraits soundlessly back on the dresser and tables. Once more, I felt rooted and safe.

I'm not sure how many more snows fell that winter before my worry fluttered again, this time flapping with a force that knocked me off my legs. It wasn't long. On a chilled day in early March, I stood with Barbara Ann on the curb of the school parking lot, waiting for my mother to fetch us in the car. She was taking forever, and, out of sheer boredom, I was counting patches of black, wet soil blossoming through thick pads of snow. My mood was dark. I had been invited by my friend Darlene to her house for the afternoon, but when I asked Mama for permission that morning, she said no. Instead, we were going on a long blurry car ride to a place I'd never been.

When Mama pulled up in the Chevy at last, I crawled into the back seat, my fingers aching from snowballs and my toes throbbing in the damp, dark hollows of my shoes. My petticoat was ripped from playing Keep Away at recess, and Mrs. Jean, my kindergarten teacher, had made me stand in the corner for *heaven knows what*.

"Are we going home?" I asked, fidgeting myself into place.

"No, we are not." Mama clipped her words, her eyes darting to the rearview mirror, her mouth flattening into a red-lipped line. Her neatly combed curls were so dark they shimmered, blue-black in the afternoon sunlight, softly brushing against the deep pink of her collared coat.

I blew out my cheeks and flopped against the seat. Barbara Ann twisted her neck around from the front seat, scrunching her brows at me.

I'm thirsty, I mouthed.

She jammed a finger against her lips, beetling her eyes, then snapped away again, her ponytail whishing against her collar.

Mama squeezed the wheel in her slender fingers and pulled out into traffic. Beside me, Roddy stared out the window and hummed, his corduroyed legs straddling a wad of toys. For what seemed a thousand miles, we rode in silence, with me slumped against the door and my head propped against the window. I didn't ask where we were going, or why. I sensed something shadowy driving the car, something that had to do with Roddy, but I wasn't sure. There was a raggedy feeling about my mother, a skittery fear. Her eyes darted around like sparks, touching us, *one-two-three*, then *zizzing* away.

When we pulled into an enormous parking lot in front of a big yellow building, we inched past a sign I couldn't read. Circling, tires sloshing the snow, Mama turned into a space and then suddenly jammed on the brakes, bucking us around in our seats and nearly mowing down a motorcycle tucked out of view.

"Dear Lord," she whispered, her eyes skipping around the car, checking each of us. Her words stunned me—I had never heard her take the Lord's name in vain.

Shakily, shifting the lever on the steering wheel, she reversed and backed out, inching slowly down the next row and into another spot. At last, she shut off the engine.

For several moments, we just sat there. Mama opened her pocketbook, pulled out a Kleenex, and blew her nose, then looked out the driver's side window. Her lips moved, but I knew she wasn't talking to me, or Barbara Ann, or Roddy. After a minute, she dabbed at her eyes and reached into her pocketbook for a compact, slipping open the latch and peering into the little round mirror. With her free hand, she plucked at her curls and bit each lip to bring back some color. Then, she clipped everything back into her pocketbook, dropped her eyelids, and bowed her head.

I wondered if I should pray, too, but I didn't know what to ask for. Instead, I dropped my chin and half-closed my eyes, listening to the rushing sound of melted snow running under the car; we must have parked over a drain since the noise roared beneath me like a river of rapids. Barbara Ann swiveled her head around just far enough to peep over the seat at me, glance at Roddy, and face forward again. After a long while, Mama raised her chin, pushed a deep breath through her lips, and reached her fingers for the door handle.

My mother must have sensed the hardest moments of her life were not yet behind her. She knew how bad fortune could roam in and out, having herself survived a childhood laced with hunger and fever. In time, I would learn that she was born in the darkest hours of the Great Depression on Christmas Eve, 1930. The town where she drew her first breaths, Chavies, Kentucky, was deeply buckled and lurching from the times. The coal industry had collapsed, severing the lifeblood of the mountains and triggering a desperation and vulnerability that would define the first years of her life. When my mother was nine, she nearly died, flattened for the better part of a year with rheumatic fever, a killer in those days. Penicillin was far from finding its way into the hands of doctors in remote parts of the country.

When I imagine my mother, a slip of a child, ill and swallowed in her bed, I see her legs, spindly and rustling like saplings beneath the covers. Her feverish cheeks, flushed bright red, are heightened by the odd pallor ringing her mouth. In the weeks ahead she would skirt even closer to death, plummeting into "side pleurisy" and double pneumonia. The story of her survival would come to me in small episodes throughout my life, revealing that, like all children who fall ill for long stretches of time, she learned to be alone in that room. By the time she emerged from her bed, she had let go of her childhood.

Sitting in the frigid car with the engine ticking and my mother praying, I understood none of this at five years old. Only that my mother was troubled and, in some way, deeply frightened. I sensed she feared something close by, something that lurked in these buildings.

The car door scraped open in her hand, shrieking against grit and winter rust. She stepped out into the parking lot of Denver University's neurology clinic, hoisting Roddy onto her hip, stepping awkwardly around snow piles and stumbling once when she came to the curb. In my mother's wake, Barbara Ann and I shuffled up the sloppy steps to the building, slipping inside the heavy front door. We trundled down a wide hallway with too many rooms; suddenly, Mama and Roddy vanished behind a doorway, leaving me and Barbara Ann standing out in the cavernous space.

Uncertain, I took in the long corridor and dark benches running up and down the center. Barbara Ann tugged on my jacket sleeve and we backed into the only empty bench spot left. I squished myself between her and a large billowy lady on my right, who was cradling a little girl too big to be held like a baby. The girl's bony arms and legs spilled out from her mother's lap and her head rolled around like a cantaloupe. I looked away, shifting my eyes and spotting a boy a few spaces down, pretzeled into a wheelchair, chin wobbling and sparkling with drool.

"Stop staring," whispered Barbara Ann. "It's rude."

Packed so close against her, I couldn't turn to see whether she was angry.

"Where *can* I look?" I asked.

"Down."

A sharp bark bounced off the ceiling and ricocheted around the room, causing me to flinch and cover my ears. Craning, I peered around to the right, casting my eyes down the row of benches. There, crouched at his mother's feet, was a little boy, a smidgen older than Roddy, his teeth clamped down on the webbed skin between his forefinger and thumb. Blood was smeared on his lips and slathered all over his chin. His mother pulled his hand out of his mouth and glanced around, her eyes landing on me.

Startled, I tucked myself back against the wall. Beside me, Barbara Ann's nose was deep into *Highlights* magazine, her pencil scratching about the page. I dropped my eyes, folding my fingers together in my lap. My chest felt hollow and dank. There was something about the boy's cry; it had a flattened tone, like a bicycle horn, a familiar sound. Roddy wasn't like this boy, he didn't chew on his hands, and yet, a deep unease entered me. An oily and ominous thought. *Could this be him?*

For the first time, I felt afraid for Roddy. Pulling my knees up close to my face, I stared at one kneecap, strips of pink skin running angrily across the top where I'd pulled off a scab. Touching my lips to the raw skin, I closed my eyes and stayed there, jostled by the little girl's melon head bump-bumping my arm. I didn't know if a few minutes passed or an hour.

When Mama finally came back out the door, Roddy still on her hip, her eyes weren't right. Her mouth was white. I scrambled off the bench after Barbara Ann, scuttling past the cantaloupe girl and bloody boy. The sharp, cold air hit my face when we stepped outside and I clattered my way down the steps, keeping my eyes fixed on the tick-tock of my shoes all the way to the car. I couldn't know that what had whitened my mother's face, the thing she'd heard in that room, was not only shocking but wrong: that my brother had been born with cerebral palsy. She wouldn't hear the right word—autism—for another two years.

On the way home that afternoon, Mama drove with her head propped against the left window, as if it were too swollen for her neck to manage. Beside her in the front seat, Barbara Ann watched the road, glancing sideways every so often, her dark ponytail a worried swish back and forth along her collar. Beside me, in the back seat, Roddy made his funny whispery noises.

"Shh, *huh*, shh, *huh*." The seat wiggled with his rocking back and forth. His hands flapped, as if he were saying bye-bye to the back of Mama's head.

Reaching across the seat, I pressed both of his hands into his lap until they stilled under my palms. If I could get his body to stop flitting around, maybe everything would be okay. But when I let go of his hands, off they went again, beating against the air like two fat-bellied birds. Their fluttering, which had always made me giggle, now made me tired, and I turned my eyes out the window.

My family was in trouble in so many ways. We were in the wrong place and the wrong time, driving home in an era that could not and would not help us. Nineteen-fifty-seven was far too early for help or understanding. We didn't know how to intervene on my brother's behalf, nor would we until it was too late. My mother, barely twenty-six, was far away from her own mother, who might have helped her weather the worst of this shock. And my father, by nature, was tightly wrapped, not a source of comfort for my mother or any of us.

Faith deepened our plight. My parents fiercely believed in the will of God. They were born-again Baptists and we all lived by the language and literal teachings of the Bible. If a bad thing happened, like a brain-damaged child, it was God's plan and we weren't really meant to question or understand. This alone would deter my parents from pushing past their own bewilderment and seeking the help of a family counselor or a gathering of like-stricken parents, anyone who could help them see this wasn't tied to God or sin or immoral behavior.

And finally, my parents were mountain people, meaning they were both proud and especially prone to shame. Where they had been raised, deep in the Appalachian Mountains, the only reason for a "retarded" child was inbreeding, a condemnable thing relegated to whispers and averted eyes.

That evening, the rooms of our duplex took on a dusky gloom. Mama's voice murmured behind the bedroom door, talking with my father on the phone, across the yawn of miles where he was away on business. She emerged with swollen eyes, and at the supper table she strained forward in her chair, tearing up when Roddy wouldn't pick up his spoon. He wailed and slapped at his bowl until it splattered to the floor. Ashen, my mother lifted her spoon and fed him from her plate.

Later on, I washed the dishes in silence beside Barbara Ann. Instead of slipping outside for another hour of play, I followed her down the hallway, tiptoeing to the door of the nursery. Hovering behind her, I used my sister as I would the rest of my life: as a scrim to soften the scene before me.

Inside the nursery, my mother cradled Roddy, rocking and rocking. Her back was toward us and her face turned away. All I saw was my brother's fuzzy hair, sticking up beyond the blanket, *whiff-whiffing* in the back-and-forth breeze. My mother didn't lift her eyes or to tell me why she was humming in a mournful voice, and I didn't ask. Every time she rocked backward, a tiny silver-framed photo on the edge of the lamp table blinked into view. I knew its every detail. Centered in the oval was my mother, dressed in her satin bridal gown, holding onto my father's arm, radiant, her eyes bright and face flushed in high spirits. She was eighteen, and my father, twenty-four. A wry smile touched his face, barely visible, as all of his emotions and fatherly affection would turn out to be. Side by side, they swept down the aisle toward this life.

I couldn't have known what I do now: that along with her delicate straight nose, her high intelligence, and her faith in heaven, my mother carried on her wedding day a desperate dream for a fresh and wholesome family—one in which everyone was healthy and well-behaved and, above all, the opposite of what she'd known. When she had lifted her high cheekbones and flashed the photographer that dazzling smile, it was as if the camera were a doorway, opening to the place she'd imagined all those childhood fevered months: her place of dreams.

Now, standing in the doorway, watching my mother rock my baby brother and cry, as she would many times in the coming months, I knew something happy had left our family: a kind of hope—a life we were supposed to live.

Chapter 3

Back Seat

Mostly in the dark hours of night, when Barbara Ann, Roddy, and I were asleep, my parents fought behind closed doors. Their muffled voices, pitched and rumbling, occasionally rattled the wall next to my bed. The only daytime signs they were cracking under the weight of their lives and the thickening horror that nothing was going to fix my brother were their features, deadened for several hours, sometimes for days: my mother's mouth, altered and frozen into a pursed, colorless beak, my father's jaw set, his lips grim. The clink of dishes and silverware and the *whah* of a door opening and shutting were the only sounds in our silent home. If voices arose, it was to instruct us to do chores or to call us to supper. Barbara Ann and I whispered and tiptoed during these times. If we wanted to talk, we wrote it down and passed notes to one another. The silence was like a dense body in the room, a corpse at the table.

After one wordless supper, during which Mama did not touch her food, my parents herded us into the car. Winding down the long driveway of our duplex, we turned left, toward the city. No one said anything. No one cried. We simply drove.

I did not know what was felling my parents. Roddy didn't look ill; he looked the same as ever, porky and giggly. I didn't know what babies were supposed to do, so nothing about him looked strange to me. This would hold sway for many more months until finally his lack of words would prove to me that something was gravely wrong.

On that first evening drive, I knew to stay quiet. Neon lights squiggled from signs and placards, endless strips of stores, car dealerships, Chevron stations. We slid past them slowly, making our way through traffic as if we were on some kind of sluggish barge and my father was steering us downriver to some distant shore where people were happier. From the middle of the back seat, I could see only partially out of either window and lost track of our direction. I didn't know we were driving in an enormous circle, lapping the city, east to Sheridan, north to Colfax, west to Kipling, and south again, to West Jewell.

At some point, a look must have passed between my parents since, without warning, my father eased the Plymouth over to the right lane and turned out of traffic. Alarmed, I sat up straighter and peered out the front window, afraid we had arrived at some sort of hospital where we'd have to wait for hours while a doctor examined Roddy. But it was only a Rexall drugstore. My father put the car in park and my mother got out without a word, went in, and came back with a bottle of Bayer aspirin. Then, we went on.

I understood aspirin was not the reason for our drive. It was the way my parents did not have to explain why we were spending an evening on the road. I didn't mind that we were in the car, in the dimming light, driving aimlessly. It was a relief to be sandwiched between Roddy and Barbara Ann, where I couldn't move or make noise. Better than tiptoeing around the house, where I invariably shut a drawer with a bang, or dropped a tube of glue, or accidentally tripped over Roddy, whose wail sometimes brought me a wordless swat from Mama's hand.

I lost count of how many times we set out after supper and meandered through the streets of Denver. Being in the back seat with the disheartened emotions of my family swirling around me, unspoken, swamps my memory of Jewell Avenue. My parents didn't go out by themselves, did not hire a sitter and get together with church friends or chaps from Martin Marietta, partly because they couldn't afford to do so, partly because neither one of them could manage the laughter and jolliness of others. The drives were the way they dealt with despair.

If I remember any small break in my parents' gloom it was on Sundays, the only time we drove up Sheridan and got out of the car. Alameda Baptist Church was the one place my parents sighed into some sort of comfort. After service, they lingered in the front entrance, talking and smiling with the pastor, my father holding Roddy in his arms, my mother looking pretty in her hat and dress.

"Mighty fine boy you have there, Brother Ray," said the pastor, pointedly. "Mighty fine."

"That's the truth, meat on his bones," answered my father. "Ticklish too." He wiggled a finger in Roddy's ribs, triggering a baby giggle and a burst of smiles.

Barbara Ann and I ran around on the front lawn, but never far from my parents. I wanted to hear their voices and see them smile. I drank it in with the resilience of a six-year-old so it would last the rest of the week.

Not surprisingly, my mother needed more comfort than a single sermon on Sunday could offer. When her grief swelled beyond her ability to manage, she clustered us into the car and took us on a different ride. This happened only a few times, the first being in the late afternoon, with light dimming over the rows of ranch houses in a dense suburb north of the city. My mother was behind the wheel, and Barbara Ann and I were in our school clothes. We pulled into a driveway and Mama got out of the car.

"Can we come in?" Barbara Ann asked with her usual gutsiness

"No, stay here and watch your brother; don't get out of the car." Mama said.

She looked tired, gray swags under her eyes. I watched her circle around the front of the car and knock on the front door.

A silhouette appeared in the doorframe and I recognized Mrs. Hays, Barbara Ann's Sunday school teacher. She was a warm older woman who had five children of her own. Pushing the screen door wide, Mrs. Hays waved and smiled to Barbara Ann, and then, with a kind look, she put her arm around my mother and steered her into the house.

"Why are we here?" I asked from the back seat.

My sister knew more than I did. Unlike me, she paid attention and observed.

"Just because," she said, not unkindly.

I sighed and opened my box of crayons, flipping through the pages of my coloring book until I landed on the fairy godmother *shu-zam-ming* the pumpkin into a golden coach. This was the way I nudged time along, sinking into the comfort of blues and purples, the rage of red and orange. I chose colors carefully, submerging in the task of coloring and forgetting about being trapped in the back seat of a car for an infinite amount of time. When Roddy fussed I handed him burnt sienna and a Big Chief tablet, and he scribbled like there was no tomorrow.

When Mama emerged again from the house, I glimpsed her puffy eyes before she slipped on her sunglasses. For a moment, she sat behind the wheel, looking out the side window. She was grappling with the skids of young marriage, three children, and the aftershocks that came with my brother: doctors, tutors, dead ends. Now, even the car key gave her a hard time, eluding her as she rummaged in her pocketbook. Finally, flinging the purse aside, she turned to my sister.

"Oh, Barbara Ann," she said, her voice tangled up, "all I've ever wanted was a family that was happy."

Right there, out loud, was the truth I feared: we were not a happy family. A sensation spread through me, a thickening in my arms and legs and up my collarbone into my throat. I didn't know there was such a thing as claustrophobia but I felt something squeezing my chest. For the first time, I wanted out of the back seat, out of the car, and also, in a deep and hidden part of me, I wanted out of my family.

Chapter 4

Home to Hazard

Rustling my ten-year-old legs, I lifted a crushed cheek from my pillow. Hot, soaked air pushed up my nose, filling me with the smell of rotted leaves and honeysuckle. A tiny shoot of pleasure sprouted in my chest. I knew instantly where I was: deep in the South, burrowing far into the Appalachian Mountains, toward my grandparents' home.

"Law sakes," my mother sang out from the front seat, "I'm a wreck." A coal stone bounced off the hood of the car and she flinched, hands leaping up to her breast bone.

This was how I knew we were getting close to where I was born. My father's veined hands steadied the wheel as Mama fussed at the coal truck up ahead. In another curve or two, the town of Hazard, Kentucky, would emerge from the crumpled mountains, its plucky houses hanging off the blasted cliffs. Taking us there was a curling road, barely wide enough for the rumbling coal trucks puffing and swaying like black elephants up the inclines. For the better part of two hours, we'd been inching along, the steam of the mountains swirling around us.

"Not long now," my father said, with satisfaction.

I huffed; he'd said this three times already. Now that I could smell Hazard, I couldn't wait a moment more. For my family, Kentucky was an oasis—a place of respite and ease born from belonging. My parents missed this in Denver, especially my mother: the relief of being surrounded by family. For her and my father, and already for me, Hazard was more than simply home. It was a place to shake off the wariness of the world and find reprieve from the constant vigilance and worry around my brother. In Hazard, my parents had been exceptional, smart, good-looking, elevated, most likely to succeed—unlike they were in Colorado, where all of their promise had crashed in on them. I couldn't say this, even to myself, but I sensed a softening of strain and self-consciousness in Hazard, and a peace of mind that had been a part of their marriage for a small while, before malady arrived.

Beside me in the seat, Roddy whined, rubbing his face. He was six years old and seemed as fed up as I was with this rambling. Sandwiched between me and Barbara Ann, he snorted, flutter-kicking his pale legs and feet, his bare toes pink and puffed in the heat. For a few seconds his hands flitted around his mouth and then tangled together in a squirmy knot of fingers as he grimaced and twitched his head. Who knew what was really in his mind? He had no words, and I'd given up on him ever saying anything. His eyes were no help at all, darting to and fro. His funny growling noises were all I had to figure out what he was feeling and how he was sorting out life. Right now, he might be thinking we were going to drive forever and never sleep in a bed again.

I dipped my nose toward his head: a sweet, tangy whiff, like Juicy Fruit.

"We're going to see Grandpa," I whispered.

For a half second, he quieted his legs and tipped his chin my way.

"Pineapple upside-down cake," I sang, wiggling my hips.

He hummed, a small buzzing sound rising from his throat, like a cicada's.

"Soon," I said.

We were now three days on the road, nearing the end of a trip from Denver to Hazard that marked every summer in my memory. My parents traded off the wheel throughout the night, and by day, Mama handed soft, Saran-wrapped cheese and lettuce sandwiches, sweet pickles, and peeled Sunkist oranges over the back seat. I didn't know it at the time, but we were just short of being poor. My father, recently out of the Air Force, was laboring at the bottom rung of an engineer's ladder, and my mother, bowing to the customs of the times and my father's desires, and also my brother's needs, had abandoned both her college studies and any thought of working outside the home. All of this meant our back seat was the closest thing we would get to a motel room for many years.

Part of me knew something my family never said aloud: that even if we had mounds of money to spend on motels or restaurants, or on fancier excursions, say to Carlsbad Caverns or Disneyland, we still wouldn't go. We had my brother and he wasn't meant for those places. Roddy was someone we couldn't hide, and we didn't try to— he went everywhere with us—but because of him, we were different. We didn't go on spontaneous adventures or try out new playgrounds or restaurants. Young as I was, I knew that being out among people was painful for my mother. Whenever we did venture to the Denver Drumstick or Big Boy, everything started out okay as she clustered us to the table and fussed at us to put our napkins in our laps and keep our elbows off the table. But within a few minutes people began to glance our way and linger on Roddy, his hands fidgeting for no reason, his eyes darting up and down at his plate, his voice a bundle of grunts and shapeless flat noises. I heard Mama explain to the waitress how Roddy was "different." Sometimes, if the order was delayed and he was too hungry or tired, he'd haul off and wail like a giant toddler, and we'd have to leave, sitting in the car while they wrapped and bagged our meals.

It was a relief not to go to those public places. Instead, I learned to relish the tinier pleasures of our road trips. A few hours ago, we'd entered the deeper parts of Kentucky and temperatures had sweltered up in the nineties. That's when my father swung the car into a forlorn Phillips 66. Lassoing my belly, he'd lifted the weighty red lid of the Coke machine, holding me over the frosty smoke. Plunging in my fingers, I hauled up a bright orange Nehi, pressing it to my temple as he swung me back to the ground. *Ffffft*, the top popped away, and I opened my throat to a bubbly tang.

Now, with the empty Nehi rolling at my feet, I sat up and scrubbed my fingers in my hair, pushing my tongue, gummy and unwashed, over my teeth. The final mining turn-off was behind us, and the walls of kudzu were giving way to the rooflines and storefronts of Main Street. I felt a new ping of joy.

"Here we are," Barbara Ann said, in wonder.

Dark-haired and olive-skinned, my sister was the opposite of me. At thirteen, she had already sprouted the long limbs that would carry her into womanhood. She pointed out the window where the First Baptist Church of Hazard was coming our way. Its promenade of steps, bleached white in the hot light, led up to the glory of polished wooden doors and, even higher, to a peak of stepped brick, which took my eyes to heaven.

"See?" I said softly into Roddy's ear. "Mama and Daddy were married there." I wanted him to stop his rocking and notice the moment—to share it with me. The First Baptist Church of Hazard was the most sacred, mysterious place in my heart. One day, I believed, I'd sweep down the aisle in my own wedding gown.

Roddy's nose followed my arm out the window and, for whatever reason, he complied, puffing up his ribs and twisting to see what was there.

In another minute we turned, tipping up a steep hill, and at last we were there, on High Street. My father parked and turned off the engine, and I craned my neck to read the big blade sign on the side of the brick building: "Combs Furniture." That was my name up there, where everyone in Hazard could see it. The painted glass beckoned in gold letters and, underneath, two enormous doors stood open to the street, their wooden edges worn and rounded by customers' hands.

Untangling my legs, I jumped out to the blistering curb. Hop-scotching around in my bare feet, I slipped on my flip-flops and then headed straight through the big doors to the store's sprawling inside. For a few seconds I paused and swooned, partly from the sight, and partly from the sudden swell of aromas. The air stirred with heat and the heady scents of walnut and cedar, mixed with the sweet pungency of my grandfather's tobacco. Hulks of furniture, thick-legged and heavy, clogged the floor clear to the opposite wall, pocked by floor fans swiveling and whirring in a vain effort to battle moisture and moths.

"There her be," my grandfather said. His voice, mumbly around his pipe, rose from somewhere within the maze.

I squinted, looking hard to find him. His footsteps emerged from the deepest part of the store, coming up from the damp stone cellar, where, for a time, he'd harbored his prized chickens until Grandma couldn't stand them anymore. Now, I spotted him, soft-shirted and baggy-legged, standing in the center of the room where a mess of catalogues and invoices weighed down a thick slab of table.

Plunging into the maze, I chose a winding path around bed sets, bureaus, lamps, and all manner of sofas and chairs. Beneath my feet, ancient floorboards kindled in a bright crackling of sounds. When I reached him—my Papaw, my father's father—I threw my twiggy arms about his neck and hugged, not knowing what to say. In my few years alive, I'd figured out that Papaw never said much, nor hugged readily. Still, I relished stepping into his world, so mysteriously different from my own. It wasn't only the sweet and musty aromas of the store, or the bittersweet taste of poplar honey I'd soon sample from his beehives, or even Grandma's savory shucky beans and red velvet cake. It was deeper. I felt easy and protected here and, though I didn't know at the time how to account for it, I felt cherished.

Daddy called, "Hello!" and, in the next moment, Barbara Ann and Mama and Grandma were all there, bunched in a huddle of greetings. The pent-up energy of the trip tingled down my arms and legs, and I itched to scamper about the store. Barbara Ann, largely broody and remote these days, was too much of a lady to be silly, so my eyes danced over to Roddy. He was huddling close to my mother, pulling on his bottom lip. He had soft cheeks and light brown hair clipped in half-moons around his ears. A cowlick sprang from his crown like a spit of wheat grass. His eyes flitted left, right, and then caught on me.

I ducked behind a rack of linoleum rolls. Stretching my lips wide, I sprang above the rack and flashing a rubbery smile, before plummeting back to a squat. He giggled.

Because Roddy didn't have words, I delighted in making him laugh; not that he didn't have a language of his own—grunts, lip pops, and whispers came from his mouth—but I already knew those weren't for me. They were sounds for his inside room, where he went without me. His giggle, on the other hand, meant he was here with me, at least for a little while.

Hunching, I scuffled behind the rack to the opposite end and crouched again. Through the gap between linoleum tubes I spotted the melon of his belly pushing out against his shirt and the flushed pink of his neck and chin.

"Hi!" I screaked.

Startled, he whipped his chin around, tracking my voice, and this time, he burst into a happy chortle.

"Where is she?" I heard my mother say softly, conspiratorially. "Where's your sister?"

He fussed for a minute. I knew he wanted to stay put, huddling beside my mother. But then I heard what I'd been hoping for: his funny flat steps coming after me.

At a much earlier time in his life, when he was nine months old, Roddy had opened his small throat and said "Dada." So normal was this event and so natural its timing on the baby chart that my mother didn't call me in from wherever I was playing. When I think of it now, I imagine a tender and private moment for my mother, with fingers of light spilling through the one window of the nursery, dappling Roddy's rumpled PJs and the comical sprout of fuzz on his head. As with so many things taken for granted in life, the wonder of that moment didn't fully register with my mother, or any of us, until it was gone. Though Roddy chirped "Dada" once or twice more, his speech vanished by his first birthday, as swiftly as it had arrived. He had not said a word since.

"Hi, hi, hi," I sang out again, stuffing my face into one end of a linoleum tube. My voice bounced down the ten-foot tunnel and burst out the other end. Roddy's footsteps halted somewhere over by the cellar. For several seconds the floorboards were quiet. I was about to give up when, suddenly, his steps blasted alive again and, this time, they churned straight for me. In the next instant, his face appeared in the opposite end of the tube. Eyes crinkling, he peered down the tunnel at me.

"Hi," he said.

I gasped, my breath hard and sharp. *Did he say something?*

The corners of his mouth fluttered up and down, as if uncertain where to be, and then at last, he gave me a shy, flirty smile. I yanked my head out of the tube and whipped my eyes around the room. Barbara Ann was dreamily fingering wallpaper samples lining the far wall. She hadn't heard, nor had my parents and grandparents, who were still chatting busily in a cluster by the stairs.

"Mama, Daddy!" I called out. "Come here!"

I scurried in a circle as if chasing my tail, and then sprang up again, crying "Hi!" at the top of my lungs.

"Hi," Roddy said back. Just like that.

A splatter of clapping burst from Barbara Ann as she abandoned the wallpaper and ran for us.

"Did you hear that?" she called out.

The floor rumbled with footsteps as the grownups came to life. My mother's eyes lit up and a girlish laugh sparkled from her throat. My father smiled, and my grandparents nodded and chuckled, their eyes rounded with surprise.

Dipping and springing like a Jack-in-the-Box at my end of the rack, I messed with my timing to surprise Roddy anew. Sure enough, he chirped "Hi," as effortlessly and thoughtlessly as any boy, as if he had been speaking forever. His word was bright and startling. I wanted to catch and hold it in my hands, to keep it safe and flashing inside a jar, where I'd have it forever.

He said "Hi" one more time before he turned his head away and ignored me. By then, it didn't matter. He had spoken, proving that he was like me, he could talk. Drawing in a breath, I thought, *He's not retarded anymore.* My ribs felt like balloons and I could barely balance. I didn't know this was the airiness when worry leaves your heart—when sadness lifts from your shoulders and, suddenly, you believe you won't have to carry it anymore.

Everything rushed to me all at once: the way Roddy was going to be from now on. He'd say everything he hadn't said so far, like all little brothers who couldn't keep quiet, pestering me to teach him things, like Checkers and Go Fish, and he'd ask little friends over, telling lame jokes and making me roll my eyes. Better still, he'd come to school with me, cute as a teddy, holding my hand from the bus to the kindergarten room, where I'd dust his fuzzy head and squeeze him goodbye—as if neither of us had ever belonged to a disabled family.

In the showroom, cheeriness swirled all around me, and the air buzzed with a rare liveliness, a feeling that stayed with me through the afternoon and evening as we drove the few miles to my grandparents' farmhouse. That night, around the supper table, my parents lingered over a second slice of lemon pie, and then we all drifted outside to the porch, the evening light closing in lazy folds around us. Roddy chose his favorite spot on the porch slider, next to Grandma, and the two of them rocked happily, back and forth, while Barbara Ann and I ran willy-nilly up the steep hillside, catching fireflies blinking in the black night.

At the top of the hill, I paused, breathless, gulping in warm wet air and looking down on the porch with its globe of light. I imagined hundreds of Roddy's words flashing out from the dark hollows and pinging around everyone's heads. In that small moment, I believed in miracles—the kind in the Bible, when a loaf of bread breaks into a thousand pieces.

Thrusting my hands into the night, I cupped and closed my palms around a sparkling fairy-fly. Her wings buzzed, making me laugh, and when I parted my thumbs, there she was—twinkling, and wondrous.

Chapter 5

Jesus Is Calling

Papaw's rooster bellowed in the early morning dark. I burrowed deeper under the quilt, tangled in the smell of cedar and clove and the flush of damp leaves coming through the window.

"Hop up and eat some Cheerios," Barbara Ann whispered, jiggling my shoulder. Mama rustled outside in the hallway, packing jars of fresh honey and rattling bags of shucky beans into our suitcases.

My doldrums over leaving Kentucky were softened only by my new companion, too precious to pack away in my suitcase. "Cornelia" had come to life in my own hands the week before. She was a homemade ragdoll, the only sort of doll my grandmother, Mamaw, ever had as a child growing up on a farm. With wonder, I had followed Mamaw's amused instructions, and, swiftly, Cornelia had emerged from measly things found in the kitchen and yard: her body a tubed and folded dish towel jointed with rubber bands, her eyes and nose nothing but touches of charcoal, her red lips a finger brush of blackberry juice, and her hair a globe of corn silk, the same reddish-gold as Mamaw's soft cap of curls. I imagined lifting Cornelia's rag body out of her Kleenex box and holding her aloft to the gasp of my new fifth-grade class.

Twisting around in the back seat, I wagged my fingers at Mamaw and Papaw standing on the porch steps. The car tipped forward down the steep driveway and Papaw's scuffed, brimmed hat sank below the crest of the hill.

In the first of many shifts the year would bring, I found myself two weeks later riding on the school bus, all alone. For the first time in my life, Barbara Ann wasn't beside me. She'd mounted a different bus that morning, riding to her new seventh-grade life at the junior high school across the street, a life I couldn't imagine. Even more troubling was the surprise that Mama wasn't with me either. As I'd crunched on my toast that morning, she'd reminded me that Roddy was starting school, too, a special one, far away—meaning she wouldn't be able to drive me on my first day, as she'd always done. Now, butterflies batted soft wings against my ribcage. I squished myself against the bus window and imagined her driving with Roddy somewhere on a long stretch of highway.

When we arrived at Bear Creek Elementary, I climbed off the bus and stood on the sidewalk, gaping. One hand clutched my lunchbox, and my other arm encircled both my new notebook and Cornelia's shoe box, crushing them against my chest. A wave of kids and parents parted and surged around me, moving toward the front door. I felt lost in a place where I wasn't informed, where everyone else seemed to carry a mysterious set of instructions not in my hands. *How did everyone know where to go?*

Puffing in tiny breaths, I moved forward, my feet carrying me up the steps and through the front door. My belly stirred, as if I'd eaten a plateful of watery scrambled eggs, a sensation I'd later come to know as panic. Flitting my eyes from face to face, I looked for someone I knew. A whispery memory brushed my ear: Mama saying the fifth grade was so big this year they'd had to open two new classrooms. *But where?*

I swept along with the other kids past the cafeteria to a great intersection of corridors. Straight ahead was the kindergarten, so I veered right, down the hallway where I remembered Barbara Ann's fifth- and sixth-grade classes had been. The crowd thinned around me as kids and mothers arrived at doorways and vanished inside. I hoped something would sort out by the time I reached the exit sign at the far end of the hall. But even as I plowed on, I sensed something awry: the kids around me barely came up to my shoulder. No one was my age. Dread rose in my chest as I neared the end of the hall and slowed to a halt before the last door. Taped on its face beside the tiny slit of a window was a brightly decorated piece of construction paper, announcing "Mrs. Robinson's 4th Grade."

My stomach clenched and I backed against the cold cinderblock wall, flattening my shoulder blades and pressing everything—notebook, lunchbox, and Cornelia's cardboard cradle—to my ribs. The box's edges gave under my sweaty palms. From somewhere down the hall, a door clicked and the sound racketed toward me. Then, all fell utterly silent.

If I were my friend Natalie, who'd never been afraid of getting into trouble, I might have rapped on Mrs. Robinson's door and demanded to know where she'd put my fifth-grade class. Or if I were Lily, my friend from Sunday school, who came from a big, noisy, forgiving family, I might have giggled in a spurt, thrilled to be missing a few minutes of sitting still, and hummed a silly song for as long as I dared, before Mrs. Robinson opened the door.

But I was me: a shy, observant child, sensitized to shame, who already wore a layer of uncertainty from fuzzy forces I didn't understand. In my family I'd learned there was little room for missteps; the stress was too high; mistakes often drew a sharp swipe of words and sometimes a swatting hand. Clemency was for other children, not for me.

I don't recall how long I waited there, my ribs moving beneath the cotton of my new blouse. When Mr. Tony, the gym teacher, lumbered in from the baseball field and boomed in his deep voice, "Are you lost, young lady?" I nodded without looking at him. My eyes hitched onto his big sneakered heels, and I followed him out the door and around the side of the school, where we entered a hastily renovated building. There, I stepped from behind him into Mrs. Larson's fifth-grade class.

The flat speckled tile stretching from the door to the first row of desks looked like the wilderness to me. I clopped across the vast expanse with my strange shoebox cinched under my arm, aware of the pack of eyes tracking my journey. Thirty-five faces, most of whom I didn't recognize, watched as I slid into my desk.

"Well!" Mrs. Larson exhaled an exasperated puff of air. I ventured a darting glance upward. Her clipped black hairdo, blunt at the jaw, turned away from me.

"All right then," she went on. "Let's start again. Who would like to share a summertime story?"

Cornelia's box rested on my lap. I was glad to feel eyes slip away from me and back to Mrs. Larson. If I hadn't been so anxious to impress her, I might have rested for a moment, taking in my surroundings. Long enough to notice everyone's blouses and shirts bore brightly colored nametags: badges of goodness handed out to those children who, unlike me, had arrived on time. Instead, I slipped off the crumpled lid from Cornelia's box and plumped up her silken hair. Then, I raised my hand.

Mrs. Larson's dark-rimmed eyes swiveled as she panned the room, fixing on my hand poking up like a periscope among the sea of heads. I wasn't prone to sharing my stories, partly out of wisdom. Young as I was, I knew moments in my family weren't meant for telling: my mother heaped on the floor, my brother's flapping, the yawn of silence in our home—these weren't for others to know. But now I had a bundle of good stories. Cornelia's for one, and then Papaw's beehives and chickens; and maybe, if there was time, I'd even tell them about my brother's miracle, his first word. My heart thrummed, and I shifted to stand up.

Mrs. Larson's gazed at me levelly from across the room. She was young and smartly groomed, with pale, powdered skin and thin, ruby-painted lips. Her white blouse, cool and crisp, was buttoned high to her throat. As she folded her arms across her chest, the sunlight glinted off a tiny glass button on each cuff. The room was quiet, and somewhere, a pencil rolled off a desk, pinging to the floor. I blinked and glanced away. When I looked back again, the point of her chin thrust toward me, and she tilted her head, first one way and then the other, aping a kind of foolish and exaggerated search for my name tag.

"Well, now, seeing that you don't have a name, young lady, how do you expect me to call on you?"

Clots of heat sprouted under my collar and bloomed upward to my ears. I stared at the cover of my notebook. Its illustrations of clouds ran down the left side: cumulus, nimbus, cirrus, and, in the bottom corner, a blackish-yellow storm cloud that looked like a dark smear.

"That one there's a supercell," Daddy had told me the night before when I'd padded out to the garage to show him my new notebook, the one I'd chosen out of all the others. Daddy knew everything about clouds, why they formed and how they warned us. The supercell, he'd said, was liable to drop a twisting tail to the ground, and then coil and thrash the dirt all the way to your feet.

"If you ever see one of those," he'd teased, looking up from his workbench, tapping the cover, "pick up your heels and run."

Mrs. Larson's pinpointed heels pivoted on the floor, and I listened as her heel-toe, heel-toe crossed to the far side of the room.

"Now, who do we have over here—Lynette?" she read from a name-tag somewhere near the far wall of windows. "What a pretty name."

With a happy rustle of petticoats, Lynette stood up. She began her story, her words muffling in my ears as if the air were full of cotton. My eyes slid from my notebook into my lap where Cornelia gazed up from her blue-padded box. Her eyes looked like two tiny pinholes. With one hand, I shifted the lid out from underneath her and slid it closed, across her face.

The rest of the school day blurred by with a shuffling of books and papers, a writing of numbers, a fleeting breath of fresh air on the way to and from lunch. When I arrived home, I put Cornelia's wrinkled box away in my closet. Then I peeled off my naked blouse, still without a nametag, and stuffed it into the hamper. Mama was lying down in her room, stilled under the covers, a washrag covering her eyes. I paused for a moment at her bedroom door, barely able to make out her curved form through the shuttered dark. I didn't go in. Instead, I turned and followed the sound of marbles plunking through holes and scurrying down chutes, pulling me into Roddy's room.

What could I have said to my mother, anyway? It had begun to dawn on me that she was no longer available to me and might never be again. In the way that children know things, I knew her sadness had grown to be the biggest part of her, much bigger than I could be. How was I to explain that I missed her, and because she hadn't been with me, I'd faltered, setting off a cascade of consequences that ended with a sharp and searing rebuke? I couldn't sort it even to myself: why Mrs. Larson would swing her eyes around the room and not only pass me by but mock me, even though I had something good to say, something proud to tell the world. If I'd tried to tell Mama what happened, she'd only doubt my story. As a rule, she and my father always sided with grownups.

I found Roddy sitting on the floor by his bed, riveted to his favorite toy: a wooden marble chute crafted by my father. Constructed of six grooved dowels, the contraption provided a zigzag joyride for each marble, starting from three feet off the floor and, a few seconds later, spitting out the bottom, thrilling Roddy to no end with the tumbling and rumbling. He swung a fistful of marbles up to the chute's mouth and plunked them, one at a time, down its throat.

"Hi," I sighed.

He didn't look up. He was too busy buzzing like a current. His legs, stretched out straight, jittered like two metal rods, rigid at the knees and bowed upward, his ankles and feet fluttering an inch off the floor.

I didn't have the energy to make him say hi to me. Instead, I folded my legs down to the floor, settling myself at one end of the chute so I could catch the helter-skelter orbs as they spit out at the bottom. I wished I could ask him things. Like, how was your first day? Did *you* get a nice teacher? And why was Mama in a dark room, stirring now, from the sounds of it, and rising long enough to shut her bedroom door?

Years beyond that moment, I'd know that despite Roddy's "hi" that summer, he was headed into a miserable year. My mother had already sensed what would prove true: his new school would utterly fail him. Not only would he lose his "hi," but he would also backslide in other ways, wetting his pants again and refusing to get dressed. Mama would finally discover halfway through the year that he'd been parked in a class for deaf children.

Scooping up marbles, I sensed Mama's door would stay closed until my father came home. I didn't have to get up and tiptoe over to its brown face, or lay my ear up against it to know she was kneeling beside the bed, her elbows softly denting the mattress, her slender fingers clasped and pressed to her brow in prayer. I knew enough to leave her there. If I could have slipped under her bed, I'd have heard her whisper, "Dearest Heavenly Father, forgive me my sorrow, my weakness. Help me."

Though I wasn't certain, I felt something new brewing in my mother. Her sadness was taking on a new energy, slamming doors and bursting through the cracks of our afternoons and weekends. Some days she prayed in her room, but other days she grabbed a hair brush or a yardstick, lined us up and spanked us, one by one. Saturday was her blackest hour. In the far reaches of the house, her anger gathered like a distant thunder, at first nearly inaudible over the roar of the vacuum cleaner, her words tangled and swept away in the din. Soon, the vacuum would snort and root its way around the living room baseboards, round the corner, and burst into the hallway, snarling its way to where I scurried about with my dust rag from table to lamp to baseboard.

Somehow, the crushing tedium of housework, with its endless renewable whine, ignited my mother. A poorly folded sheet corner, a scantily dusted window sill, a wet towel dropped in the dirt on the way to the clothesline were slips she couldn't bear from me or Barbara Ann. She told us we were quick-brained girls who ought to learn on the first try, unlike Roddy who needed endless repetition just to get his pants zipped up and keep his fingers out of his food. I believed my mother. She shouldn't have to teach me over and over, like Roddy. I knew I tore her patience into thin, ragged shreds.

A few months later, on a Saturday in December, I was fumbling with my bed, botching the sheet corners. They were supposed to be done with hospital edges, the clever lift-tuck-fold-tuck that cinched the sheet corners like cupped hands around the mattress, the way

Mama had taught me. But my fingers fumbled and it came out wrong. I heard my mother knocking about in the living room, the uncoiling *whip-whip* of the vacuum cord, the quick bite of a plug thrust into the wall. In the next instant, the Hoover's *vroooom* shook my ears.

Clawing at the cotton edges, wadding and shoving them deep into the fissure of the mattress, I felt a pinch of tears prick my eyes. My mother's voice sputtered up like sparks above the vacuum, reaching my ears in short hot bursts: ". . . you girls need a blistering . . . within an inch of your life . . . I'll give you something to cry about. . . ."

I thought of running to Barbara Ann, knowing she was nosing along in the next room with her dust mop. I imagined her pushing the handle in quick, tight strokes and then, as my mother came into the room, snapping to attention, saluting, and then bowing her head toward the floor in one fluid motion, offering her bottom up for whacking and saying, "Go on, Mama, get it over with."

But I didn't have my sister's courage. Abandoning the sheet, I flashed across the hallway, lunging into the bathroom and shutting the door. Thumbing the lock, I backed away, scooting my haunches onto the toilet seat. On the other side of the door, the vacuum burst from the living room, rumbling and whacking down the hall toward me. By the time it reached the bathroom door, I'd slipped off the toilet seat and stood, blue-legged and trembling, with my hand cleaved around the cold chrome of the toilet handle.

"Who's in there?" The door knob rattled.

Silence.

"Answer me!"

"I am."

"What? What are you doing in there?" Her words coiled and squeezed through the wood fibers of the door.

I cocked my wrist and flushed, letting the whoosh and pebbly gargle do its best to back me up.

For a moment, I heard only the open-mouthed roar of the idling vacuum, and then my mother's voice again, saying, in a knowing tone, that if she caught me dawdling she'd give me *what for*. These last two words punched from her throat and hit the door, *pow pow*. Then, I heard her throat catch, as if someone had clamped her windpipe, but only for an instant. The motor revved up again and growled away, first into Roddy's room and then into our girls' room, where it faded behind the door.

I held my breath. I knew my faulty sheet corners were only seconds away from discovery, and I'd only a fraction of time before my mother would holler my name. This time I'd have to give in, open the door, and stand before her. But several moments passed and, finally, I realized she'd stopped vacuuming. I heard only the rasp of the Hoover as it stood still, waiting.

Cracking the door, I saw Barbara Ann, a few feet away, tiptoeing toward our bedroom door. She had on her straw "coolie" hat, the one my father had brought home from some office party long ago. Barbara Ann had started wearing it on Saturdays so she could amuse herself during my mother's rants. If she got caught in a room where my mother was vacuuming, she only had to dip her chin ever so slightly to make my mother disappear. Now, as I came up behind my sister, she lifted one finger to the wooden door, and softly pushed.

The vacuum came into view, abandoned at the base of Barbara Ann's bed. It was an upright with a long belly of a bag, and its pig nose, still vibrating near the floor, rattled little bits of paper and dirt. On the bed was the body of my mother, flung backward. Her face was turned to the wall. Both of her hands were clasped over her chest, heaving up and down with her breath.

Barbara Ann spoke softly, "Mama? Are you okay?"

Our mother didn't move. The up and down of her ribs was the only sign she was alive. I sensed she didn't hear us or want to know we were there.

After a moment, Barbara Ann took a step further into the room, reaching her hand toward the vacuum and flipping it off. Its gears groaned and, with a long keening sigh, it fell silent. She waved me backward and we shuffled out into the hallway, pulling the door closed with a soft click.

Seeing my mother splayed that way was like seeing her fall again—as she had so long ago, folding to the ground at my father's feet. Something had broken in her then, and now, I saw she was still broken. A glimmer of something that would take me more years to fully understand glinted in my mind. It wasn't so much me or Barbara Ann she was railing at; instead, she was lashing out at her life. The unfairness of being trapped inside a place she hadn't foreseen and that now yawned before her like a vast stretch to the horizon. Between here and the end of her days lay the relentless needs of a disabled child, and the fear that maybe she didn't know how to be a mother or how she would ever help her son.

I couldn't do more than simply sense this about her, and I didn't want to know more. The deeper I saw into my mother, the more hopeless I became. By January, I no longer wanted to go to school (thanks to Mrs. Larson, who continued to ignore my raised hand, call on Lynette, and tell me sharply to wait my turn) nor did I want to be at home. I gave up on all of the days of the week, except for Sunday. Though the Sabbath carried a trying set of givens for me—scratchy petticoats, severe ponytails, hours of hard, cold sitting—it was the one place where life wasn't muddy with confusion. I didn't have to figure out how to make my mother happy or how to follow Mrs. Larson's rules. There was only one rule and it was clear: I simply had to believe.

In March of that year, with snow deep on the ground, I sat fiddling with the tissue pages of my Bible. It was 10:30 in the morning at Lakeridge Baptist Church, and I sat in the third pew, listening to my mother sing. She stood at the pulpit in her lavender print suit, taking deep breaths and sending out song. She had a beautiful voice, a euphonic, sweet soprano that fluttered over the congregation. As always, I was vaguely startled to hear her sing, aware I was seeing and hearing a part of her that wasn't really mine. Though we had a piano in our living room at home, my mother rarely played, nor did she teach us children's songs or ever burst into happy lyrics herself while moving through the rooms of our house. It was only in church that she turned into a songbird. My father, who was tone deaf and couldn't for the life of him hold a tune, was the one much more likely to burst into song while strolling through our house, belting out Mel Tormé songs or his favorite. *Oh, Danny boy . . .*

"Blessed are we to have beautiful voices in our flock," Pastor Bill said, as my mother stepped down from the pulpit and slipped into the pew beside me and Barbara Ann.

I shifted and sighed. The hard oak pew pushed against the knobs of my spine, and my bottom felt bloodless and numb. Barbara Ann nudged me, sliding her New Testament into my hands, the fancy one she'd gotten for her thirteenth birthday. It had illustrations of Jesus in Gethsemane, feet smothered in lambs. But not even this seemed enough to hold my attention.

Glancing around, I spotted Ruthie Belcher, a girl my age, further down to my left, leaning forward in the pew. She gave me a moist smile, her pale lips parted and pulled slightly downward, as if each corner of her mouth were tacked to her chin. Her cheeks were spongy and her skin was a faint, whispery gray.

I smiled wanly and looked away. Ruthie frightened me. When she was a baby, she'd caught a bad case of measles and the high fever had burned part of her brain. Now she had epilepsy—not the quiet sort, but big, rocking fits that knocked chairs and crashed plates and sent her head and spine slamming to the floor. Only last week, during Wednesday evening fellowship, I'd heard a commotion back near the potluck table, and a plate of brownies had skidded off the table cloth and bounced into shards and crumbs. Jumping up, I saw grownups huddled around Ruthie's chair. All I could see of her were her shoes trembling near the floor.

Now, I scooted to the edge of the pew and stared down at my feet. Lately, my own body had started to do strange things. Yesterday, I'd learned that I was having night terrors, scrambling up in the middle of the night, talking and yanking at Barbara Ann, entreating her to go with me somewhere, and then fleeing into the darkened hallway clear down through the living room. I had no memory of doing such a thing, and still wouldn't have known if Daddy hadn't teased me as I had headed off to bed.

"'Night, S'marge," he'd said, his pet name for me coming over the top of his newspaper. "No more of that running around, right?"

Confused, I'd stood blinking in my PJs, heat crawling around my ears.

"You don't remember?" Mama said, her tone light and doubtful, taking my shoulders and turning me toward the bedroom.

"You had a nightmare," Barbara Ann whispered as we trundled down the hall.

My stomach shifted as I shuffled beside her.

"How do you know?" I whispered back, looking at the floor.

"You were screaming. A lot."

Mortified, I slipped into bed, and Mama shut the light, retreating back down the hall. Barbara Ann said into the black silence, "You've been doing that all week."

I didn't answer. Instead, I packed my stuffed animals three deep on either side, pulled the covers up to my chin, and turned to the wall. I didn't want to know something or someone could be inside of me, someone hidden, whom I didn't know, and who got me up in the middle of the night.

Now, a folded note slapped my elbow and bounced onto the pew seat. I darted my eyes to Ruthie, knitted my brow, and shook my head, fiercely, long enough to see her eyes dim and her face drift back out of my sight, behind her mother's shoulder. I knew what the note said. It was inviting me over to her house after church. I didn't want to go. Not now, not ever. Her house was too much like mine: somber, silent, a carpet of sadness throughout the rooms.

Pastor Bill's voice wound down, and I knew without looking that he was raising both hands, lifting us to our feet.

"All ye who are weary, Jesus softly calls . . ."

I stood up, the congregation rattling around me, my limbs tingling as blood crackled through my veins and woke the wooden parts of me. Suddenly, I was aware of everything beneath my skin, my bones and blood vessels, and thick tangles of nerves. I didn't know I was clutching the hymnal with both hands and staring at the cover until Barbara Ann pulled it from my grip and hastily started flipping to the right page.

"Softly and tenderly, Jesus is calling, calling for you and for me . . ."

Barbara Ann held half of the hymnal toward me, and I took hold of it as Mama's voice lifted again into song. I felt myself lean toward the longing of the words, the tender lilt of the notes rising off the page. Everything was held within: love and tenderness, safety, a blanket of soft dreams.

"Come take your savior's hand, He's holding it out for you . . ."

A rustling beside me and a change of bodies bumped my arm. I felt Ruthie materialize beside me. She'd switched seats with her mother and now she pecked at my arm with her finger. I twitched my elbow away from her but tore my eyes off the hymnal, following her finger now poking downward to the floor. There, her foot was pressed up next to mine, our ankles all but touching, and our shoes, polished white, polka dotted and bowed, were exactly alike, as if our feet belonged to the same person.

"Whatever your troubles are today, whatever darkens your soul, hand it to Jesus . . ." crooned Pastor Bill, extending the traditional call to sinners to come forward and be saved.

I wanted to be as far from Ruthie Belcher as my feet could take me. For a blinding moment I sensed that, beneath my skin, she and I were exactly alike. We were bundles of nerves and bone, with a spongy orb of brain stuff that might burn with fever, or as Roddy's had, grow wrong in the womb.

I pushed the hymnal into Barbara Ann's hands and shoved past her and my mother, stepping out into the center aisle. It looked like a smooth runway, a wide slide toward a place without holes or questions. My feet flew past the pews and headed toward the altar.

Pastor Bill's eyebrows lifted as he saw me coming. Leaning down, he took my hand, enveloping my fingers between his palms, like two soft pillows.

"What brings you here today?" he murmured into my ear.

I lifted my lips and whispered, "I want to go to heaven."

To another life—to safety—was what I meant to say.

"And what must you do before you can enter the Kingdom of Heaven?"

I told him the answer, the one that would get me into heaven.

"I accept Jesus as my Savior."

He nodded, pressing my hand and guiding me over to his side. I stood, pushing back tears, swallowing hard at the knot bouncing in my throat. At last, here was what I needed—protection from the fits and forces that sent me stumbling through the night.

Chapter 6

Monkey Bird

Early on, I learned how to move through our house without making a sound. I didn't know what to do for my mother, covered as she was beneath the bedspread, her face blanketed with an icy cloth. If I knew anything about her headaches, it was that the smallest sliver of noise plunged like a knife blade into her temples and for hours she needed the black silence of a tomb.

One Sunday afternoon in June, I slipped through our screen door with the softness of a thief. Better to be outside where I couldn't disturb Mama. I was about to turn eleven and my early birthday gift, *The Adventures of Lassie*, was tucked under my arm. It was my very first hardcover book, a gift from my parents, and I wanted not only to escape the dark entombment of the house but also to find a special place to settle in and open to the first page.

Heading in my usual path, around the garage, I was drawn by the buzz of cicadas and darting flashes of dragonflies crisscrossing the half-acre field beside our house. We lived on a two-acre lot far out in the country, just past a bend in the road. Ours was a small ranch house painted soft lavender, the color my mother loved. The house itself wasn't much to see, but for me it was a glorious place. A wild, weedy field circled around the back, and in front, shielding us from the occasional ambling car, were four towering cottonwood trees. Their cool promise of shade and secrets harbored in the ditch at their feet drew me down the driveway. In no hurry, I zigzagged, watching the dirt puff up around my feet, unaware that within minutes I'd discover a way to fly.

My favorite cottonwood wore a raggedy lightning scar down one side. Reaching its trunk, I pressed the open face of my palm against its gray furrowed chest. Its years of growth pushed back against my hand, and for several moments I didn't move. I sensed something, my first inkling there were things in the outside world I might go to for comfort. Leaning in, I lifted my eyes and saw the lowest branch flexed like an arm, dipping just deep enough for me to leap and grab onto its elbow.

Swiftly, I glanced over my shoulder at the house, darting my eyes from window to shuttered window, and confirmed no one was watching. I didn't know if I was allowed to climb; the rules of what girls could and could not do and how they must behave, especially Baptist girls, baffled me. Already, I had learned what I needed to do to have adventure: namely, act fast and stay out of sight. Tucking my book into my waistband, I planted my feet at the edge of the ditch, hinged my knees, took a deep breath, and sprang up, flailing my spindly arms for the sky.

The rough bark of the branch burned my palms as I squeezed and dangled there for a moment, high above the earth. Then, clenching my belly, I swung a scabby leg high enough to plant one heel in the V of the trunk and hooked the other leg up over the limb. In another moment, I was up and scrambling higher, three branches more, until I reached an upper leafy platform. The flat bench of the branch fit my haunches like a saddle, and once I settled into place, my spine pressed back against the trunk, I sank into the scents of moss and bark, the tingle of leaves dancing along my ears.

Up here, the world was mine. Swooping my gaze back and forth, I scanned all there was to see beyond the borders of my yard. To my left was the rumpled rise and dip of the pond basin across the road, unseeable from the ground; straight ahead of me, the shallow slope of valley spilled down toward Bear Creek; and on my right, farthest away, was the Devil's Backbone, a bony spine of rock rising from the prairie, and behind it, the hulks of mountains.

Giddily, I closed my eyes and inhaled the smell of leaves. I felt like a tree dweller, capable of knowing everything that birds, monkeys, and flying squirrels already knew: that human troubles were small, little more than faint scratchings in the dirt. Hordes of grownups could shuffle beneath me and never know I was there. The limbs of the next cottonwood were so close that if I were to leap gently, barely lofting off my perch, I could float and land comfortably in its arms, leaves holding me like water, washing me in green light, catching my fall. The rough and ugly edges of the roots and ground below would be a million miles away, no threat to my airy bones.

"Margie Ray?" I heard the screen door crank open.

I held my breath. My mother's darkly coiffed head popped out from behind the screen door and swiveled as she scanned the yard. Her eyes were hooded and her lips colorless. Seconds passed. I knew she couldn't see me, and for a moment I considered staying quiet, foreshadowing what would grow into a deep pattern.

"Yes, Ma'am?" I said, giving in.

Her head flipped to the left where the gas tank hulked behind a bundle of shrubs, and then she looked back down the driveway, brow furrowed at the road, before she finally stepped through the door onto the porch and looked up.

"What are you doing up there?"

"Nothing."

"Well I swear, how did you get up there?"

"I climbed." A twinge of attitude edged my words.

She came out into the yard and headed down the driveway, a laundry basket full of wet sheets on her hip. I sighed and pulled my feet up into a squat, already anticipating her command for me to climb down.

Below me, she halted, put down the basket, and straightened up again, blocking the sunlight with one hand on her brow. The light glittered off the leaves and tossed shadows across her face. I still couldn't make out if she was in her dark mood. I blinked and pushed my bangs out of my eyes.

"Well," she said, peering up at me, shaking her head.

The light shifted, and suddenly I saw her mouth was soft. Surprised, I smiled, and then, just as quickly, touched my fingers to my lips. Her eyes held a yearning. In a moment, she dropped her gaze and stood in the heat, hands propped on her hips, looking out across the field. She chewed on her bottom lip, as she often did when she was somewhere else, and I thought, even if I swung from my knees, she might not notice.

A scamper of air lifted and twisted her hem, then dropped it, and twirled away up over the rise to the pond. Finally, she sighed and glanced up at me again.

"Well, be careful up there," she said, hoisting the basket onto her hip.

I watched her disappear around the house and then bob up again, farther away, at the clothesline. I sensed some kind of moment had passed between us. A kind of generosity I couldn't define. Something about my perching in a tree had lightened her spirit. I didn't know that she had been a tomboy before she fell ill with rheumatic fever. She wasn't allowed to climb trees or run with her brothers after she recovered. But before, as a seven-year-old, she had once slid between the legs of her older brother to make a backyard touchdown.

Settling into my treetop perch, I opened my book and began to read, beginning the first of many afternoons I would spend above ground. In the weeks to come, I simply left gravity behind, crawling up the same trunk three more times, until I'd mastered it, and then, I took on the other trees. Each one demanded a new cleverness, a renewed courage for finding my way up the fat barrel of trunk to the first branch; and then a careful patience for the next footing, the next grip and tug on a branch before trusting it with my weight. Slowly, I learned climbing trees was a kind of talking—a back and forth between me and the tree. If I paused enough and listened, I could venture out on raw branches as far as I dared, halting and gasping as they bowed and sprang under my weight. Every branch was like a dipping and swooping bird taking me out to another part of the sky, showing me yet a new view, a different angle of seeing.

As I gained confidence, I packed more than a book to take up into the branches: Ritz crackers and Kraft cheese slices, half an apple and a box of raisins; boldly, though disastrously, I once pushed my luck and taped a Coke bottle to my ribs with an ace bandage. It plummeted from my squirming ribs and shattered on the rocks below, startling me enough to lose one hand's grip for a few seconds as I wildly clutched at the air. My heart fluttered and sank when the screen door opened. Should Mama see me now she would change her mind and take my tree away. Instead, it was Barbara Ann who scurried toward me, rustling open a paper bag. Without looking up she squatted, plucking the angry shards from around the rock and dropping them into the bag, then sweeping the tinier slivers away with a floppy shredded branch she pulled out from the ditch. Quickly, rolling the bag, she stuck it under her shirt and glanced at me long enough to make sure I had my grip.

"Don't climb without your shoes on," she admonished over her shoulder as she zipped around the garage and disappeared, ferrying away the evidence that would have gotten me spanked.

After that, I carried only dry things up to my perch, special things I knew wouldn't break if they fell: my Bible, which I didn't open; and my diary, which I unlocked before starting upward, slipping the key under the cool hand of a rock, for safety.

By the end of July, I mastered climbing every cottonwood except one. The fattest and tallest stood alone on the opposite side of the driveway, its lowest branch far above my reach and its bark void of footholds. When I wrestled a boulder in from the sloping field, rolled it into place, and leaped straight up off the rock with my fingers open, I managed only to bloody my fingertips as they grazed the branch and to twang my ankle on the hard ground below.

Thwarted, I gave up on the last tree. Earthbound for two weeks with my swollen ankle and a driving summer rain that pelted the roof and windows, I stayed indoors, imprisoned. On the last Saturday of August, when I finally was able to lace up my sneaker and head back outside, the summer was all but gone. On the way to my old favorite scarred tree I caught sight of something new on the lone, fat cottonwood that stood by itself, silent and stubborn—the one I'd despaired of ever scaling. I stood and stared. There, marching up the trunk, was a set of wooden stepping stones, each secured by a single nail. Like a wonder of nature, they had sprouted overnight. The first was the height of my kneecap, and the last one nailed far above my head, where the tree's branch forked from the trunk and arched into the sky.

Where had they come from? I peered over to the front door of my house as if it had the answer, squinting in the hot light. No one was there. Shyly, I reached out and touched the block at my eye level. It was just the size of my grip and, when I tugged, it held fast. Lifting my right knee, I planted my sneaker on the lowest step and bore down hard, and then I shimmied upward, hand over hand, easily arriving at the platform of the branch, christening this final tree, my last frontier. Broader and more solid than any of the others, this branch benched me on its back comfortably, and I sat, swinging my feet and scribbling in my diary. *August 23. Up in the clouds. Want to live here forever. Signed, Monkeybird.*

Later, after my mother's call for supper and my climb down from the clouds, I dawdled in the doorway to the living room. My father sat in his wing-backed chair, reading the paper, and didn't look up as I sauntered in and perched on the edge of the couch.

"Daddy?"

The paper crumpled and dipped below his chin and his face appeared.

"I climbed the big tree out there."

He folded the paper into his lap and looked over his glasses at me. "You did."

"Yes."

"The last time I looked that branch was too high for you."

"Nope," I giggled.

"Huh," he grunted, dropping the corners of his mouth. "How 'bout that."

Pleased, I turned and ran down the hall to the bathroom and washed my hands for supper.

I'm not certain when my father first saw me struggling with that cottonwood. Perhaps the day I missed the branch and twisted my ankle, or the two Saturdays before, when I'd stood at its base, puzzled, staring up at its branches reaching to the sky. I don't know when he resolved to help me; perhaps when he saw me slump away from the tree with my bag of crackers and my book, defeated. As was his custom, he observed things from afar, rarely commenting on the goings on in our family.

Not until years later, after we had moved away from the cottonwoods, would I fully know why those nailed wooden steps meant so much to me. In a home like ours, I rarely felt seen, except when being punished. I couldn't have explained it then, but I knew my father had seen me. He was not an effusive man, but with the trauma in our family, the anguish of my mother—her sadness and headaches—he had closed off even further, numbing himself to stay strong. I was not aware of his sorrow then. Not until I became an adult would I learn that he had cried over Roddy. Through what must have been the fog of his disappointment and worry about both my brother and my mother, he noticed my quest and sense of failure. He must have known what was at stake. My climbing that summer was more than a childish desire to turn into a monkey or a bird. It was the first flight above my family's pervasive sense of sorrow; the beginning of a life-long quest to turn from what had happened to our family and run, and climb, and fly—what a lot of children do when they wake up in a family they don't understand and cannot change.

I couldn't have said it even to myself, but my heart knew. When my father chose and trimmed pieces of wood thick enough for my fingers and toes, and, when I wasn't looking, eyed the trunk and hammered each rung into place, he offered me his hand.

Chapter 7

Among the Dead

Not long after I ran down the aisle that Sunday and accepted Christ as my savior, I was zigzagging with my best friend, Lily, through the maze of marble and granite slabs checkering her front yard. Lily was ten years old, like me, and also small, with slender birdlike features and a zest that would one day win her a state beauty crown. She and her large Baptist family lived in the middle of Fort Logan National Cemetery in the southwest corner of Denver County. Their small, white clapboard house, bursting at the seams with six children and two parents, doubled as an office for her father. As cemetery sexton, he oversaw the business of proper military burials and caring for 160 acres of land marked for eternal sleep.

I didn't know then that only soldiers rested beneath my flying feet, or that the herd of headstones stretching away from us in three directions tapped out a rhythm of war dating back a hundred years. To me, this was like any cemetery, jumbled with all kinds of death and diseases, and anyone lying here was a Baptist, so, pleasantly, they'd all made it into heaven.

"Stop," I shouted, thrusting myself against a dark gravestone. Pressing into the cold granite, I leaned forward and puffed.

Lily halted, trotting backward and hitching her flank up on the other corner of the stone. Together, we wheezed in the soft warm air. From where I propped, I could look out across an acre of open ground, newly cleared and tenderly planted. A downy green brushed the land clear to the top of the hill. That area wasn't cordoned off, but we were forbidden to go there. Deep and gaping holes in the ground waited for new bodies, and if we came too close we could slip over the sides. A backhoe, miniatured in the distance, hunched near a pile of tarped dirt, and I saw, not far from its quiet blade, a new crop of crisp white headstones. I'd counted four the last time I was here, a mere week ago. Now, there were seven more, eleven in all: simple and unadorned, each chiseled with a single cross.

"What are those new ones?" I asked. "Over there."

Lily, still breathy, didn't lift her chin or look to where I was pointing. "They're from the war," she said, exhaling on the word.

A flare of alarm licked around in my chest. *There was a war? Where?* I couldn't fathom that there was a smoldering in another part of the world, a vague skirmish in a murky place I'd not yet heard of. Within three years, Vietnam would flare into a hot white roar, and body counts would bloat into the thousands, engulfing all of Fort Logan's open ground. But here, in the older, sleepy part of the cemetery, death felt as outdated and benign as the stones.

In part, I felt protected from death. I believed what my parents had taught me: Jesus held the tickets to everlasting life and now that I was baptized, I had one in my hand. I felt invincible and at the same time a little baffled. If it was so simple to get into heaven, why didn't God just let everybody know? And why were we Baptists the only ones in the know?

"Come on!" Lily snapped up and pushed away, zapped with new energy. I sprang off the stone, dashing after her down the main promenade. Paved wide enough for hearses and caissons, it felt like a raceway. If there were any tragedies, they lay fathoms below us, and in the sharp outlines of bright midday, I could run safely among the dead and go untouched.

"Do Catholics go to heaven?" I shouted to the back of Lily's sweater, which flapped and twirled like a scarlet cape. We were still in our Sunday best, our hard-soled heels churning on the pavement, crinoline and dotted Swiss swirling around our knees as we sped past thick slices of mottled marble.

I often seized the moment when I was with Lily, peppering her with questions in a ravenous way. I was starved for understanding and to make sense of life's rules. So little of it made sense to me. I knew as a Baptist that not everyone was going to heaven, and from what I could tell, Catholics were getting themselves kicked straight down to hell.

"Nope, not going to heaven!" Lily shouted, veering onto the grass and waving me to follow. A few feet more and she whipped her head sideways, flinging the sins of Catholics over her shoulders. "Idol worship!" she shouted over her left shoulder. Then over the right: "Praying to Mary!"

On her heels, I curved in and out of gloomy shadows and called out, "But aren't they baptized?"

"We-e-e-ell, it doesn't count. It's just a sprinkle," she said, lifting her palms up as if to say, what are they thinking?

I was incredulous. Even I knew you had to be dunked all the way under water or you weren't getting past the Pearly Gates.

"You mean they're all damned?" I trilled after her.

She slowed so I could catch up and then shrugged her shoulders up and down, up and down, staring at me bug-eyed and paying no attention to where her feet were going. Giggles bubbled up from my throat, escaping into the air as she twisted frontward and pulled out in front of me.

We rounded the corner plot and headed toward the distant shade of a shaggy willow. The toe of my shoe clipped her heel and we both slammed down, skidding on our bellies, skirts and petticoats whirling around our lopping legs. Rolling over onto my bottom, I sat up, calves splayed, a dirty green smear of grave grass etched across the white belly of my blouse. Blades lay flattened in a chaotic swath across the grassy plot, as if each of us had landed a prop plane.

I knew Mama would chide me when she saw my dirty blouse, but for the moment I didn't care. This is why I craved coming here: Lily and her siblings indulged in abandon and hilarity, and Mr. and Mrs. Sparler burst out laughing at their children. That never happened in my family.

At the farthest edge of the graveyard, just short of the brick out-building full of digging tools and machinery, we sprawled and caught our breath. Towering nearby, higher than the flat roof and reaching all the way to the branches of an overhanging elm, was a mountain of soil.

"What's all that?" I asked, squinting and shielding my eyes.

Lily followed my finger pointing to the mound. "Oh," she said, shrugging, "that's the leftovers."

"Leftovers?" I thought of refrigerated gravy and old chicken thighs.

She sighed, rolling onto her back. "From the graves," she said.

"How come it's sitting out here? Why don't they put it back in?"

"It can't all fit back in, silly. There's a coffin in there."

I sat for a moment staring at the enormous pile. It had a special name in the graveyard world: *spoils*. Though I didn't know the word, I knew that pile was more than a pile. It was a mound of death. I imag-ined scaling the crumbly sides, wondering if I could make it to the top before sinking into its soft folds, the clods plugging my mouth.

A shudder went through me. Death felt closer and larger and more permanent, and, even though I had been baptized and given a sure spot in heaven, it frightened me. I peeled my eyes away from the pile and read the name incised in marble behind Lily's back. "Colonel Robert Burien," it read. "Died with honor, 1943." An uneasy aware-ness came over me. A person lay right beneath me. His gravestone had sculpted grooves and a lilting curve to the top. Right in the cen-ter, gazing down at me and draped in hooded folds, was the Virgin Mary, mother of God. Her palms were open and beseeching, as if she were asking for a hug.

"Oh my stars," I said, a tiny choked sound, "he was a Catholic!"

Lily looked up. She was picking grass out of her hair, and her brow was scrunched into a little peak above her nose, both corners of her mouth dropped into a fish-lipped frown.

"So?" she said.

"Is he still burning?" I asked, not wanting the answer. Maybe I'd gotten some part wrong; maybe he hadn't gone to hell. He was a hero, after all. In some deep place I smelled a schism. How could God burn a hero?

Lily's eyes wrinkled as she looked at me. Then, she blew out her cheeks, a little wheezing noise, and shifted her eyes away. Lifting her gaze slowly to the sky, she raised her palms, higher and higher, and, just as she tipped backward, her legs flying into the air, she chimed, nonsensically:

"Bori-yori-yoring?"

I squealed and collapsed backward onto the tickly grass, my feet flying in the air, like Lily's. Side by side, we laughed and rocked, our cotton petticoats flapping like white flags. To anyone watching we were irreverent hooligans, worthy of a scolding and a stinging switch or two, rather than what we were: two little girls in an open-hearted moment of admitting how hopeless and baffling death was to us, no matter how many times we asked the sky for answers.

We went on like this until, suddenly, out of nowhere, a loud voice bounced off the tombstone into my ear.

"How dare thee!"

It was a deep voice, oddly muffled, as if coming from behind a wall. I jack-knifed up to a sitting position, twisting around to stare at Lily. For all my laughter, I knew I was taking liberties: running in my dress clothes, flopping around on the ground, not keeping my legs together, all vaguely attached to whether I was a good, clean girl, and worthy of heaven. Now, someone had caught us.

Lily grabbed my arm and pressed a forefinger across her lips, waving her other hand for me to follow. I crouched in a bent scurry behind her, over to a towering stone fat enough to hide us both. Lily stretched high, while I squatted low, our stacked heads cautiously peeking around the stone, like two blond owls.

"Blaaah!" A figure lunged toward us, grunting and snarling from behind a wobbly mask. Bulging from the center of its rubbery forehead was a single bloodshot eyeball.

"Cut it out, Billy," Lily screeched, darting away from her brother's stiff-legged stomping. She glanced back at me, delighted.

"Rrrrarrrr," Billy bellowed. "Ye sinners!" At fourteen, he was nearly as tall as a man. His two long arms flailed about as he clomped one way and then the other, his enormous hands clutching fistfuls of tangled branches and vines, as if he'd just torn a path through the swamp.

"Whoever he touches goes straight to hell!" cried Lily, taking off.

This was what I adored: unabashed flailing, screaming, heart-stopping fright, which dissolved into laughter—things I never got at home. I knew what I needed, though I didn't know why. Mirth was something I craved. With Lily, I could throw off the sorrow that pervaded my life, the stiffness of my family, the imperative for me to be an obedient, compliant child. When I visited her house, I lived inside a family I wanted: the Sparlers were messy and noisy, and had a zaniness that overjoyed and soothed me. With them, misbehaving wasn't about sin but about grabbing hold of being alive.

I ran, zooming around Billy Cyclops, just to catch his eye. I heard his "Huh?" and then his roar as he started after me. Picking up speed, I headed right for the outbuilding and that big mountain of spoils. At its base, I didn't stop, but launched right up the side, churning my legs like pistons, faster than the soft earth could swallow me. In seconds, I'd not only arrived at the top but vaulted off its summit, grasping the lowest branch of an overhanging elm and swinging up to land in its saddle.

Below me, Billy was getting nowhere, high stepping and struggling to back out of the dirt pile before he sank to his thighs.

"Dagnabbit!" he muttered, pulling off his mask and stumbling backward until he was on flat ground. He glanced up at me and said, "Rarrrr," like a big kitten. Then he brushed off his pants and loped away.

From my lookout, the eleven new gravestones were only tiny pinpricks of light. I could see all the way to the house, where Lily was looping around and speeding back toward me, and Mrs. Sparler was hollering out the front door, calling us in to supper.

It wouldn't be long before my mother drove up and I'd have to go back home, back to my life with my brother and the gloom. But not yet. Inhaling, I felt the breath in my body—the *Here and Now* of it. I knew I was alive and in another moment, as we gathered around the table for supper, scampering in from all parts of the house and yard, holding hands and saying grace and then passing milk and mashed potatoes, it would feel like forgiveness for tearing across graves, for leaping over stones, for giving in to abandon. For laughing at all.

Chapter 8

Put 'em Up, Boys

Before the year ended, Lily vanished from my life. She went away with her family to a higher-paying cemetery in hot, dusty Texas. Texas was like the moon to me: unthinkably far away and barren—a vast open plain riddled with cracks and parched weeds, and trampled with a lot of weary cows groaning and moving toward silly-named towns like Amarillo. I couldn't imagine Lily being there, nor could I understand how to go on without her.

The first Sunday without Lily I slumped in my scratchy dress, head propped on one hand, my mouth dry and quiet. My gaze flitted around the Sunday school room like a bird trying to keep twiggy feet from sticking to icy surfaces: the bare cinderblock wall, the worn piano, and finally, the aluminum window sill. Outside, gusty squalls shifted around the church yard, brushing bald spots into the snow and flinging ice grains onto the sidewalk.

Mrs. Desmond cleared her throat with a two-syllable "uh-hum," delivered like the swish-swat of a broom. My gaze yanked from the window to the front of the room where she pursed her lips.

"It's a glorious day for the Lord. Now, Margie, stand up and try that again, in a big voice."

I slid off the chair and straightened my knees.

"Arise, shine, for thy light has come," I recited, thickly. "Isaiah, 60:1."

My lungs felt flaccid as old balloons. Mrs. Desmond chuffed and pleated her lips in a show of disappointment at my lack of enthusiasm, motioning me to my chair.

Try as I might, I couldn't rally. My head rested like a boulder in one hand, the hour oozing from the clock above the piano. I raised my hand only once, and then only feebly. For the first time, I wasn't sure of the right Bible verse.

Later on, after worship service, I slid from my pew and tunneled through cheery wads of grownups, moving down the back hallway, through the nursery, and out the side door to the parking lot. The dry February wind scraped its bony fingers down my neck and inside my unbuttoned coat, chilling my belly and ribs. Still, I ran for the car as if it were an outpost. I wanted nothing more than to be alone.

The car door handle crackled under my mittens, shedding ice chips as I yanked it open. I slipped inside, scooting down onto the floor, my coat bunching around my ears. Wedged there, my spine against the wheel well, I opened the pages of my Bible to the Book of Psalms. I didn't yet know I was a lover of poetry, or that my passion for Psalms, with their singing forms, was less about worship and more about the grace of sonnets and couplets; how the cadence of words was a windy musical flight, lofting whenever I turned a new page.

Bless the Lord, O my soul . . . You set the earth on its foundations, so that it shall never be shaken . . .

Briefly stretching my neck above the seat to confirm I was truly alone, I scrunched back down and read the lines aloud. They were even lighter in my voice, lifting from the pages like ribbons, fluttering about the car, weaving in and around one another, so that when I reached the last word, I felt I'd flown on a carpet, woven by rhythms, to somewhere warm.

"There you are!" cried my mother's voice.

The Bible jumped in my hands. Through the window she was looking at me with an edgy mixture of pique and relief. She opened the back door and hoisted Roddy up onto the runner.

"What are you doing out here?"

I shifted from the floor and reached for Roddy's hands, guiding him into his seat. The door slammed. My mother got in the front, took off her gloves, and looked over the back seat.

"I've been looking all over for you. Why didn't you tell me you were coming out to the car?"

When I didn't answer she motioned me forward and felt my forehead.

"Ruthie Belcher was looking for you. She's invited you over for Sunday dinner."

I lidded my eyes and sank back against the seat.

"I don't feel well," I said, not looking at her.

"Hmmm."

I'm *empty* is what I'd meant to say, what I would have said if I were years older and understood loss and its stages of grief. No one had asked me if I missed Lily. I hadn't even asked myself. I just knew there was a new hollow in my chest. Time seemed more like a slow being, circling me, moving the clock's hands in increments or not at all. There was a time when I would have arrived last to my car, sneaking instead with Lily into the church kitchen for stray cookies, or ducking behind the altar to peer in the Baptismal. Or plotting to ride home with her, tangled among the Sparlers in the back of their station wagon, planning abominable snowman games. Now, all I wanted was to be invisible, to ride away before anyone invited me to play.

At home, I lay down long enough to fake a nap, and then cased around for a way to fill the long Sunday. Dragging my chalkboard out of my closet, I rattled its easel down the hallway. I wasn't sure what my mission was, but I headed for the living room, maneuvering around Roddy and his precision convoy of Hot Wheels and Tonka trucks lined up, bumper to bumper, in the hallway. He'd been there for an hour, aligning axles and bumpers, his bottom stuck in the air, his face close to the ground. Now, as I stepped over his puppy body, I saw the line of the convoy was dead straight, just like Daddy's pencil lines on his airplane drawings.

Feeling lifted by this somehow, by the promise of it—Roddy had such precision so he must a smart boy—I set up my chalkboard at the edge of the living room carpet and pulled over a single chair. Then, I went into the kitchen to butter some Honey Grahams and swizzle Hershey's into two glasses of milk: one for me and one for Roddy. My mission was taking shape: I was going to teach Roddy and fix his trouble once and for all.

I couldn't have known my brother was a small but clear dot on one extreme end of the autism spectrum, the opposite end of high-functioning so-called Asperger's. None of us knew then: not my parents, not even Roddy's teachers at the Wallace School for the Handicapped. Like most autistic children born into the world, Roddy was no savant, nor a high-functioning star. He'd come into life with a labyrinth of disabilities. His oddities, so familiar to me—the darting gaze, his flapping hands, his odd rituals and slurry words—so flummoxed his teachers that they shuffled him from one placement and classroom to another.

These details weren't part of my world at the time, but I sensed them, partly because of my own suffering in Mrs. Larson's class. Roddy's welfare, I reasoned, rested with me at home, rather than out in a world full of mean teachers. All his brain needed to catch up with mine was practice, like learning to tie shoes, or ride a bike, or scale a fat tree. Once he got a hang of it, from someone older, someone like me, he'd always know how. He'd never forget again.

"Mama, he did it!" I called out to the kitchen, where my mother was frying up a chicken. Not fifteen minutes had passed since I'd coaxed Roddy to sit in front of my chalkboard and we'd plunged into our first lesson. "He counted all the way to ten!"

"Is that right?" She turned from the stove, tongs poised above the sizzling pan, a faint, soft smile on her lips. When I saw her face, a note of hope around her eyes, I felt a triumph that kicked back at the world.

I know now a deeper thing ran beneath that afternoon. I was beginning to grapple with hopelessness and anger. With the powerlessness I felt in the wake of my mother's sorrow and my brother's troubles. For all my seeming patience and benevolence, my efforts to help Roddy were a way to thumb my nose at life's wrongdoing.

When I softened my tone, pointing to the numbers and sounding them out carefully for Roddy, gently clapping and saying, "You're so smart," again and again, no matter how many times he had to start over, I was taking a kind of revenge. I was being what Mrs. Larson wasn't, and what every child instinctively knows a teacher should be: kind, and willing to see all the way inside a child and to honor the treasures found there.

When Roddy sagged on the third round of numbers, I put down my chalk and carried in the tray of buttered Honey Grahams, and we ended our school hour munching together. And when he slid off his chair and tunneled back to the hallway with its soothing lines of cars, I let him go.

I didn't know then that my anger was an egged creature, small and contained inside me. It was quietly growing, gaining enough strength to puncture its shell. I wasn't aware it existed in me, or that I shared it with other children whose sisters and brothers were afflicted in some way. I hadn't a clue how fiercely it would emerge and drive my life.

Later that spring, my anger cracked through for the first time. I was sitting with Roddy on the school steps, counting sprouts of green nosing up around the concrete. Beside me, he munched saltines and made funny crumb-filled sounds. We were waiting for Mama to get through with my end-of-the-year conference with Mrs. Larson.

Part of me was nervous. I had little hope my conference would turn out well. Mrs. Larson was bound to spill all of my misdeeds: the time I tossed a scribbled note to Bethany with the right answers so she'd stop making frantic faces for help; the time I horsed around with Russel in art class and jammed a pencil clear through the soft pad of my little finger; the time I told Lynette to "shut up, we've heard about your new horse a million times." I knew I couldn't take these things back, and I felt a turgid rumbling under my ribs as if I'd eaten something rotten from my lunchbox.

Wrestling off my spring coat, I flopped over onto a slender patch of cool grass. A mad flurry of trembling blades caught my eye and in the next instant a roly-poly bug crawled onto my finger. When I tapped its backside it curled sweetly into its own self, rolling like a gray bead on my palm. I wondered if somewhere in the universe, some place where life was different and fair, people might be fashioned this way: born with their own armor and a way of enfolding their tender parts against the fierce outside.

Tipping my hand, I rolled him back to the grass, and then, I lifted my head. Something was odd. Roddy wasn't where he should have been, on the step, a few inches from me. A little spear zipped around in my stomach and my breath pattered as I twisted around, sitting up.

At the far edge of the parking lot, a bunch of boys clotted around the fire hydrant. Sniggers loosened like rocks and rattled from the circle all the way over to where I was. And then, a word spit from the cluster of boys into the air.

"Retard!"

Unhinging my knees, I bounded off the step, churning my feet across the twenty steps to the curb, boring myself through the clump of bodies, straight into the heart of the circle. There, Roddy huddled against the hydrant, dipping his chin to his chest, his little body slumped and motionless, except for the fingers of one hand mauling his bottom lip. I flipped my body around, straddling my legs and jamming a fist into each hip. I knew Roddy loathed being touched, so I stiffened my spine, creating a mica thin pane of space between us. The circle pressed inward, the boys' bodies purposely close. One boy, bulky and oversized, towered over my head.

"You leave my brother alone," I hissed up at his chin.

"He's a dummy," said the boy, pressing in and staring down at me.

"You're a dummy. Look at your face—you dumb dope."

Part of me watched these words spit from my mouth, hot and coming fast, at once exhilarating and fierce. I felt a soup of bad words boiling inside me.

"Fat lips!" I said, pushing up on tiptoe and pressing my face close to his mouth. His lids fluttered. I saw I'd hit a weak spot. He was a swollen-featured boy. I punched again.

"Blubber face. What's the matter, you got the mumps?"

I'd be whipped if Mama heard me, but I couldn't stop. A fury cracked deep inside me, elbowing its way up my throat. I felt breathless, now that I had my enemy—this big, lunky boy, whom I could slap with my words.

In that moment, I felt something sure—something I hadn't realized. I'd been waiting months for this boy, for a fleshy bad person, someone who was my brother's enemy, and mine. Someone I could punish.

Though Roddy had no way of telling me outright, he'd been sending signals all winter that he was being bullied at his special school. I'd come home from my own miserable day in fifth grade to find him in his bedroom facing no particular direction, arms stiffened and held straight out in front of his body, palms up and flattened, fingers curled into what I guessed was his version of boxing fists.

"Put 'em up boys," he said to the wall.

Another time, I looked up from the kitchen table and caught him peering around the doorframe. His flat hand was smashed against his face, palm outward, and he was staring with one eye through the webbed V of his thumb and forefinger, as if through some stubby, telescopic instrument.

"What's he doing?" I had whispered to Barbara Ann. She was sitting across the table from me, surrounded by encyclopedias, scribbling a report on Mount Vesuvius.

"I think he's scouting for danger," she mused, pencil poised above her notebook, discreetly glancing over to where he was peeking around the door. "He's some kind of spy."

Roddy wasn't looking at either of us, but seemingly at the refrigerator, or maybe the stove.

"Who's his enemy?" I whispered back.

I wanted to believe Roddy wasn't dealing with anyone or anything crueler than I'd ever experienced. I couldn't fathom anyone being mean to a child like him. No one in my circle had ever done such a thing.

For a few minutes, Barbara Ann and I both watched Roddy scan the kitchen for enemies, as if we might gain a clue.

"I'm not sure who it is," she'd said, finally.

Now, inches from this big boy's face and smelling his Beefaroni breath, I was sure. Even as he blinked at me, I wanted to sink my teeth again, gouge deeper with a harder word, something searing and foul. I found it stored inside me, lodged in a dark place where I thought I'd forgotten it—a word uttered once by a loud-mouthed boy behind the door of the boy's bathroom.

"Asshole!"

Spitting it out, I tasted ugliness, the kind that left bitterness in the mouth.

In the next instant, Mama was out the front door and the boys disintegrated, scattering in all directions.

"What did I just hear you say?" She gripped my arm and smacked my bottom, yanking me to the car.

Not long before, I'd have been mortified, cringing with shame to be spanked out in the open. Even in that moment, part of me flushed. But in a deep and secret place, I felt good. It was the price I had to pay for committing a sin for a good reason, by choice. As I rode in silence all the way home, tying and untying the bow on my blouse, I knew, for the first time, why swear words were in the world. There were times when only they would do.

Chapter 9

Aileron

In the warm, thinning light of summer evenings in Colorado, I knew where to find my father. Once our supper table was cleared and I'd dust-panned the crumbs away, I reached for the kitchen door knob.

We lived far out in the country beyond a bend in the road. It was a place of virtues for me, a wandering child of ten, prone to loneliness and reverie. At twilight, when chiggers and mosquitoes forced me indoors, I sought out my father's domain: our two-car garage.

Daddy's VW Bug, painted sky blue, always greeted me as I swung the door wide. Not two feet away sat Mama's finned white Fury, both cars side by side, the way my parents would be throughout life, an inseparable fleet of two. Despite this, I believed my father belonged to me. I was most like him, taking after his side of the family: my blondish hair a whisper of his mother's; my nose and eyes a regeneration of his aunt Malta; and my middle name, Ray, was the same as his first name.

One summer afternoon, I pushed open the screen door to the garage and, for a moment, paused, dizzied by the pungency of warm engine oil, gasoline, and treaded rubber. A funnel of soft light fell through the only window, and there, half-perched on a stool, my father curved like a fishing pole over his work bench, casting and dropping his fingers into a pool of parts and bits that seemed from another world: model-pins, X-Acto blades, ball-headed studs, swivel socket links, stabilizers. Dust motes swirled around his dark thatch of hair, curling upward to the ceiling where a flock of delicate model airplane skeletons dangled from the rafters, covered in sleek flawless skins of brushed reds and buttery yellows. Though meant to float on the air like prairie birds, Dad's airplanes, with their tissued wings and opaque membranes, appeared more to me like pterosaurs: mysterious, primal creatures taking shelter in our garage.

Though I didn't recognize it then, I sensed my father's awe. Aviation was a youthful and evolving dream in 1962, with nearly a decade to go before Boeing would fly its first 747, ferrying crowds of people across unfathomable miles as easily and comfortably as Chevrolets. Nearly as many years would pass before Neil Armstrong scuffed his boot in the dust of the moon. Flight and its mystery were imaginative and visionary, and, in the case of missiles and booster rockets, heroic and powerful.

My father didn't look up. I stood for another small moment, the door half-open, and inhaled a deep whiff of glue and wood dust, my lungs billowing and folding like bellows. In the next half second, a clattering sound exploded behind me from the back corridors of the house. Quickly, I pulled the door shut as the noise tumbled up against its hollow core, muffled and fierce. In a distant bedroom, Roddy's fists and heels whirled and pounded, bits of gears and toy parts scattering and crunching under his heels. The fury of his barking gave way suddenly to the deep thumping sound of his forehead, deliberate and unhurried, banging the wall. *Bong, bong, bong.*

My mother's footsteps hurried through the distant hallway as her voice rose and sank. Daddy's face lifted to the window, his hand stilled midair, a tube of epoxy balanced on his fingers. I knew he was waiting, listening like me, and Barbara Ann in some other part of the house, her bedroom maybe, holding her palomino mare and the big chestnut stallion still on the pasture of her bedspread. Each of us paused, stalled long enough to measure whether the evening could go on.

I carried only one word for my brother, then: *retarded*. Other words would rise as I came of age, obscure terms I didn't understand. What I knew was that he was a shy boy with a funny, flat-footed run and a loppy smile, and what was wrong with him had moved into our home like a seizure, unpredictable and baffling, thinning my mother's smile, rimming her hazel eyes with tears, and bowing her head in prayer.

A silence fell in the garage, a dense lack of sound. After another moment, the silvery tube in my father's hand resumed its journey downward, delivering a bead of glue into the waiting dihedral of the wing. Pushing out a puff of air, I shifted my weight away from the door and slapped my flip-flops down two steps to the concrete floor. Dodging the VW's fender and sidestepping the lawn mower, I came up to my father's side. He tugged a tall stool out from under the table and held it steady as I climbed on. Then, he chose for me a grainy square of sandpaper and a slender piece of soft white wood.

Balsa was an essence to me: a silky slide beneath my thumb and forefinger, a tangy citrus inside my nose. Its delicate airy thinness, when trimmed and deburred, could catch the edge of the wind and wing to the sky. I was finally old enough to build my own plane, and the piece my father handed me was not just any scrap, but my first wing, with a trailing edge and elliptical curve that could part and shape the air.

"Easy there," he advised.

I halted, mid-stroke, the heat from my vigorous sanding wafting up from the wood.

"But you said it's supposed to be thin," I protested, my voice reedy and high. I was an impatient learner with a penchant for perfection, and the tyranny of my expectations made me anxious and accusatory.

"Well, you're right there."

He paused, measured and unaffected by my distress, an approach that would both toughen and alienate me at different points in my life. I waited, jiggling my knee as he finished fastening a miniscule wire inside his fuselage.

At last, he straightened, satisfied with his handiwork, and turned to me.

"Can't flatten that wing, though," he observed. "It won't fly."

Taking up a pencil, he sketched a few strokes on the white paper surface of the table. Quick and clean, in a draftsman's hand, a wing appeared. Cutaway on the side, its elegant swell on the left edge spilled down to the right, sloping and vanishing into a mica-thin trailing edge. Three more pencil strokes and the wind arrived, slipping over and under the wing. He stretched his long arms up above the storage cabinet and brought down a wing in progress, shifting it in the light so I could peer down its length and register its curve. Then, he propped it in front of me and turned back to his fuselage.

It was the beginning of my long journey toward acquiring patience and the beauty of fine skills, neither of which came to me without struggle. As it was, my plane slowly came to life and, by summer's end, I was in the Volkswagen alongside my father on the way to a model airplane contest on the flat plains of Colorado Springs.

Feather-light, weighing less than a gram, my hand-launch glider rested in my lap, its thin fuselage like a glass straw in my fingers, its stabilizer barely thicker than a shaving. If not for the spotty brushes of red paint covering its surface and trembly black numbers I'd painted across the left wing, I wouldn't have believed it was there. Unlike Dad's plane, mine hadn't a hefty engine, or even a contraption for a catapult launch; it was too simple even for ailerons, the little movable flaps on wings that turn a plane into an acrobat.

"How do you say that again?" I'd asked a few weeks before, deflated to learn my plane was too young for loops and flips. Daddy had stopped tamping down his tobacco.

"Ay-ee-le-ron," he had repeated, holding his pipe a few inches from his mouth. "Tricky word. It's French, I believe."

"What's it mean?"

"'Little wing,' I reckon."

Hearing this, my head felt lighter. I caught the word out of the air and gave it to my plane, knowing she would need all the cleverness and French she could get. If my Little Wing were to have any hope of climbing into the sky, it would come partly from luck and partly from the strength in my arm and angle of my wrist as I flung her upward. Once airborne, she'd be on her own, up to the fate of fancier forces I didn't fully understand—downwash, drag, wake turbulence—all of which meant she'd either spiral upward, catch the wind, and glide slowly back to earth, or cut a half slice through the air, stall for a miserable moment, and plummet straight down as if shot from the sky.

Daddy pulled the VW into a dirt lot next to a crowd of other cars and we got out into a vast empty field. The sweep of space rushing all the way to the horizon made me teeter for a moment, and I stood pressed up against the car while Daddy unloaded our tent and cooler. Holding my plane, I didn't move until he called me to come on. Cars were pulling in all around us with trunks swinging open and car doors slamming. Boys tumbled out and followed their dads, toting tool boxes and radio control gear. Here and there, moms clipped alongside with plaid thermoses of iced tea and brownie-stuffed Tupperware. The air rustled with excitement, and we were surrounded by a pageant of airplanes, all graceful and long-winged with sashes of black and red adorning the wing tips and rudders.

In the bright bald daylight, Little Wing looked blotchy and small. Waiting for Daddy to set up our tent, I tucked her under my sweater and, once the tent was anchored, slipped her inside behind the cooler. Unknown to me, this was my pattern, a tendency to shield imperfection. For as long as I had been alive, whenever people stared at Roddy as if he were an animal, I had shifted my body in front of him. I did this now for Little Wing, stepping between her and the world's eyes, which I knew could penetrate and wither. In the shadows, she wouldn't have to feel shaky about who she was.

With her tucked away, I stepped back out into the sunshine and settled myself on the blanket next to the tool box. Its stepped layers hinged open to a treasure of doo-dads. Daddy sat in a webbed beach chair, fiddling with his remote controller, and I took up doing what I loved best, fishing out the parts and pieces he needed: a spool of thin wire, needle-nose pliers, the red-tipped cap to the glue.

"Howdy there, Ray," a man hollered out, pulling up to our tent. He had a paunchy middle and a round, balding head that looked pink and sore from the sun. "Heard you brought my oldest boy some competition today."

I looked up, shielding my eyes, squinting in the glare. A gangly boy with a head of dark, wiry hair shuffled just behind the man to a big-footed halt. And buzzing lower down near the man's thighs was a younger boy, a Shorty Pants, with a rooster cowlick that sprang from his head, like Roddy's. He was pitching a plastic toy plane from hand to hand, throttling the air with a whining engine noise and then plunging its nose in a low-flying death dive.

"Well you heard right, I reckon," my father said. He stood up from his folding chair, wiping 3-in-1 off his fingers, and held out his hand. Everyone knew my dad. He was a champion flyer, and our rooms at home were lined with his gleaming, spired trophies. "This here's my daughter. I expect she'll give you a run for your money."

The man let out a delighted "Ha!" His moustache split above his teeth as he grinned and shook hands with my dad. His eyebrows danced up and down and his pupils darted about, searching for my plane. Then he clapped a hand between his older boy's shoulder blades.

"Hear that, Buddy? There's a girl at your rudder!"

A small pulse of uncertainty penetrated my chest and lapped once around my ribcage. My heart did not like this man. His arm shot out and caught Shorty Pants in a neck hold, and he scrubbed the boy's hair with a knuckled hand as he snorted and caught my eye. He winked, the drop of his eyelid like a small, quick cut. Then he looked over at my dad.

"You've got a son too, don't you Ray?"

I dropped my chin to the tool box, where screws and bolts lay bunched in their bins. The air thickened suddenly in my ears and I felt something heavy pressed on my chest. Glancing sideways, I brushed my eyes across Daddy's face. A shadow flickered across his eyes.

"Yes sir," he said. "I do." His voice was not his own. Its color had shifted slightly, as if dampening down a shade. The man didn't notice.

"Still too young to come along, is he?"

The smallest of minutes passed. I thought of Roddy. If he were here, he wouldn't be bombing a toy plane. He'd be hunched beside me on the blanket, his little boy legs stretched out from his shorts. He'd be pulling on his lip, making his washing machine sounds like he does: hissing at first, then a low chugging in his nose, tongue thrubbing far back in his throat, followed by a *shush shush shushing* and a whispery trail of *rrrs*, and, finally, a whiney *yi yi yi yi yi*, meaning he'd come to the spin cycle, at last.

I picked up a bolt and turned it with sweaty fingers. Out of the corner of my eye, I glimpsed a rag in my father's hand wiping slowly down the leading edge of his wing, then his fingertips running back over the same edge, as if he were checking for splinters. I wondered if I could see inside my father's head, what would be there? Would it be crowded like mine, tangled with all the things you couldn't say?

"That's right," he said, finally.

When my father spoke again, he remarked on what a good day it was for flying. Then the boy's father said, "May the best man win," and they turned away.

I watched them go, the man's arm draped over the taller boy's shoulders, Shorty Pants running backward in choppy steps and jabbing his toy plane in the air as they disappeared into the sea of tents. In their wake, a voice rose from some deep place within me and broke the surface of what I feared. *Daddy doesn't have a real son.*

I gasped and jerked my eyes to my father's face, to see if he'd said this. I knew he hadn't. I got up and went into the tent, sat down in the shadows next to my plane, and wrapped my knees in my arms. My head, wobbly and heavy, lay like a stone on the knobs of my kneecaps. I couldn't say how long I stayed there, feeling a murky and shapeless regret that I was a girl. When I heard Daddy calling me to fetch my plane and come on out from the tent, I stood up, knowing I was different. No matter how well I threw or how lucky I got with the wind, I would never be a boy. And I sensed that I could never fill that space for my father.

When I stepped squinting into the sunlight, my dad was shaking hands with a man holding a stop watch, and I knew it was my turn to fly.

"Aren't you going to time me, Daddy?" I whispered up into his ear.

"No. No, that wouldn't be right," he said, matter-of-factly. "It has to be official. Go on with Mr. Small here. He'll record your time."

I moved off our blanket as if stepping into the deep. My courage slid like water down my legs.

Mr. Small explained I'd have three tries. To my dismay, the three would not be done all at once, but with an hour break in between. This was in favor of fairness, mixing up the breezes and elements like a deck of cards so that no one had an unfair advantage. But for me, who wished for a hasty finish, it only served to make me miserable.

Mr. Small may have sensed my distress. He was soft-spoken and kind as he led me beyond the tents to a marked-off space in the dirt and repeated the rules to me before walking a few paces away and holding up his stopwatch.

"Okay," he said. "Give it a whirl."

I turned Little Wing onto her side and placed the pad of my forefinger in the notch Daddy had carved in her wing right next to the fuselage. My other fingers slid down to the blob of clay that protected her nose, and squeezed. Looking out over the field I took a deep breath, and then another. Finally, knowing I couldn't wait any longer, I jumped into a sideways slide and whipped my arm in a low scoop, as if flinging a rock across water, winging the plane off my fingers.

Little Wing spun upward and vanished into the glare of the sun. I huffed and closed my eyes, hunching up my shoulders. I didn't want to see her drop like a stone and already I could feel a sting of tears under my lids. Mr. Small said nothing, and I guessed he was feeling bad for me. When finally I glanced over, he was standing still, stopwatch held out in front of his white collared shirt, looking up.

I frowned and lifted one hand up to shade my eyes, tilting my head back. High overhead, Little Wing hovered in the same spot, caught for a moment in a gust of air that pushed directly on her nose. Then just as suddenly, she sighed and slid forward, floating for several yards before dipping slightly and gliding for several more, then lifting gently and bobbing, as if I'd taught her how to dance. Unhurried, she circled and floated the way she was supposed to, and just when I thought she was coming down for a landing, she lifted her nose one last time and skimmed along the cheat grass another two yards before a tuft reached up and caught her, bringing her to rest.

Mr. Small clicked his watch and wrote down a number, which, by day's end, landed me a second-place trophy.

If I were any other child, I would have celebrated. I'd have held my trophy and paraded it to the car, tracing its wooden spire and flashy golden wings, exuberant and chattering. I'd have insisted Daddy swing into the A&W on the way home so I could order a vanilla shake and French fries, even though it was getting dark and Mama had a pot roast warming in the oven.

But there were so many reasons I couldn't rejoice. I wasn't a boy, and because of this, I didn't belong in this world of airplanes. Tangled in with this new realization was a harder truth: Roddy could not belong, even though he *was* the boy.

Riding along in my lap, her nose scuffed and her fuselage cracked, Little Wing likely knew what would, in the end, prove true. I would not go on to be a champion flier. Beyond that day, I would abandon her to my father's workbench.

Chapter 10

Split Levels

S pring came early the year I turned eleven, startling the buds into quick, hard blooms and rattling me with sneezes. I pushed my fists deep into my eye sockets and rubbed, viciously, feeling my eyeballs slip around like grapes.

"Don't," Barbara Ann whispered. "You're only making it worse."

We three—Barbara Ann, Roddy, and I—sat in the back seat, riding with our parents to the Goodings' house for supper. We'd been driving for an hour, coming in from the mountains and making our way through the streets of Cherry Creek.

"So what," I said, darkly.

I felt vengeful, the way allergies always made me feel. The fact they nested only in me, not Barbara Ann or Roddy, darkened my resentment. They were a part of my father I didn't want and couldn't give back. Pushing my face into a frayed wad of tissue, I rode on, too puffy to care where we were going, even as the car rounded into a driveway.

Barbara Ann nudged me and pecked a forefinger on her window.

"Look, it's a tri-level!" she whispered, breathy and awed.

I looked up through the windshield. The house before us was like nothing I'd ever seen. Not at all like our house on Lamar Street, a single flattened ranch. This one split into all kinds of levels, each with different-sized windows, plus a crazy mix of roof lines. It looked very cool, and suddenly I was filled with a longing that was new to me. I wanted to have it. To be a person who might live there.

Scooting after Barbara Ann, I crammed my wet Kleenex down into my purse and paused in the driveway with the rest of my family, straightening myself. I wore a new set of pedal pushers that zipped up the side and a stretchy blue headband I'd found in J. C. Penney's. My mother raked her fingers through my bangs. "Tuck in your blouse," she said.

Only a few fuzzy things were known to me about the Goodings and why we might journey all this way for a visit. Jeanette and Bill Gooding came from a time in my parents' lives I couldn't fathom, before I was born. They were Kentuckians and shared with my parents a Southern upbringing in the dense, drenched hills of Hazard. Like my father, Bill Gooding had emerged from the University of Kentucky an aerospace engineer, and had left Appalachia, wending across the country to the echoing plains, where he, too, was now building rockets at Martin Marietta.

"Well hello-o-o," Mr. Gooding said, pushing the screen door, arching it wide so he could see us. We were in suburbia, a mysterious land to me, void of cottonwoods and weedy fields, and full of soft clipped yards and houses stitched together by fencerows and sidewalks: a giant quilt of families. "Come on in. I'll hold the door."

Mr. Gooding looked like my dad, clean-shaven and lean, with a crisp-collared shirt and steady eyes. We clacked up concrete steps to the porch into a flurry of handshakes and tittery greetings. Mrs. Gooding joined in with a high sing-song, coming down the hall as we stepped inside, slipping off her apron and touching her short brown curls.

Behind me, Roddy was twitchy and I felt him tether back on my hand. Halting on the threshold, I waited as he sorted out which foot had to go first. In that early time, Roddy's rituals were mere glimpses of what would come later, when he was a young man, when he would pass whole mornings tapping his toothbrush, chopping in tiny steps down the hallway, freezing in doorways, incapable of skipping any of his ordered movements or complying with my pleading and pounding on the bathroom door. In the Goodings' doorway he was still a young boy and needed only a minute to switch his feet twice, and then, at last, step across the threshold.

The house was warmed with sunlight and smelled of pot roast. I looked around in wonder. Everything was wildly different from our house, where you tramped from the porch straight into the living room. Here, we stood in an open entryway, and all around there was a dizziness of directions. To the right was a living room, softened in creamy carpet and spilling backward toward a dining room and a long, clothed table, set for supper. Straight before us were two flights of stairs, inviting a delight of ideas. One flight led down six steps where it disappeared into something called a "den," Mrs. Gooding was saying to my mother. Or you could choose the up flight, lofting to where I imagined the bedrooms might cast a sky view over the backyard.

Staring up to the landing, wanting to fly there and look around, I gasped. A tiny figure was standing up there, a young girl. She was dressed in a daisied jumper, with a lacy, collared blouse underneath. She had a slender, heart-shaped face and blondish hair that feathered across her tiny nose. She tipped her head sideways, taking each of us in, her bright silvery eyes flitting about like fairy wings.

"Hi, hi, hi," she called out in a light voice. She sounded like a bird. Like a chickadee.

Hopping down the steps, her dress fluffing about her knees, she landed at the bottom a few inches from me and sang out, "Ta da!"

"Here's our Sarah," said Mrs. Gooding, sending up a clatter of chuckles from the grownups, a kindness of sound.

I blinked and looked away. Something was wrong. My eyes scuffled back to Sarah and, in a flurry of glances, I took her in. Her neck was bent sideways as if a hard swat had sent her head slamming down to her shoulder and everything had simply stuck there. Her toppled head, glued to the hunched knob of her shoulder, swung and pitched whichever way her shoulder moved. Beneath her shoulder waved an arm, which was less an arm and more a shriveled wing. Though its parts were all there, it looked as if someone had thrown it into a hot wash, shrinking it a size or two, her muscles shortening into taut bands that now held her elbow and wrist in bent and permanent angles. It looked like a turkey wing.

A hot flush came over me. I felt my lungs, like two huge petals, curl inward. She said something to me but I didn't hear. Her limb flung outward, sending her five fingers, which were pink and fluid, swimming in the air, like little eels. Rummaging around in my head, I felt for the right word and then hauled it up from a deep, muddy place. *Deformed.*

"Supper first, Sarah. Then you can show the girls your room," Mrs. Gooding said in a smooth and liquid-y voice, as if nothing were raw and sore in the room.

I looked for Barbara Ann, but only caught the back of her brown curls as she fell into step behind the grownups, heading to the dining room. Still holding Roddy's hand, I hung back as Sarah swiftly moved in front of me. She was a head shorter than I, though her mother, only minutes before, said she would turn thirteen on her next birthday. Down below, her legs and feet moved just like mine, carrying on as if nothing were amiss, and her one good arm, the left one, swung a good rhythm by her side. But everything else looked crunched and cuckoo, as if she were being silly, bent sideways like that, like a broken stalk.

I thought suddenly of the stonings in the Bible. How they bent people over. It was as if one of those stones had reached out of the sky and stricken Sarah; not a bull's-eye, as if God had aimed well, but off to one side, just enough to hurt her. From all I could tell, He had missed her brain but had still made a mess of her.

As I slipped into my supper chair, I held my eyes on my plate, relieved to feel Barbara Ann settle in by my side. The beefy aromas comforted me. Aside from a mound of pot roast steaming on the table, I smelled the smokiness of shucky beans and the buttery warmth of Sunbeam rolls. I knew my father was happy; he loved these foods. The Goodings were Baptists, too, and "Our Heavenly Father" resonated over the table in Mr. Gooding's deep voice. I was grateful for grace, for the few moments of blindness.

When I opened my eyes again, I caught my breath. There was Sarah's arm, inches from mine. She'd sat in the chair on my left and was passing a bowl to me filled with white fluffy potatoes.

"Mother mashes a good potato," she said, giggling. "That's what my dad says."

The bowl looked massive and fragile, like a baby in her arms. She squeezed it like a vise, her shriveled limb and hand turning blotched and blue as they braced hard against the bowled glass. Twisting my ribs toward her, I shoved my palms beneath the bowl. My breastbone bumped her head with a soft *bop*.

"Oops," she said.

She didn't let go even though her was head was torqued sideways and around the bowl, as it had to be, and her nose was nearly smothered in the pillow of potatoes. She angled her eyes upward, toward the top of her head, wrenching them high in her eye sockets until they caught hold of my face.

"Take a big scoop. We have lots!" she said.

Quiet settled around the table, the sound of people paying attention while pretending not to. I couldn't seem to move. My head felt dumb with confusion. *Should I do as she said? Let go of the bowl and scoop out a helping?* I didn't know how to be around her. I wasn't her sister, growing up beside her. I knew all about Roddy's affliction, which was inside. Hers was outside, where I could see it. It was like a bright hot light that stunned me, making me wide-eyed and stupid.

"Time's a wastin'," Sarah said, her voice still light but with a slight twinge.

My armpits felt damp. I'm not sure how many seconds passed before, finally, from the far end of the table, my father's voice stirred.

"Hurry up that bowl. I cain't eat 'em if they're cold."

Chuckles fluttered in the air. Though I blushed, I felt something unlatch. The Southern ease in my father's voice, the drawl he rarely used, brought Kentucky into the room. I heard my mother's girlish laughter. Though I was too young to know why, I sensed a lightness in my parents, as if they'd both shed heavy coats at the door, the heaviness they usually wore by being the only ones with an afflicted child.

I drew one hand from under the bowl and hurried it to the spoon, scooping a blot of potatoes onto my plate. In the next moment, Sarah released the bowl into my hands, and I narrowly had time to pass it on to Barbara Ann before the rolls came at me from Sarah's side, and then the hot bowl of gravy. Sarah chattered and ate as fast as anyone, spearing her beans, cutting her roast, pulling apart her cloverleaf roll and buttering it with swift swipes of her knife. She was vivacious and confident and she hadn't a drop of shame. I thought, *She doesn't know she's crippled.*

When Sarah asked to be excused to show us her room, my armpits felt dry and cool again. A kind of relief moved in, and I slid easily off my chair and up the six stairs to where she slept. Barbara Ann and Roddy came, too, and we clustered down the hall into her room.

It was light blue, like a pale western sky, with two windows dressed in white curtains, each trimmed in deep ruffles. In the shy way of girls, Barbara Ann and I made our way to her bed and perched on the edge. Sarah flitted about to all the surfaces, plucking glass figurines from her bureau and sea shells from her windowsill, bringing them over one by one. She liked having us there. The air warmed with her chatter as we turned her treasures in our hands. Then, she brought out her box of sixty-four Crayolas and thick pads of paper.

Barbara Ann drew a Palomino mare, the horse she kept wishing for. I, on the other hand, drew a seahorse and a funny tangle of lines that was supposed to be seaweed.

"I like that blue. It's a fishy blue," said Sarah, looking at my paper. "You don't have to go to the ocean to see the ocean."

I looked at Sarah's creature-hand flying over the paper, her wrist curled, her fingers tangled around the crayon as if she'd captured some prey. The white surface of her paper blossomed with intricate flowers and lacy vines, her colors, like nature, all in their place, neatly within the lines. Not five inches away, Roddy's soft, perfect fingers gripped the red crayon, all five pads choked up around the red knob. He was scribbling, senselessly, his page growing into a muddy blot.

"Wow," said Sarah, glancing at Roddy's page. Her face was full of wonder. "That's a whole bunch of colors."

Roddy's eyes cut sideways. The ends of his mouth hopped in a smile.

My hand felt suddenly leaden. A thought rose like a web of heat, prickling up through my arm and into my face, wrapping around my head. It felt like it grew from deep inside my nerves. There around the table, in all of our crayons, in all of our arms, even mine and Barbara Ann's, I saw something startling, something yawning and wide. I'd known it for a long time. *I had been spared.*

I felt a hot panting in my chest, as if a puppy were in there. I had never asked why. I looked over at Barbara Ann, her head bent over horses and dreams. Smartly, her fingers entwined brown and red crayons, tips together, brushing the rump of her mare with an arty chestnut blend. *Did she know she had been spared?*

I faltered then. I knew what it was to be the sister of a damaged boy, but this was something altogether different. I had a strange feeling inside of me, an inkling that I was seeing something I shouldn't, that wasn't good for me or for my family. Something I suspected and didn't want to know. I felt sick to think of it. *Maybe God didn't have a plan. Maybe we were all just accidents.*

The room stretched away from me, as if I were no longer seated there at the table, but streets away, looking into the window of this house and into this room with four children sitting here together, two of us with God's bruises.

I didn't like thinking this way. I blew out my cheeks and stood up, moving to the door, hearing my father's words: "If you see a supercell comin' at you, pick up your heels and run." Barbara Ann looked up, and Sarah, too, following me with their eyes. I was nearly to the stairs when I heard Sarah coming after me with all her might.

"Let's play tag!" she called out, rushing past me to the stairs. "Follow me!"

I didn't know why I'd been spared, and why Roddy hadn't. I didn't know the words "arbitrary" or "fluke," but I didn't need to know. I sensed them and was frightened by what they insinuated: God was either out of control or careless or just plain mean.

As I ran out after Sarah into the evening light, I ran away from my troubled thoughts. Thankful to pant hard and run fast, feeling my legs speed me along, around the swing set and through the baby aspen trees.

By the time we got back into our car, night was upon us, deep and unbroken. Sarah ran to the end of the driveway, waving, her good arm stretched high overhead, her small hand open and rippling in the moonlight. Her other limb stuck out like a wing, balancing her, keeping her upright.

In the darkness of the car, my hand lifted from my lap and touched Roddy's knee, like a soft cloth, patting just enough times so he knew I was there. "I'm sorry," I whispered, not knowing if he heard me.

I didn't know, as we drove away, that Sarah, years from then, would eventually marry and have a child. I didn't need this knowledge. Already, I sensed from the blossoms on her paper, her quick smart wit, and her small happiness hopping there in the driveway that she might have a chance for a full life.

Between her and my brother, I knew who was the luckier. On the way home, I prayed hard for any baby about to be born. *If you must, God, if you must smite a baby, then please aim poorly: strike bone, knock the neck sideways, shrivel the arm. Amen.*

Chapter 11

Mercy

On the hot slab of our driveway, a snake looped its sheathed muscle into a triggered pile, ready to fire. It was a small rattler, diamond-backed and delicate, its tail-tipped rattle barely larger than my toenail. I was eleven years old on that cloudless, blue-lit morning, and dressed for worship in a blue gingham sundress and pearl-button sweater. I had never seen a live viper, and I gazed down at its fluid fury, struck with wonder. My father held out a long-handled hoe, pausing long enough for me to curl my small fingers around the handle, then stepped back.

"Aim behind the head," he said.

The snake hissed and flared. Its dry, husked sound scraped in my ears. Moments ago, its beaded back had been stretched along a crevice in the concrete when I'd stepped from our patio to the car, clipping its tail. Each of us, reptile and child, had flinched and reeled, wondering what in tarnation the other was doing there. From the far side of the yard, my father had lifted his head, dropping the hose and moving toward me as if he were meant for this moment, hoe in hand.

"Don't dally," he said.

My hands gripped the wooden shaft. A dry breeze fingered the edge of my dress as if plucking it off my knees and out of the way. If bitten, I knew what to do: scalpel a crosshatch over the wound, suck venom into my mouth, spit.

Days before, I'd unfolded these instructions along with a bevy of snake bite tools out across my bedspread, fingering the tiny cutting blade and suction pump. They felt clever and important—part of my new life. We'd just moved from the outskirts of Denver deeper toward the mountains, and our new home sat on a raw, unsettled tract of land tucked behind the Devil's Backbone, a sharply crested ridge of earth shoved violently upward fifteen million years before. The neighborhood was largely untamed, vastly treeless, with stretches of prairie short grass broken by iron-stained rock formations pushing to the sky.

Though I'd always lived in the country, I knew this was a wilder place. I felt its intersecting and conflicting desires. The high-pitched cries of bobcat and coyote pierced the night outside my bedroom window where, barely a century ago, Ute and Apache hunted elk and deer. Within sight of our back patio, a natural wind-carved cave of rock reached three hundred feet skyward and once sheltered the Ute Indian Chief Colorow and his band of braves hiding out from government troops. Just beyond the road's curve to our lot, ruins of a stagecoach stop lingered among the scrubby pines and newest crop of cheat grass.

I felt my father's eyes on my back, urging me to act. If I hadn't been afraid someone could die—Barbara Ann, who steadied my world, or Roddy, who couldn't help who he was—I might have refused. I didn't know the coiled creature at my feet would as soon slither off into the weeds than strike me. Or that I was a bulky and inedible enemy, largely a waste of hard-won venom. In that moment, I felt only the adrenalin of survival laced with a dread of snakes.

Beware the serpent in the Garden. I heard Pastor Bill's voice fill my ear, as if I weren't here, but instead surrounded by our Baptist sanctuary, and these rustlings were not from a snake's tail but the pages of my Bible parting beneath my fingertips. *Be ever mindful of the Devil's disguise.*

The hoe in my hand flailed upward and dropped. The blade struck hard, dinging the concrete, at once shooting back into my palms a repellent mixture of hard surface and soft, violated tissue.

"Don't let up," my father said, behind me.

I clung to his clarity. His words held a certitude that came from deep in the Appalachian Mountains, where he was raised and slaughter wasn't pondered. In the depths of winter, when ice and floods wrapped the mountainside, sealing off my grandparents' dirt farm, the act of slitting a pig's throat or gunning an egg-thieving weasel was second nature. It kept the family fed and stirring. Eliminating predators and foragers, even raccoons and stray dogs, added up to another month of provisions. Coexistence was not something my father could imagine.

White-knuckled, I bore down, blade pinning the spine just back of the jaw. The body writhed and flicked. I squeezed my eyelids. Sourness seeped onto my tongue. I didn't know things fought so hard to live. Apart from flies and biting sweat bees, and one black widow spider that died with a swift clomp, I'd never assaulted a life before. *Please*, I whispered to myself, sensing, even as the tendons knotted in my hands, that releasing now, mid-death, would mean a harsher suffering. When finally the hoe pulled away into my father's hand, I opened my eyes.

"Stay back from the head," he ordered, propping the handle against the garage door and moving purposefully inside.

At my feet, the body lay blunted and unfurled. The head was gone. For a hurried moment, I scuffled along in a half crouch along the edge of concrete, brushing my fingers over the tender sprouts of grass and weeds, soiling the ruffled hem of my dress as I dragged along, searching for the triangular skull. At last I found it, cloudy-eyed and open-fanged, in the outlying gravel where my father had kicked it. Its jaws, I knew, could still bite, so I pressed my hands, tightly curled, to my chest as I bent over. I saw right away that it was no longer interested in me. Bone-white and covered in dust, it was already part of the ground.

"Young lady, what on earth are you doing? I can see your underpants."

Springing up, I blushed and yanked at my hem.

At the edge of the patio, my mother stood in a lavender suit and pillbox hat, a slender hand folded around her Bible, surveying the mess. From behind her shoulder peered Barbara Ann, leggy at thirteen, brunette and soft-curled. She was a girl of serious expression and she chewed at her cheek, moving her dark eyes from me to the hoe to the chopped snake. Partially hidden in her shadow, Roddy tilted his ear to one side, whispering to himself.

"Well, I declare," my mother said.

In the next instant, my father stepped from the garage, toting an old broom handle and a two-by-four. Wordlessly, he tweezed up the beheaded snake and gaited off to the field. I watched him go, striding by himself. He didn't call for Roddy to come along, the way a father might with his son. Roddy wasn't a boy who scampered to his dad, or toddled after him out to the garage, or tromped off with him to do away with snakes.

Barbara Ann's glassy-bottomed shoes racketed across the concrete and she came up beside me. Together, we watched as my father crested the distant rise, paused, and flung. The lithe loop of tissue, for a brief moment, revived, arcing with a languid twist through the air, as if it might sprout feathers and soar off to the nearest peak of Colorow's Cave. When, instead, it dropped to the weeds, my lungs slumped inside me.

"Oh," Barbara Ann said, her voice soft and startled.

"Well now," my father announced, striding back, "she killed her first rattler."

For a half second my mother looked pleased as she clipped around to the driver's side, opening the car door and steering Roddy inside. Stopping before me, my father held out his two curled fists and said for me to choose. When I tapped the left, his fingers opened to a scaly bundle: three horny rings, neatly necklaced, capped with a tiny fourth, the end button every rattler has at birth. Gently, I lifted the rattle with my thumb and forefinger, transferring it into my palm like an eggshell, afraid I'd crush this last part into powder.

"Hurry up now. You can wash your hands when we get to church," my mother said.

Cupping my hand and holding it chest-high, I climbed into the back seat. Part of me thrilled at bravery, facing down a fanged creature and coming out alive. I imagined a half hour from now, holding up my treasure in Sunday school, the boys fidgeting and reaching for it. I knew I'd keep it close to my ribs as I told my story.

Barbara Ann retrieved and slid my pocketbook onto the floor at my feet, then handed me a hankie from hers before getting into the front. My door clicked shut and my father turned from the car, his shoulders swaying from lanky strides as he moved back across the yard, taking up the garden hose and his quiet hour of chores before joining us later, for sermon.

As we drove from the driveway, I cradled the rattle in my lap. It was airy and weightless, like a bone.

"Remember what God calls this, children?" I could hear Mrs. Desmond say, her hand on my shoulder. "What does God say we have over animals?"

Dominion.

I whispered the word, its syllables riding over my tongue and through my lips like an echo, as if coming from a distant past and part of the world. It sounded like "kingdom," and "chosen," and "everlasting." Ringing words that held sway and made sense of suffering.

Still, something shadowy shifted in me. Pulling my eyes from my lap to the window, I gazed at the ditch grass and sage blurring past, and beyond, to the hogback, its long spiny backbone of rock rising and twisting alongside the car. Lately, I couldn't sort the questions bothering me, ones I didn't know how to ask. If I'd been older, I could have turned from the window, opened my mouth and said, "But why? How is slaughter godly?" Young as I was, I could only wad my worry inside my ribs and let it tumble there. The Bible seemed more and more to me like a book of blood, with animals and people falling alike. Even Noah seemed a sorry keeper of life. His big-bellied ark shut against slashing rain, bobbing in rumpled waters, stuffed with two of every beast, dry and breathing inside. What of the others? I wanted to know. The unchosen? Those threes and fours left behind, soft-nosed and bumping against the bow. Why all of those deaths? I'd dreamed of those animals, hooves splish-splashing. When I turned once to a center spread of cow bodies in *Life* magazine, bloated and floating down the Ganges, I thought of Noah and his ark. The way life looked when it was discarded.

"Did you say something?" my mother asked from the front seat. Her gloved hands turned the wheel, fluttering over and under one another, like doves.

"No ma'am," I said.

I had never questioned these things before. Always, I'd trusted what my parents believed: that cruelty was a part of life, of a just world—things had to be this way. How else to make things behave—and how else were we to stay alive? It was impossible to tell a snake to retreat and leave me alone—its brain was too small; it didn't know what was what.

Still, doubt swam around in my belly like a tiny minnow, fluttering against the walls. It was alone in there, in a place it didn't belong. As we turned off our dirt road and headed east out of the valley, I took the hankie my sister had given me and swaddled the rattle inside, folding in the corners and rolling the cloth into a puffy cocoon. Then, I let out a small breath and closed my eyes. I thought of the snake's startled surprise, the tiny frantic flame of its tongue, and, then, its helpless, conquered head. It stirred in me a memory I didn't want: of another particular day, another flurry of death. I pushed the memory back again, shutting it away.

"Do animals go to heaven?" I asked, opening my eyes.

My mother's ear angled toward me.

"No, honey. They don't have souls."

"They don't?" I said.

Barbara Ann's fingers reached back between the seat and the door and yanked, one-two, on my ruffled hem. We're Baptists, her tug was telling me, in case I'd forgotten; doubting God's rules is a sin. The car slowed as my mother paused, looking both ways, and then moved onto the main road that took us out of the valley.

"Haven't you been listening in Sunday school?" she said, finally.

Silence.

"They're not in God's image, honey, you know that."

I'm not either, I thought. God was a man, a giant who swirled around in a lot of folded fabric—a mighty two-legged being, who, once shaved and trimmed, would look like my father.

"Is that their fault?"

My mother's chin darted up. Barbara Ann's fingers yanked, harder. A tiny pop sounded in my ears as a stitch of my ruffle gave way.

"No-o-o," my mother said, her patience pulling on the word. "They don't have the brains to understand."

"Their brains aren't big enough?"

"Mmm-mm. And not the right kind."

I turned my head from the window and looked over at Roddy. He had his spy hand pressed up to his face, peering with one eye through the wedge of his thumb and forefinger. He was making his sounds and rocking. *Whomp whomp whomp*, he bounced off the seat, little puffs snorting from his nose.

I thought over the truths of heaven. You needed a big brain to get in, a people brain. But also, it had to be stuffed with the right thoughts, the beliefs inside your head. Otherwise, how to account for damning the Catholics and the Jews?

"Does Roddy have beliefs?" I asked.

My mother *tsked*, glancing disapprovingly in the rear-view mirror. Barbara Ann didn't look around. Her fingers let go of my hem and slid back to the front seat. I lurched onward.

"Does he have a soul?"

As soon as I let go of these words, they flew like windy seeds around the car and I couldn't catch them back. My breath caught in my throat. We reached the bottom of the off-ramp and my mother pushed the lever into park, then twisted quickly to look at me, eyes darting back and forth between my eyes. She didn't say *how dare you wonder if your brother is human? How could you?* But I felt her fury like a heat, and if not for the seat back separating us, my leg would burn with the sting of her palm. One day, I would understand her. Why she couldn't, at times, bear the world with its gray areas and complexities of belief. There was too much complexity already in our family, too much disappointment and confusion around my brother. I knew only that she had misunderstood me. *Is Roddy safe*, I'd meant to ask, *from a choosy heaven?*

I dropped my gaze into my lap and then out the window. I didn't yet know I was a doubting, inquisitive, resistant child—a rebel as it would turn out, destined to challenge the arbitrary lines of any heaven. This part of my nature had only begun to stir.

She slipped on her sunglasses and turned back to the windshield, easing the car back onto the road. When we pulled the car into the church parking lot, I got out, trailing after Barbara Ann and my mother, who was holding Roddy's hand. Once inside, my mother paused at the door to my Sunday school class and lifted one hand to my face. Smoothing a stray curl behind my ear, she said, in a softened voice, "God forgives those who can't understand," before turning and moving on with Roddy down the hall.

Though I felt relief at her words, I didn't feel comfort. I went in and chose my seat, without fanfare. When Mrs. Desmond, minutes later, announced show-and-tell, I kept my hand down, holding my rattle beneath the table, deep in its burrow of cloth. I sensed it was asking me for this, for a closed-in darkness.

On the way home, after sermon, I said I was tired when my mother asked, "Why so quiet?" But once in the house, I slipped from my gingham into pedal pushers and headed for the back door. Barbara Ann looked up, quizzical, as I brushed past. She was camped beside a plate of Honey Grahams and two iced teas (one for me), and her long limbs spidered around the funny pages on the living room floor. I said nothing. I couldn't explain. Something inside me was rumpled and unquiet.

At the end of our driveway I turned, opposite from where the snake dropped to its weedy grave, and headed instead across the field where our cambered lot sloped down to the dirt road. My breath steadied as I took in the wilderness. The sweet tang of prairie grass mingled with a toasted coconut smell I'd know one day was the sap of ponderosa pines warming in the sun. From farther away, gusting down from the escarpments, came a loamier smell, of needled trees and buried roots. I thought of that cottonwood tree I'd once scaled at our old house, spending a long afternoon in its branches, surrounded by the touch of its leaves. But even as I wished for its height, I realized it wouldn't be tall enough for me today. I needed something higher.

At the edge of the field, I stepped into the dust of the road and followed its puffs, veering off onto a smaller path. Riding deep inside my shirt pocket, the snake rattle knocked out a tiny rhythm on my breast bone. Though I didn't know why or how, I knew I needed to mark the snake's death.

When at last my feet slowed to a halt, I stood at the mouth of Colorow Cave. Its enormous crescent-shaped maw arched overhead, and I felt suddenly as if I'd paused in the opened mouth of a whale. I'd only been here once before, never alone. Light spilled down through the water-carved cleft in the roof, splashing on the flagstone floor and illuminating the sides and back of the cave with its crenellated walls harboring bats and pigeons.

What was I here for? A voice, a soft footstep, the smell of horse? I didn't have native ancestors to teach me how to honor a death. I didn't know what I expected to feel or what I should do. Arching my neck back, I loosened my tongue and clucked into the air, startling a swallow that flew from the shadows and spiraled up through the rain-carved crevice in the ceiling. Its tail feathers vanished like black points into the sky. Suddenly, I saw where I wanted to be.

Turning on my heels, I exited the cave and circled to the right, picking through scrubby pine, searching for a place to hoist myself up. The cave's roof slanted like a giant ramp, starting low on the front side and sloping up toward the back, where it peaked several hundred feet above the ground. If I had any hope of mounting the cave, I'd have to bushwhack through some brambles and find a foothold somewhere along this front face.

Stomping my way into the bushes, I was elbowing branches aside, scratching my face and forearms when, suddenly, I stopped. A deep-throated drone pulsed inside my ears. In a split second, I knew it wasn't human. Yanking my eyes about, I looked left and right, glimpsing a blur of color, and then, holding still, spotted a sparkling orb of green. I gasped, holding my breath, enchanted. *What was it?* Thumb-sized, it hovered no more than six inches away, upright, gazing straight at me. A hummingbird, I marveled. I'd never seen one before. Its throat, a deep rose, and the iridescent green of its crown startled me. Darting once to the left, then right, it met each of my eyes. I didn't move. The world was utterly quiet. I knew I was being observed. It whirred around my shoulders and then back to look again on my face. When at last I blinked, it disappeared.

A puff of loss escaped from my throat and I swiveled my chin to one side and the other, searching for its fluorescent whir. I had never been close enough to a wild animal to see its consciousness. More than its beauty, I wanted to feel its curiosity again, its measure of me. For those few shimmering moments, I had slipped behind its eyes and was looking back at what I must have seemed: a large featherless thing, agile but earthbound, less marvelous and beautiful. *What am I to you?* I wanted to ask. *What do you call me?* I stared again at the spot where I'd last seen it hover, willing it to reappear, but, instead, I spotted the foothold in the rock-face I'd been hoping for, a rain-carved gully wide enough for my shoe.

In another minute I was up on the roof, pushing my feet against the iron-red rock, heading straight up the incline. I practically ran, like a goat up a gentle mountain, hopping small crevices and scrambling with my hands and feet. As I reached the uppermost edge, I halted, just short of where the rock fell away. Holding my breath high in my chest, I inched my feet to the edge, keeping my eyes down on the red-scuffed toes of my shoes, afraid the slightest extra movement might send me, footless and gripless, into the open air. At last, I lifted my chin.

"Ah!" I drew in a sharp breath.

Everything about my axis vanished. Space swooped away from my feet, rushing across the valley clear to the foothills, wrenching and breathtaking. The earth opened in every direction, hazing into the sky, the horizon gone. To my left and right, golden fields stretched and rippled in waves, and there, in the middle, impossibly small, floated my house, its dark roof tiny and rafted in the sun-fired ocean. The sight stilled me and, at the same time, plunged me backward.

I knew, now, what was bothering me most: a fear summoned by the snake, not by its fangs, but by its death. I'd come here to reckon with it, and I could no longer hold off the memory of one afternoon, on a particular Saturday, right after we'd moved. The image of Barbara Ann, pale and breathless, coming into my bedroom, flooded my mind.

"Daddy found the babies," she had whispered, flicking her fingers as she stood there, as if burned.

"How do you know?"

We'd kept our secret, a pink and sightless tangle of fourteen babies in our hamster cage, for nearly a week. This was the third litter, one my father had forbidden.

"No more," he'd said, hard-jawed, after the second batch had been ferried out to friends. Wedging a wooden divider down the middle of the cage, he'd banned Whiskers to one side and Millie to the other.

Their scratchings—Whiskers raking and gnawing at the wood, Millie pacing frantically along the wooden wall—weakened us. They were the sounds of sadness. We knew nothing of hormones or bad timing. One afternoon, home by ourselves, Barbara Ann and I had lifted the furred bodies out of the guillotined cage and placed them together in the wheel barrel, free to waddle and wrestle, we thought, harmlessly, for a short while.

When eight weeks later the babies arrived, we dove into fluffing up the shavings around the nest, plucking up a wobbly straggler when it toddled out from under Millie's pillowed belly. I couldn't say what our plan had been. We hadn't had one, beyond a vague reasoning that if we stretched out our secret, long enough for fur to sprout and eyes to open, the babies would grow too cute to do away with. Shifting the cage deeper into the basement, we created decoys of noise, setting up our homework on the card table, ironing, sweeping surreptitiously.

My father rarely went to the far side of the stairwell, even on a weekend. His workbench kept him for the most part on the front side, directly in front of the door. Still, when Barbara Ann and I left our vigil on a Saturday morning, shopping with our mother, he must have heard something out of the ordinary that breached the rustlings of his workbench: a new muddle of movement. Little stars of sound.

"How do you know?" I asked Barbara Ann again, standing still, my legs surrounded by shopping bags, dumped and unopened.

She didn't answer. On some level, I believed our father would forgive. Partly because we hadn't meant to disobey, and partly because, I believed still, his heart was the same as mine.

We stood, not moving, and listened. The cage, directly beneath my bedroom floor, whined open and snapped shut, followed by my father's shoes tromping up the steps leading to the yard. He didn't stop to put on his boots, even though it was March, the ground chilled under a blanket of late snow. The basement door slammed hard. Neither Barbara Ann nor I went running down.

I didn't ask how they died. Barbara Ann, later, went down alone, peering into the cage, confirming what we knew was true. Summoning enough courage, she'd approached my father's bench.

"They're gone now," he'd answered, sanding a piece of wood, not looking up.

Turning, she'd gone to the door and climbed the steps out into the yard, far enough to see his footprints marking a path out into the snow, before coming back in and closing the door.

Standing, now, on top of an ancient cave, troubled and wondering, I couldn't erase the scene I'd conjured in my mind during the weeks that followed: my father, far out in the snowy field, stomping the babies, the shock of black hair flopping as his shoulders snapped forward, driving his heel deeper into the earth. Had he done so? Even as I wondered, a far more weighted question entered my heart. What was his dark anger? Did he know that stomping on our hamsters would wound me and my sister? His aloofness to their suffering made me feel alone.

Balancing there, perched at the edge of the world, the ground dropped away from my feet, I felt the different levels of life push up against my shoes. I was going against my primitive brain, trying to break through to broader ways of seeing the world, to understand the death of blind, tender rodents, to determine my place in the universe.

Reaching down into my pocket, I drew out the rattle and placed it into my palm. It felt like an old thing, fragile and everlasting. With one finger, I touched the papery rings, the hinged joints movable but silent without the muscle of a tail. A kind of knowing arose in me. I felt I knew something about snakes. They wanted to live as much as I did.

It came to me, what I would do. I'd honor this death the only way I knew how. Carrying the rattle home, I'd find the smallest of my jewelry boxes, the white one with its blanket of cotton. Lifting the lid, I'd move aside my birthstone pearl, and lay beside it the rattle's rings.

I felt some comfort, then. With funneled fingers, I slipped the rattle back into my dark pocket and, one foot at a time, stepped away from the edge. Turning, I eased down the keeled rock, knowing I was returning with new bundles of nerves, a re-circuited heart. As I touched ground, I paused long enough to mark the gully point in my mind; then, I stepped again into the field.

I couldn't have known this fully, but I was moving toward wisdom and who I was going to become. I was beginning to touch what makes up a soul. These moments—the hummingbird, a spate of senseless snowy deaths, and the untimely fall of a reptile—had opened a path for me I now chose to turn down. Away from dominion and judgment. Toward mercy.

I am a creature, too, I thought, pushing through the long grass home, stirring, with each step, a soft rustling sound—a rattling of grass.

Chapter 12

Laundromat

A mile or so out of downtown Hazard, Bea's Laundromat sagged off the back of a Phillips 66. Little bigger than a shed, it offered six worn washing machines pushed against the back wall, three dryers, two of them broken, a cement floor with a gritty drain, and four sorry kitchen chairs clustered in the middle of the room. Water stained the concrete, meandering in a slow ribbon across the floor, puddling in the corner. I trailed my sister and mother toward the back, set my basket on the floor, and stood up to assess the situation.

"Don't," my mother whispered. "That floor's filthy." She swooped up the basket and put it on one of the dead machines.

At eleven years old I had never seen the inside of a laundromat. As frugal as my parents were on my father's salary, we were never without our own washing machine. Neither were my grandparents. Both sides of my family in Hazard had the very best of GE and Maytag: washers, refrigerators, electric stoves, huge hulking freezers.

Still, even the best of machines broke down, and a few days into our summer visit the wringer washer in my grandmother's basement had made a raucous noise and conked. We were still waiting for a repairman. So here we were, on a Saturday afternoon in sweltering humidity, with a wicker basket and two pillowcases full of sorted shorts, sheets, underpants, Roddy's corduroys, and my father's shirts.

"Start the machine before you put in the soap," Mama instructed, still speaking in a low tone. "And don't crowd the clothes."

She was murmuring for a reason. There was another family in the room and we didn't want to know them. A noisy passel of kids, two in dirty diapers, three others in worn T-shirts and ill-fitting pants, all of them barefoot, orbited around their mother who was parked in one of the chairs. The mother's back was to me, but I could see she was colossal, fleshy-armed, and moist. Her sleeveless, faded housedress was soiled around the collar, damp between her shoulder blades, and darkened beneath her armpits with great wet half-moons. A thin gray crust discolored her elbows. An angry hot rash huddled in the folds of her neck, yawning and chafing whenever she shifted in her seat.

In a hard-scrabble mining town like Hazard, most everyone was either poor or poorer. Your station in life was determined by your whiteness, your cleanliness, whether you went to a Baptist church or not, and especially by how you spoke: your grammar, your choice of words. How fiercely you flattened your long *i*'s and clipped your short *e*'s from "get" to "git"; whether you said "ain't"; how loosely you drawled. One way meant you were backwoods, reclusive, tobacco-spitting. It meant you bore too many children, many of them slow, most of them inbred, all of them dirty.

I avoided glancing sideways, studiously dropping underpants and pajamas into the washer. Suddenly, behind me, one of the toddlers slipped in the puddle and slammed her mouth on the concrete. Gasping, I twisted around and covered my mouth. The little girl lifted her head and howled, her face blotched with muck, her lips and tongue split and beading blood. The mother cranked around in her chair.

"Git her up," she said, thrusting her chin.

I wasn't sure whom she was ordering about. My body instinctively moved forward but an older child slid out of a chair and padded over to the toddler, lifted her up, swiped her bloody mouth with a soiled shirt hem, and walked back to the chair. The toddler stood sniffling for a moment, fist in her mouth.

I didn't understand the ways of the world, how babies were made, how children were born. Like most girls born in the Fifties, I made it up. I had decided every girl had a certain number of seeds in her stomach and, magically, when she married, these seeds sprouted into babies. I still believed this, though I sensed there was something missing, something I was ashamed not to know. My mother had not told me why "napkins" were sold in bathrooms or why they cost a whole dime. Once, I'd blurted this question in a restaurant bathroom and she had giggled and glanced at Barbara Ann, yanking on the towel dispenser. They had shared a conspiratorial smile.

Blankly, I hoped I didn't have as many seeds as this woman. She must have sensed I was staring at her because she shifted around and looked in my direction. That was when I saw him: the teenage boy in her lap. He lay cupped like a baby in her arms. He was about my size, but so thin I couldn't fathom his years. He flailed like a large stork, stick-legged and loose-winged, his head lolling to the side. His parts meandered around as if they didn't know how to position themselves. His skull was shaved and pocked with scars, his mouth smeared with baby food. As I stared, his eyes rolled back and he shuddered.

Queasily, I glanced away and then back again. What would I do with such a child—who kept growing but couldn't feed himself or walk? When would I ever put him down?

"Margie," my mother said. "Pay attention here."

Startled, I turned and slotted the coins, triggering whooshes of water. Barbara Ann nudged my arm and handed me a pillowcase stuffed with pajamas and petticoats. Her lips held the pout she had worn all morning since arguing with Mama about mascara. From all I could tell, Barbara Ann hadn't even noticed the flailing boy.

"Okay, girls, I'm going around the corner to the Piggly Wiggly," Mama said, her tone both brisk and oddly sad. "We're short on detergent."

I glimpsed her face. She was pale and her eyes were moist and tinged with something fragile. Whenever my mother was doing household

chores she looked weary and downcast. But this was something different, something that had nothing to do with laundry. It was a look
of nausea and pity stirred together—the look she had worn for so
many months when my brother was a baby.

I sensed, as profoundly as any child could, why my mother was
troubled. There, in Hazard, she was surrounded by her deeply
Southern hometown, where belief prevailed that the kind of people
who bred retarded children were low and uneducated, whose bad
behavior and foul natures led to illness and plague, who were careless and unscrupulous, whose children were ignorant and soiled. They
looked like this family taking up the chairs, mixing blood with germs,
bedraggled, unclean, squalid, wretched.

Part of me understood why my mother left for the Piggly Wiggly.
Why she didn't come back until the dryer was done and Barbara Ann
and I had folded all of the clothes. She was a born-again, devoutly
Christian, clean, educated woman and, still, she had birthed a retarded
child, just like this behemoth of a woman with her piteous boy.

Over in the corner, the oldest girl bent over a bucket sink and
spigot. She had a washer board, against which she rubbed a colorless dress. I sensed she was my age. Her flimsy hair fell over her face
and she didn't bother to push it back. Strands clung to her cheek
and lips. I realized that she, her mother, and her siblings were not
here for the washing machines at all. They couldn't afford the necessary coins. Instead, they had come in here for the plumbing, the
running water, so they wouldn't have to go down to the banks and
suds-up the river.

I closed the machine and felt its agitation shudder up my arms.
The wash drum shimmied like a big bottom, getting on with the
task: loosening the grip of dirt, scouring soot and squalor out of our
twisted threads and Perma Press.

Casting around for a seat, I saw only one chair was empty, shoved
aside by the mother so her boy's flailing toes wouldn't wham its hard
edges. A *Family Circle* lay on the seat, wrinkled and manhandled. I
left it alone and instead hoisted myself up onto a washing machine
beside Barbara Ann, hanging my legs over the side, my sandaled feet

far from the dirty floor. There, I waited for the cycles to wring the last load, and for my mother to return.

It wasn't until I had switched all the loads to the dryer that the woman finally hauled herself and her boy out of the chair, swaying heavily from his weight and her own. I did not see her tenderness or realize that she'd carried her son a mile or more so he wouldn't be left alone for the afternoon. The way she held his head aloft and turned her body so he could see where they were going was lost on me. As she lumbered out the door and headed down to the river bank, I thought only that I did not want her life. Nor did I want my mother's. If there was any way to keep my seeds from sprouting I was going to make it happen. From all I'd seen, it was best not to have children at all.

Chapter 13

All God's Children

The air stank of fish. It was Friday and I scuffled after my friend Natalie, pressing my lunch box to my chest, veering around the hot lunch line and weaving in and out of chairs to the cafeteria's far end zone.

"Why do they have to eat fish on Friday?" I rasped, cupping a hand over my nose. My fingers smelled blissfully of pencils and glue and a faint swirl of Dentyne.

"Who?" Natalie wore a madras skirt that flung about her knees and her long, roped braids swished on her back like saucy tails. She chose an empty table and sat down, flipping open her lunch box and peering inside.

"Catholics," I whispered, my eyes darting around.

"How should I know?" Natalie dug out a package of Hostess Sno Balls and shredded off the cellophane. "That's what Catholics do."

Biting into the pink mound, she lost track of me for a few seconds. Her eyelids fluttered and her cheeks puffed with cake.

"How come?" My voice was high and pickled. Even now, at eleven years old and in my last year at Bear Creek Elementary, I couldn't add up the pieces of life. I wanted answers. Scraping out my chair, I tugged my skirt taut and sank down on the shivery metal.

"Maybe it's a punishment," I said, flinging the thought out in the open.

Natalie looked up at me, coconut whiskers around her mouth. She chewed, regarding me curiously, as if I were an odd specimen.

How had I arrived at this notion? I knew only that fish was a dreaded meal to me, dry and clinging to my throat, tasting of dirt and minerals. Even fish sticks, masked with bread crumbs and slathers of ketchup, were tolerable only with macaroni and cheese maneuvers following every bite.

Years from then, after I left home and the Southern table of my family for the Eastern seaboard of New England, I'd learn fish could be a delightful meal, with wild swings of flavor and tenderness. The ocean's bounty, in the end, would become my favorite cuisine. But then, in 1962, the thawed and over-cooked halibut sliding off my mother's spatula always felt like penance.

In my child's mind, my distaste for fish and what I knew of Catholics were woven together like bad threads in a carpet. Few Catholics went to my school, so there was little to unravel my confusion. I knew of only one Catholic boy. Buddy Gaynor was a foul-mouth who startled me. Without warning, he'd lunge at me at recess, agitating rocks and dust and snorting as he spun away. I couldn't see that he wanted my attention, that he liked me and didn't know any other way to show it. I felt only disrelish for him and his habits. Once every year, he came to school with a smear of ashes on his forehead, a dirtiness I wanted to wipe away.

"You're mixed up," Natalie muffled, spraying dark crumbs. She held her forefinger in the air, swallowed, and took a drink of chocolate milk. "They eat fish so they *won't* be punished. When they sneak bologna or hotdogs or something like that, they get into big trouble."

She put down the Sno Ball, tore open her Lay's bag, and snapped a chip onto her tongue.

"You mean if they eat meat they've committed a sin?" I flipped my palms up, exasperated.

"Yep. Bologna's the Devil or something."

I'd never heard of anything so foolish, or as worrisome. I ran my eyes around the room, scanning the hot lunch line for Buddy Gaynor. He wasn't there. Rising out of my chair, I craned my neck to see over to the boys' table, and sure enough, there he was, in the midst of a huddle, saying something he shouldn't and triggering a rumble of sniggers. His hands flew up and I saw they were empty. I'd heard he always skipped lunch on Fridays—that he was too embarrassed to eat fish.

Sinking back to my chair, I considered my own lunch. Unwrapped before me on a crumple of waxed paper was a soft Wonder Bread blanket covering a square of orange cheese, a leaf of lettuce, and a floppy slice of bologna. Peeling off the bread, I stared down at the pink meat. It looked fleshy and sunburned.

In the next instant, it vanished, right from under my nose. Whipping my eyes up, I saw Natalie looking dumbly at me. With a short, sharp snap of her wrists she sent my bologna straight up, launching it like a flying saucer. Neither of us looked up. We'd done this before, though always with dry wads of paper, rubbery erasers, or carrot sticks that ricocheted and bounced. Never had we risked a slimy slab of food that might stick to the ceiling.

We waited, studying each other's gaze, holding our eyes still and our edges straight. A tiny laugh moved my nostrils. Still, no bologna. Out of the corner of my eye I glimpsed Mrs. Cooper patrolling the outer perimeter of the tables in her thick-heeled shoes. Natalie drooped her lids. Still looking at me, she rustled her hand to my lunch box, pulled out a celery stick, and, flat-eyed, clamped down with a crunch.

"What's up, Doc?" she said.

I squealed. I couldn't help it. Instantly, other girls seated around us looked up from their sandwiches and demanded, "What's so funny?" Mrs. Cooper, clomping toward us, wanted to know what all the commotion was about, and just as she arrived at the end of our table, planting her bosoms before us, her fists on her wide hips, my bologna peeled off the ceiling, dropping like a wet rag from the sky and slapping me on the head.

Natalie threw back her braids and laughed, braying like a donkey.

For the first time, I found myself trundling back to the kitchen where the lunch ladies stood in puffs of hot steam and having to apologize. Then, back at the tables, I swiped from one end of the room, and Natalie the other, picking up dirty napkins and tossed bits of food. When I finally hurried down the corridor, run-walking over the slippery linoleum and making for the far end of the hall where our classmates were vanishing through the exit door, I forgot all about sorting Catholics. Natalie flipped around, pushing her bottom against the handlebar, and we spun out to the school's back lot with its wall of barracks.

Despite being tardy, I halted just outside the door, holding out my arms to the faraway mountains. It was November, Thanksgiving just over a week away, and snappy gusts of air hit my face. I took a deep breath, inhaling the clean scent of snow sliding off the Colorado peaks, finally washing the dead scent of fish from my nose. Natalie's tiny voice shouting "Come on!" spurred me back to a run. I tugged my coat collar up around my ears, speeding to the first barracks and scampering up the steps to where Mr. Hennesee stood, coatless, in a crisp white shirt and dark blue tie, holding the door.

I had begun to like school, partly because I was no longer in Mrs. Larson's class, partly because I'd discovered words and how they blossomed from my pen. But mostly, I'd fallen in love. Mr. Hennesee couldn't have been more than twenty-eight at the time. I'd glimpsed his pretty red-headed wife once from the classroom doorway when she came to school on a surprise visit during lunch. She and Mr. Hennesee stood on the sidewalk, murmuring and smiling over the fuzzy-haired baby held in her arms. All other times, though, I stashed his real life away where it didn't matter. When I sat in class, his blue-eyed gaze and clean-cut hair, his measured voice and fairness of heart, were all mine.

Now, at the top of the steps, I glanced up to catch his eye. Always, he greeted each of us as we came to the door, even when we straggled in late. But today, he scarcely nodded to me, a short curt drop of his chin with his eyes glancing to the door. My heart fluttered, instantly sorry for my bologna and bad behavior, and, especially, my tardiness to his class. Once inside, I paused at the coat hooks, staring back through the window. There he stood, on the porch, his back to me and the door, hands in his pockets, looking out at nothing.

The room was a shuffle of scraping desks and chattering noise. My seat was in the front row, directly in front of Mr. Hennesee's desk, and I maneuvered up the aisle around bumping bodies rustling books out from beneath the desks. When I reached my seat and leaned down to fetch my notebook, Mr. Hennesee moved soundlessly by.

As was true for every Friday, he paused at the front of the room, leaning his weight back against his desk. This was my favorite hour of the week, when Mr. Hennesee lifted the thick copy of *The Deerslayer* off his desk, unfolded its pages, and began reading the story aloud. Today though, he didn't reach for the book, but instead placed both hands to either side of his hips and curled his fingers around the beveled edge of the desk, as if making sure it was strong enough to hold him.

Something strange sat in his eyes. Like metal. The line of his mouth was thin. He looked like a different person, like he'd been taken ill. A shadow slid over his face and he took a breath.

"I'm sorry to have to say this," he said.

My heart dropped. He wasn't even looking at me. I had a sickening moment of regret, wishing I could turn back and undo all of the times I'd been thoughtless and late to his class. My elbows folded onto the desk top and I laid my chin in my hands.

"Our president has been shot."

A thick silence fell. No one moved. From above the blackboard, the clock tapped out a thin rhythm as if its hands were tiny sticks. Several seconds passed, and then someone, in a quiet voice, asked, "Is he still alive?"

Mr. Hennesee moved his eyes, casting them high over me and toward the back of the room. I could hear his breath pushing out from somewhere deep in his lungs.

"I'm afraid the answer is no," he said. "The president died, just about an hour ago."

Silence. Someone shifted.

"You mean President Kennedy?"

"Yes."

A leaden hand pressed on my chest. My insides yawned, as if every part of me was wondering how to stay in place. I wanted to get up, leave, tear across the street to the junior high, where Barbara Ann would be waiting to tell me none of these words were true. I wanted to get home to everything I'd left behind.

Mr. Hennesee spoke again but I didn't hear him. He turned from this black news to ordinary things, helping us move on from this moment to the next, until the bell rang and we rose from our desks. I felt myself move out to the sidewalk, falling into step beside Natalie, wordlessly, and walking to the buses. All around, bodies moved and shuffled, shoes scuffed. No one spoke.

Living as I did far out in the country, my journey home was a long one. I sat alone, the seats emptying around me, and when I stepped off the bus at the mouth of Crestbrook Drive, I felt the oddness of the ground. In the wake of the exhaust, I couldn't get my bearings. I no longer felt eleven, or hungry, or wishful. Or that I owned any of the parts I'd woken up with that morning.

Dampened and chilled, the ground pushed up through my shoes. I left the pavement and took the foot path, breaking through the field, crunching the wintered grass, brown and bent from the cold. My left foot, the one that tended slightly inward, rubbed against my shoe, but I pushed on, hurrying, wanting to get to my mother, to ask what it meant for the president to die. I wasn't aware at the time that even with my family's troubles I was a protected child: white, high middle class, raised in a home with both parents, and fairly certain that I would get a chance to live out my life. I had not been touched by war or death in my family. But somehow this felt like my death, like everyone's death.

Suddenly, as I crested the hill and my house came into view, I slowed my steps. A thought swam up before me, one I had been pushing down the whole ride home. *He was a Catholic.* A faint memory surfaced in my mind, of an evening three years before, when I'd woken in my darkened bedroom, the steady murmuring of the television seeping through the wall. A noise of despair had touched my ear, causing me to sit up and listen. It wasn't Roddy. I'd risen quickly, moving to the doorway, and peered into the living room.

The television flickered from the corner next to the fire place, and on the screen, a throng of people, wild and bobbing under placards and balloons, crowded around one man. In the next moment, his turned his profile to the camera and I saw, instantly, the face of John F. Kennedy.

A kind of horror and dread hung on my mother's face. She was standing, staring at the screen, holding her small hands to her mouth.

"What are we going to do?" she said, barely above a whisper.

My father's face was hidden. Only the back of his head was visible to me, steady and still above the horizon of the couch.

"Ray," she said, more urgently, as if he should get up and do something. Her voice caught. "We have a Catholic in the White House."

My father replied, his voice dark and derisive. My stomach fluttered as I caught only two words: *Irish Catholic.* I didn't wonder what he meant. I didn't have to ask. I knew the tried-and-true Christian we wanted, the red-blooded American we could trust, was not John F. Kennedy.

Now, as I lifted my eyes and started up the last hundred yards to my house, I felt my stomach move in a gray, watery roll. Was it possible that my mother and father would be glad the president was dead? When I stepped through the back door, the house felt empty, save for the faint, tinny sound of the radio. My mother usually called out hello from some corner of the house, and a new balloon of worry surged in my chest. Might it be possible this was a day of bad happenings, the beginning of the end, when the whole world was dying, and my mother and Roddy were already gone?

Then I heard the rumble of marbles, and I breathed. The sound drew me to the top of the stairwell and I followed it down the stairs to the basement den. There was Roddy, sitting on the rug, legs trembling, a fistful of marbles running helter-skelter down the gullies of his marble chute. My mother, a few feet away, looked up at me, the iron suspended in her hand. My father's striped blue shirt draped over the ironing board, sleeves limp and dangling over the sides. The couch was covered with orderly piles of underwear and socks.

"The President died," I said, hoping she'd say it wasn't so.

"Yes." She nodded to the radio.

I scanned the edges of her eyes and face, searching for what was there. She shook her head quietly in a way I couldn't read. Was she horrified at what the world was coming to? Or was she saying, *I might have told you this would happen*? I didn't know. She looked down again, steam sputtering from the iron.

"Who killed him?" I said, my voice high and hurt.

"I'm not sure, honey. They've arrested somebody."

I sank down into the couch, my dress wrinkling under my thighs, and looked over at Roddy a few feet away, reveling in his marbles. His hands plunged like steam shovels into the bin, grabbing bunches of cat's eyes and hauling them up to the top of the chute. Dropping them in, he fell back to his haunches, trembling and flapping as they roared down one shaft and clanked to the next, gathering speed and spitting out the bottom, missing the bin and vanishing beneath the Lazy Boy.

Twisting around, he turned his chin and the perfect swirl of his ear my way.

"Under there," he said, waving his fingers at the dark under-chair.

I moved off the couch and down to the floor, dropping to my knees and reaching my hand into the thin crevice between carpet and chair. I felt grateful. For the first time, since hearing the news, I knew what to do. Moving my hand, I coaxed each marble forward, six in all, and placed them in Roddy's outstretched hand.

"More in there," he said, pointing again.

Obeying, I bent forward, and as I did, it came to me that Roddy didn't know. He wouldn't ever have to know. For those few small moments I felt some relief, and I stayed, fetching his marbles, doing this small task and collecting comfort.

For the rest of the weekend, the concrete walls of our basement den closed me in with the death of the president. The last time my family had gathered in this room, we had come together to laugh at the First Family. My father had brought home a comedy album—a spoof of President Kennedy's New England accent and his marriage to Jackie, her breathy voice and bubbleheaded decisions around decorating the White House. They both sounded like morons. I didn't understand every joke but giggled anyway, thrilled to be laughing with my family, a rare occurrence. I kept asking to replay the record again and again.

Now, I sat near Barbara Ann, my legs folded on the rug before the television, waiting for the next newscast, my social studies book opened and papers around me, abandoned. I couldn't bear my homework. I didn't care if it ever got finished. Each time I lifted my eyes and looked at the television, there it was: everything I wished wasn't real. I could hardly look, and yet, my eyes clung to everything I saw. A scrawny man in a T-shirt, the barren room where he'd nested and then aimed his gun, and the radiant face of Jackie Kennedy as she clutched a spray of red roses, riding beside her husband through throngs of people, ten and twelve deep, toward the Triple Underpass and the man in a window.

Time moved, as if bent, from this moment through death, to when she stood, ash-white, beside Lyndon Johnson and his oath-raised hand. The lifetime in between—John Kennedy slumping forward, Jackie crawling in panic onto the back of the car—weren't yet visible to the world. They wouldn't be for five more days. Until then, there was only this: a woman stricken, her dress splattered, her legs spidered with a madness of dark threads.

I scribbled in my notebook, sliding it quietly over to Barbara Ann. She looked down at my written question, moved her pen to the page, and wrote, in finely curled letters, *That's his blood*. I read these words and glanced up, quickly, to her face. She nodded at me, her eyes sorrowful.

On Monday, the whole world felt raw and sore. In the day's bleak and chilly light, I pulled on sweat pants, wrapped myself in a woolen sweater, and went downstairs. By one o'clock, the hour of the funeral, we were all there: my mother, ironing; my father with his pipe, on the couch; Barbara Ann, sharing the rug with me, her knitting in her lap; Roddy, fussing with his marbles.

I sat with my legs entwined in the cloth of my clothes, and the tragedy rose and swallowed me; this time to a deeper depth. I felt myself there, moving into the Rotunda with its high dome of air, holding fast to the velvet rope, breathing shallowly and not wanting to be there, on this day, in this year of time. Caroline and her mother moved forward, surrounded by silence. Together, they knelt, and Caroline's tiny gloved hand reached for her father's coffin.

I knew then the depth of loss, what it looked like and how it sounded—matted, deeper than sadness and despair. I stood inside of it, in the chill, my breath visible, the echoing clop of horses in my ear, the turning of wheels beneath a caisson, the thunder of guns. Soundlessness descended like a giant net over the whole of the world.

When I looked at Barbara Ann, she had a damp Kleenex to her nose. Her cheeks glittered. I didn't turn to where my parents sat on the couch. I kept my eyes forward, all the while pushing down my sorrow, even as the black stallion appeared, riderless, its hero fallen from its back. And even in the cemetery, when they lifted the flag—folding its edges thirteen times and holding it out for Jackie.

Not until her hands reached to take it did I feel something small break deep inside me. She lifted her eyes. In that moment, through her veil, I saw the shatter of a heart. And in that same instant, I saw someone I knew. She looked like my mother had when she first found out about Roddy.

Wildly, I swung my eyes around the room, first to my father's face, dry-eyed and solemn, and then to my mother's. Held above her folded hands, my mother's face, with its thick lashes and finely drawn cheekbones, was unnerved. Tiny hairlines of pain webbed her eyes.

I turned back, and for the first time, put my head in my hands. I let go my tears, feeling a hidden part of my own heart. In that moment, I knew Jackie and her children were suffering. They mourned and feared and didn't know how they were going to live through this. I didn't want to scorn them anymore, or believe they were sinners and weren't going to heaven.

On that November afternoon, in the midst of a nation's mourning, I made up my mind to love in whatever ways I could.

Chapter 14

Pieces

Seeking privacy was a suspicious act in my household. It meant you must be up to something, which I was. I was thirteen years old and sitting on the floor in my parents' bathroom, having dragged in the telephone from their bedside table and run the cord beneath the door. Now the simple act of dialing the number unleashed a clacking sound that bounced off the commode and shower stall, making me cringe. Snatching a bath towel off the rack, I hastily rolled it up and wrapped it around the carriage.

"Hello," I whispered into the receiver smashed to my lips. "May I speak with Natalie, please?"

"Who's calling?" Natalie's mother demanded sharply.

She knew who I was, but that was beside the point. Natalie's parents, like mine, had strict rules around telephone etiquette. One was to identify yourself, in case you were a good-for-nothing.

"This is Margie calling," I said.

If my mother were listening on the other side of the door this was the moment she would rap her knuckles twice against the wood. Miraculously, nothing happened. I exhaled and waited.

"Hiya," Natalie said.

"Do you have it? Did you buy it?" I rasped, beside myself.

She didn't answer. I heard some crackling and wire rustling and guessed that she must be putting the receiver up to her record player. Yes! There it was! The heart-stopping song from a band of hairy British hooligans: "I Want to Hold Your Hand" ripped straight through the phone into my ear and down into my lungs.

I had never heard the likes of it or felt myself rising to this dangerous delicious height. I didn't have to ask; I knew this music was not allowed in my house. Gripping the receiver, I pressed it against my ear lobe, cutting off the circulation. My ear drum buzzed from the beat and shuddered with the wailing of notes.

Until then, I had only touched a piano, my fingertips lightly prancing around on the keys. I couldn't imagine twanging electric guitar strings or wildly beating on drums. In my home, music was an obedient and diligent pastime. My piano teacher, Mrs. Desmond, the pastor's wife, taught me and Barbara Ann in the Baptist sanctuary. For the first hour, I sat in the pew and killed time during Barbara Ann's lesson, and then for another hour, I sat on the piano bench myself and plucked at the keys, sending my own notes echoing through the baptistery. The melodies arising from my fingers were silly and childish, assigned from a stepladder of workbooks. They weren't meant to stir the heart.

If I were to surrender to passion, it had to be religious. Fervor was not a word spoken out loud in my house, but in church, especially during revivals, it flew around and dropped people to their knees. On my own, I had begun to learn the notes of hymns, yearning for some sliver of emotion. "How Great Thou Art" was the closest I had come to feeling my inner stirrings crackling from my heart down through my hands and into the ivory keys.

A shadow rippled under the bathroom door.

"Margie, what are you doing in there?"

"Talking to Nat."

"What about?"

"Homework."

"Well, come on out of there, then. You can jolly well talk in the kitchen."

"Gotta go," I said into the receiver, pushing the button down. The music, galloping through the wire, dropped dead.

I was becoming handy at duplicity. Most teenagers do this sooner or later, but I was particularly skilled. The façade I had created as a young child, the ability to be two people at once, to flatten my face when everyone was staring at my family, to be invisible, aloof, unaffected, when really I was mortified inside, was a skill I now applied at home. I was one child when my parents were looking and another when they were not. Back in my room, I sat on the floor and pushed my back against the door. Though I had my own room now, my territory, painted in my favorite blue with a matching eyelet bedspread, I did not have a lock on my door; only my parents had that privacy. Still, it was place of my own.

Turning my transistor radio down to its lowest volume, I jammed it up to my ear. The wild thrash of rock and roll thrust through me, awakening a new realm of senses I couldn't name. I felt like a sinner, and at the same time, good and alive. I was awakening parts of myself I never knew I had, and I wanted to know them even if I had to veil them away.

One afternoon, I came home from school and went straight to my room. I had a hard, twisted rope in my throat. Nat King Cole had just died and I couldn't bear it. I didn't want this to be true. I had fallen in love with him. To me, he was pure romance, his velvet voice and suave rhythm just as alluring as the wail of the Beatles. He was another kind of passion, the part that was quiet and just between him and me, not on display. I didn't know how to relieve the ache in my stomach except to bring him into my room. He poured over the airwaves: "Ramblin' Rose," "The Very Thought of You," "Those Lazy-Hazy-Crazy Days of Summer." Sitting on my bed with one leg folded beneath me, I spread out my homework and listened, losing myself in his voice, riding on the waves of his notes, comforted in knowing he was still reachable. For once, I didn't have to turn down the volume or push my back up against the door. Nat King Cole was not the Beatles or any kind of rock and roll: He was Perry Como and Mel Tormé, singers my parents listened to all the time, the songs of whom my father bellowed out on the way to the garage.

Just as I finished my history essay, my bedroom door flew open, banging against the doorstop. I jumped, jamming my pencil into my thigh. My father stood on the threshold, his face flushed red.

"Get that crap off the radio," he said. He spoke through his teeth, his jaw bone clamped.

Startled by the tone of his voice, a kind of dark fury, I stared at him and didn't move.

"Snap at it." He did not raise his voice. He flattened it like a blade. "Turn it off."

Struggling to understand, to make sense of his severity, I dropped my eyes, reached for the knob, and clicked. The room fell silent.

"Get out here and help your mother set the table," he said, closing the door.

A wave of hot bile came up into my throat. Acid tears burned my eyes. Ripping a page from my notebook, I slapped it down and tore at the surface with my pen—the black ink slashing across the page. I didn't know my father's disapproval lay with Nat King Cole's blackness, not his music. The sin my father wanted banished from my bedroom was the admiration I had for a black man. In 1965, with post-Kennedy civil rights rumbling in the South, southerners like my father were uneasy. He had relocated his family to white territory, outside of Denver, in a suburban white neighborhood where blacks didn't exist, where there were no overt racial tensions for him or my mother to comment on, no black faces or attitudes to deride. But the racism was there. I would not know the depths of it until I was a grown woman and my parents had moved back to the South to live out the rest of their lives.

All I knew that day was that something ugly had crossed between my father and me. Until then, he had been my ally, my tree-climbing partner, my fellow plane flyer. He had been the one who never spanked me, who never raised his voice to me. Now, I couldn't get the look in his eyes out of my mind. It burned like a hot coal.

Blindly, I scribbled as if someone else held my pen—someone or something inside me. I didn't stop until the pen tore a gouge down the middle of the paper and I threw it on the floor. Breathing, I sat, holding the paper in my hands, looking at what I had drawn: five figures, a man and woman, two girls and a little boy. My family. Words bubbled from the man, my father, a fierce tall figure standing over me: *Get that crap off the radio*. In high heels, her shoulders drooped, tears in her eyes, mouth pursed, my mother ran the vacuum, its *roarrrrrrr* jumbled with *I'll blister you!* Barbara Ann in her Chinese coolie hat, bending over: *Go on get it over with*. Roddy on the floor pushing his lady bug: *Uh uh uh*. Me standing behind a door: *I want out of my family; fuck you!*

I had barely registered what I'd done before I crushed the paper into a ball, shoved it into the trash can, fished it out again, tore it into shredded strips, folded and tore the shreds into a hundred pieces of confetti. I didn't hate my family, not my sister, or my brother, not even my parents. I just wanted to punch the unhappiness, the dearth of joy in my home. Scooping the pieces into the bottom of the trash can, I covered them with wadded Kleenex, and for several minutes crawled around on the floor, retrieving stray bits floating on the air currents in the room. As if the anger of my family, my anger, could be destroyed and pushed out of sight, as if it could be shoved into a trash can and I could be rid of it once and for all.

Over the next two days, I trudged to school and back home, barely speaking to anyone. Not even Natalie could get me to laugh. I didn't tell her what had happened; I was too insulted and embarrassed. I knew my life was choking, though I couldn't say it to myself.

On the third day, my mood started to lift. Natalie had given me an early birthday present: a John Lennon doll. I had laughed out loud at its oversized head of hair, tiny black-suited body, and even tinier guitar. He was tucked into my pocketbook and was enough joy to make me forget about the torn paper and everything on it. I got home and headed to my bedroom, envisioning exactly where I was going to display John Lennon, right in the nook of my headboard.

As soon as I stepped into my room, my stomach roiled. There it was, on my bed: the whole portrait pieced back together, an intricate tell-tale puzzle. I reached out to scatter the pieces but, instantly, my mother was in the doorway. I looked up at her. She stood with her hands on her hips, mouth set, eyes dark: the same way she had looked every time she had lined me and Barbara Ann up for spankings.

"Did you draw this thing?" she said, as if anyone else would have.

I backed away from the door. I hadn't felt the sting of my mother's whipping in a long time and didn't want to feel it again. Swiftly, I blurted the only thing I knew could protect me.

"Mama, I tore it up. I was so ashamed, I asked Jesus to forgive me."

Then I did something surprising. I burst into tears. I had shredded that paper because I was afraid of my anger, not because I was ashamed of it. I didn't know what else to do with it. I had grown up hiding my emotion, my frustration and brewing fury at what God had done to my brother, at my mother's sadness, at the silences in my home, at the joy I envied in my friends' homes. This boil of fury had unnerved me enough to be careless, to slash my feelings out on paper.

My mother hesitated. I sensed she had seen something she hadn't expected to see. Something in the drawing. She stood for several minutes in the doorway, finally handing me a Kleenex from her apron pocket. Then, she gathered up the shredded pieces, cupping them in her hands, and walked away.

In her wake, my galloping breath and heart slowed. Mixed with my calming nerves was a sense of bewilderment. The time she had taken to put all of those pieces together, to slowly assemble each character, each bubble of damning words. I bent down over my trash can and peered into its empty bowl. A stray fleck of blank paper still clung to the rim, held there by static. Suddenly I saw her moving from room to room in the quiet of the house, emptying trash cans, coming into my room.

"—ck you!" the shred of paper called out, enticing her to look closer, to lick her forefinger and tap it to the paper; and with the other hand, dig past the wads of Kleenex. Tipping the can, she dumped the contents onto the bed, a snowstorm of flakes fluttering across the quilt. At least an hour, maybe two, it would take to put it all of these pieces together, but there was time—an entire day to fill. Puzzles required only patience, an eye for pattern, and a willingness to stay with the task. She was good at puzzles and patterns. Spreading all the paper pieces across the bedspread, she flipped them up so the marks called out to each other, and then patiently—steeled by initial outrage, then disbelief, then despair—she assembled them, one by careful one. Slowly, our family emerged, so different from the dream she had imagined as an eighteen-year-old bride so long ago. In the center, there she was, wearing the crown I had drawn on her head, roaring and blistering and driving the vacuum, a broken queen.

Chapter 15

Guns in the Family

Throughout my childhood a .22-caliber rifle rested in the coat closet of our home in Colorado, its barrel propped among the sleeves of my father's raincoat and the pleats of my mother's peacoat. Knowing what I know now, how far my parents were pushed to the edge and how close they came to a breaking point, I am struck by the fact that they—that all of us—are still alive.

My father grew up shooting his own food. In the basement of his childhood home, like so many in Kentucky, a gun case held a .410 gauge shotgun, a .35 Remington, and three .22-caliber rifles: a pump, bolt action, and semiautomatic. As a child, my father brought home squirrels and rabbits, and later, as the only boy in the family, he regularly went out into the backyard pen, picked out a pig, and took its life.

One summer, when I was thirteen, I stood on my grandparents' porch in Hazard and aimed one of the .22s at a poplar tree up on the ridge. Barbara Ann stood beside me, having already hit the trunk dead on. Apparently she was a decent shot. Neither she nor I had ever fired a rifle before, and I couldn't fathom killing anything, animal or human; it just intrigued me to hit something so far away on the exact spot I had picked out. It was like throwing darts.

Pushing my cheek against the cold butt, I squinted. The slender barrel felt too thin to be lethal, but the way it shifted wildly as I tried to keep it still unnerved me; it had a life of its own. Recklessly, I fired and it bucked and rammed against my shoulder, knocking me backward.

"Don't yank on that trigger," my father said. He sat in a porch chair in my peripheral vision, stuffing his pipe. "Squeeze it, like I told you to."

His tone irked me. It implied I hadn't been listening and, what's more, I shot *like a girl*. As a budding teenager, I picked up on his condescension without being able to call it such. Don't throw, don't run, don't bat, don't fish, don't pull that trigger *like a girl*. And yet, I was a girl. Over the last year, as I had put on my first bra and wriggled into a pair of hosiery, his manner toward me had turned more and more stilted and condescending. This was the Sixties, when condescending to women was an accepted practice, and my father was masterful. I couldn't have articulated it at the time, but I knew I was supposed to endure his subtle undercutting, along with sanitary napkins, budding breasts, and wobbly high heels. It was all a part of becoming a woman. I had learned this from my mother, who wilted and shrank beneath his remarks, her only protest a pained expression that she wore through dinner and sometimes for days. My impulse, on the other hand, was to bite back. I didn't know the words "chauvinism" and "sexism" at the time—the women's movement was only stirring—but part of me wanted to shoot the gun just to one-up his attitude, to prove I could master anything he handed me.

Red-faced, I recovered my balance and wiped each hand on the seat of my shorts.

"There's the rag," my father said, nodding his head to where an old washrag hung from a nail.

The screen door whined and my grandfather joined us, settling on the porch rocker and taking out his chewing tobacco.

"Cain't shoot with slippy fingers," Grandpa observed, good-naturedly.

It was 1965, and Americans could still order a rifle by mail from a magazine, though not for much longer. The killing of President Kennedy two years before had opened a raw wound in the nation's side. He'd been shot and killed with a rifle mail-ordered from an ad in *National Rifle Association* magazine. Two more assassinations loomed ahead, Martin Luther King's and Robert Kennedy's, and exactly one year from then, a sniper would climb into the clock tower at Texas University and end the lives of sixteen people in the first mass shooting of its kind. All of these slaughters would have to happen before the Gun Control Act passed in 1968. Only then would mail-order sales of rifles and shotguns finally be illegal, and most felons, drug users, and people found mentally incompetent would be prohibited from buying guns. This new law would infuriate my father.

Aiming again, I steadied the barrel until my eye turned watery, and then, with a firm but easing pressure, I pulled the trigger. *Blam!* A bit of bark spit from the trunk.

"Yap, she nicked her," my father said, approvingly.

"Well, Ray, does she really need to be doing that?" My mother's shadow stood behind the screen door. A tinkling came from the ice cubes in her glass.

My mother rarely challenged my father, and certainly not in front of me or my sister. But she couldn't abide guns or alcohol. Both had lacerated her childhood. At eleven years old, not long after she had risen from her sickbed and had begun to believe she might live after all, a banging came to her family's front door. My mother's parents, Marguerite and Benjamin, lifted their eyes from the supper table and looked at one another. Benjamin wiped his mouth on his napkin, rose from the table, and went to the door. An urgency of muttering drifted back to the table and when Benjamin returned moments later, his mouth was thin and set.

"Get your coats on," he said to my mother and her two brothers. "You're going to Aunt Jeanette's."

"Why?"

"Don't ask questions."

The reason would come to my mother in bits and pieces over the ensuing months, hushed whispers overheard, and gaps filled in randomly by her brothers. The story of that afternoon in 1940 had begun better than most: my mother's grandfather, Carl Knox, actually managed to make it home, stumbling back up the mountain from the bar in town. He banged through the screen door of his mostly empty house. The only one home was his wife, my mother's grandmother, Bertha Mae.

Though soft at heart, Bertha Mae was a gritty woman. Married at fourteen, she birthed thirteen children, losing only one to meningitis. She sold apples and slopped hogs, sewed exquisite and sweetly designed quilts, and left her husband several times. That very morning, Bertha Mae had gathered all of the jars full of grain alcohol from Carl's hiding places, hauled them to the creek, and dumped their clear, acrid liquid into its watery mouth.

Still, her resolve must have shuddered as her husband ravaged through the house. As with all alcoholics, he wanted more, and his fury mounted from room to room as he rooted and banged about. Her fingers fumbled with the slippery cups and plates swimming around in the sudsy sink, and when he clattered down into the cellar she felt her spine jitter all the way to her tailbone. He came roaring back up the stairs like a bellowed fire and the plate in her hands dropped, splintering in the sink as she spun away. Flinging her arms up to the rack over the kitchen door, she grabbed the family rifle and ran out into the yard.

"Don't come near me!" she hollered, breathless, her voice rattling through her teeth.

Carl, halfway through the screen door before he spotted the gun in her hands, halted, surprised.

"Aw, come on, you won't shoot that."

"I will. I swear I will!"

He whooped, launching off the porch. As yet, Carl had never laid a hand on Bertha Mae, but the whiskey turned him into someone she didn't know and couldn't trust. The fury that had so strengthened her earlier in the day dissolved now in the face of what she had done. She had defied him and, more dangerously, had deprived him.

She took off down the lane, lurching as the gun butt banged against her ribs, her footing erratic and wild as she fought the binding hem of her dress.

"Don't, Carl! Don't come any closer!" she cried.

He wasn't listening. He laughed again and she heard his footfalls gaining on her. Panic rose like bile in her throat and suddenly she stopped, twisted around, aimed for his ankles, and fired.

The gun bucked hard against her shoulder and the barrel moved. She saw her husband skid and falter, then drop like a piece of sawed lumber to the dirt. He wasn't ten feet away, and she could see a black stain pooling like oil through the cloth of his pants, not down at the cuff, but higher, at the pocket of his hip bone.

She screamed, calling out to anyone who might hear, and ran toward him. The neighbors, Jim and Ethyl Everett, hurried out and across the field, but when they saw the gun, they stopped and hurriedly backed away.

"No, please stay here," she said, her voice shaking. "Help him. I didn't mean to shoot."

"Don't blame her," Carl sputtered from the ground. "I drove her to it."

By the time word arrived at my grandparents' door, pounding so hard the knife rattled against my mother's supper plate, Carl Knox had bled to death in the road.

Bertha Mae cried for days. She lost control of her bladder. Though no charges were ever brought, a heavy pall of shame lowered over the family, deepening through the funeral, darkening for weeks in the newspaper and around supper tables across town. Bertha Mae closed up the house and no one in the family stayed or settled on that part of the mountain again.

Now, years later, as I wrestled with a rifle and felt its danger in my hands, I knew this story of my great-grandparents from family members, but had no way of comprehending how close I had come to a gun death in my own generation. I did not know that sometime in the early days of my childhood, when I was five or six years old, my mother had hunched on the edge of her marital bed, her eyes raw and red-rimmed with fatigue, her nose running, her hands wringing a handkerchief. Across the room, my father had leaned against the bureau, tightly wrapped, his arms folded across his chest.

"I'm going to kill myself and take Roddy with me," she had cried through a blur of mucus and tears. She uttered this despite the trauma of her childhood, despite her ferocious belief that killing oneself was a mortal sin against God, a flagrant flouting of His right to give and take life. For her to have even thought about ending her life, and then to have uttered it out loud in the same breath as threatening to murder my brother, could only have meant she was utterly distraught. She must have believed with all of her heart that she couldn't save my brother and couldn't bear to look at a life without that hope. All of her strength and dreams rested on her Christian faith, on her trust in Jesus, and God, and the Holy Spirit, and the whole lot of it was letting her down.

My father, stilled and silent, made no move to comfort her. In the way he had been raised to weather harsh times, he flattened his heart.

"You can go wherever you want," he said, finally, his voice hard and lifeless. Unrelenting. "But he stays."

Standing on the porch at thirteen, gun in hand, I didn't know my mother had ever threatened suicide. I wouldn't know this until I was fifty, but I sensed it then. If she had walked out on the porch in that moment and announced she couldn't do this anymore, she wanted to end her life, I wouldn't have had to ask why. I knew the story, even if it was rent with holes.

I lowered the gun. The tree, pocked and shredded, looked as if it might limp away.

"Plenty more shots left," my father said, thinking me discouraged. Smoke billowed from his pipe, its sweet aroma wafting up my nose.

I was straddling myself, one foot still in the stirrup of boyhood, the other in womanhood, realizing there were parts I could not take with me. Others I did not want to carry. Having seen the bark pit and fly like a bit of flesh, I felt no affinity for this metal weapon. I didn't need its weight or its violence, not for food, or pride, or principle. I sensed its shadow, how close it had come once, and could still come, to my mother, and how, in the hands of someone intent on killing, it might not miss.

"No sir," I said, hearing an inflection in my voice that I only used in Kentucky, "I think I'm done."

Shifting the gun carefully, the way my father had shown me, nozzle down, I released it into his hands. Until that point, I'd always tried to be the son that Roddy couldn't be. A weight lifted, a part of childhood I would not take with me.

Part II

Flight

Chapter 16

Wings

A human is not meant to fly. Powerful elements work against such a thing: the weight of muscle and bone, the wrench of gravity, a woeful lack of wing. But I had discovered a glorious way around these flaws. Bearing down, my feet pushed against the trampoline bed and, instantly, I propelled upward, rushing toward the ceiling, hanging there for a pinpoint of time. Far below me, Barbara Ann looked up, positioned at the end of the trampoline, ready to stop me if I yawed off course.

This was as close to flying as I'd ever come, closer than my swings and the perch of high trees. I had found a way to leave the earth. The most thrilling moment was not on the way up, but falling back down, the luscious swoon in my belly and zing of blood up to my brain. Plummeting, as I was doing now, was a weightless, boneless rush.

"Okay, be ready. On your next bounce!" called Mark, my trampoline teacher, as if he knew I was getting carried away and had forgotten what to do. He was standing on the metal frame, ready to spring in and catch me.

This was the moment we had worked for. I was twelve years old, and for the first time, I was going to tip the capsule of my body backward, spin 360 degrees, and break out in time to save myself, all on my own: without the snug spotting belt around my middle or Mark's hands catching and putting me on my feet.

In a split second, I sank into the bed and flew up again. Breathless with fear, I flung my arms up and folded my knees into my chest. I saw nothing, felt nothing—not the trampoline, not my sister, only a black blur of sensation. My body wanted to live, to break from spinning and see the ground. A flash split through my brain to let go, to reach for something, but I clenched and crushed my knees into my ribs. The thick canvas bed pitched into view and, in another millisecond, my feet appeared, touching down as if they knew what to do.

"All yours!" shouted Mark.

I burst into a smile. Mark grinned, hands in the air, dramatizing the moment. At the end of the trampoline, Barbara Ann clapped her hands once and clasped them to her chest. I had watched her learn the trick first and was determined to master it myself. Time and again, Mark had maneuvered me through the steps, forcing my body with his hands to lift high enough, spin fast enough, keep track of up and down. It was as much a victory for him as for me, this moment when the brain and body react together and do something marvelous. His ruddy features wore the heightened joy of a teacher when a slip of knowledge implants in a student, like a new gene.

"Again," he commanded. "Do not think. Just feel."

I couldn't have been happier. I was in the bowels of an industrial park, inside an inauspicious building full of vague manufacturing. The front lobby had a towering ceiling and just enough floor space for a giant trampoline and one strip of tumbling mats. It was grimy and hot and I wanted to stay there forever. This was Mark's world. He had been a circus performer until he'd caught one hand in some sort of machine that tore three fingers from his right hand. From all I could see, his absent fingers didn't faze him. He could churn out six back handsprings in a row, starting from a dead standstill and revving into an effortless and fluid flipping machine all the way across the floor, ending with a full twisting back flip just short of the plywood wall.

I longed to learn all that he knew: how to make my body morph into a gyrating machine, working in tandem with gravity and whirling through the air. I couldn't get enough. I wanted to feel and re-feel the sensation of release. Before discovering the trampoline, the only time I had inched close to the same euphoria was riding in my father's sail plane, feeling a swirl in my stomach each time the winch cord severed its hold and he and I were there alone, with only a pair of wings and the air's breath.

Now, I was the breath. I felt light and strong in a way that was new.

"A-ha, your mother's here. One more time, for her," Mark said, gallantly.

At my budding age, I knew Mark was handsome in a worn and rustic way, and I sensed he and my mother were about the same age. He flirted with her, recognizing what I did not: that she was beautiful and sad and admirable all at once. That she deserved to be flattered and to savor a bit of joy, the moment of pleasure that every mother longs for: when her child triumphs.

Glancing over to the gaping door, which stood wide open to the heat, I saw my mother and Roddy silhouetted in the sliding light. I couldn't see her features at first, but she stepped closer, over the tumbling mat, helping Roddy negotiate the surface, and I noticed that she was pretty and blushing lightly, her uplifted eyes anticipating pleasure.

I wanted more than anything to keep that pleasure on her face. Hastily, I pushed off the trampoline bed once again, bouncing with gusto, *once, twice . . .*

"Whoa!" shouted Mark, abruptly, startling me.

I buckled my knees, giving into the bed and gravity, breaking my bounce. He had never raised his voice, but then again, I had never rocketed into motion with such disregard, ignoring the fact that he was standing on the bed. He had stepped in for this round, knowing more than I did: that the second try was the more dangerous, when overconfidence makes you careless. I had forgotten that when he was on the bed we needed to bounce in synchrony. Because of me, his body now twanged upward, arching over Barbara Ann and diving for the floor. Horrified, I gasped, clamped both hands on my mouth, and ran to the metal edge, in time to see him buckle and roll on the ground, absorbing the force as if he were a paratrooper dropping in from the sky. Rolling to his feet, he lunged forward into a round off, back handspring, bouncing out of it and landing on one foot and one knee, gesturing as if to say *ta-da!*

We all burst into laughter, surprise ricocheting off metal pipes and the corrugated ceiling. I felt a rush of gratitude and relief. I had not caused his death, nor apparently was I going to suffer humiliation for my carelessness.

"Start over," he said, trotting back to the trampoline. In a few nifty steps, he hopped back up onto the frame. "But first, say what you know."

Reciting what he had taught me, I marked out the actions with my arms, reaching hard and fast up to my ears, then just as rapidly, clamping around my lifted knee as I mimicked tucking into a ball.

"Okay, go ahead. Turn her over."

The close steamy air was thick with desire. My mother had no knowledge of this thing called gymnastics, coming as she had from the remote mountains of Kentucky. She had seen me crushed in my first competition only six months before: a merciless, all-day meet with hundreds of girls. I hadn't even made it past the morning round. Riding home in the car, my parents up front, Barbara Ann, Roddy, and me in the back, I had fought a twisted wad in my throat. My mother had reached back over the seat and tugged on my sweater; she had tears in her eyes. Pulling away, I had snapped my face back to the window. I did not want her tears; I did not want to be the one who brought her to tears. Her tears were for my brother.

Now, as I pushed off the bed once again, training my body in this new language, I felt the muscles in my thighs surge with determination. This was something I wanted, for me, and for her. Some part of me knew my mother had seen my raw ability even though I'd lost the competition. She'd gone right out and found someone who could teach me and now, here I was, mastering another world.

On three, I reached hard, resisting the urge to see the ground, and lifted my pelvis to the ceiling, drove my knees into the wrap of my arms, spinning, spinning on my own. This time, my rotation was slow and I broke out a tad early, landing in a low squat, barely sneaking my feet under me. Mike did not intervene; he backed away and let me fight for my balance and finish on my own.

I sensed my mother imagined doing what I was doing. I had her body, her petite frame, her strong thighs, and her tomboy energy. Deep within me, I had her musician's rhythm and timing. If not for her birth in the middle of the Depression or her rheumatic fever as a child, she might have been me, the one up on this trampoline, learning how to fly.

As I straightened up, triumphantly, I didn't look to Mark; I looked to my mother. There was what I had longed for and didn't think was within my reach: her face flushed with delight, her eyes tearless and full of hope—of ripe, ravishing hope.

From that moment forward, gymnastics became my second family. I stayed after school three times a week and spent two hours in the girls' tiny gymnasium. This new world dared me to find my own way around being human, or at the very least to compensate for not having been fashioned with wings or a tail. I discovered a gymnast's world, a swinging habitat where, if I was strong, agile, and fearless enough, I could choose when and if my feet ever touched down. My body adapted with thick calluses that rose at the base of each finger and beneath the hinge of every joint until the touch of my palm was like a leather glove; muscle fibers in my groin and thighs stretched into elastic strands; my inner ear turned limber and vertigo vanished. I craved the chalk-filled air and the smell of resin, the thrill of mastering each piece of equipment, and the wonder of rewiring my brain and body into a winged creature.

The state championship meet, the very one in which I had so miserably failed that first year, came around again in the spring of my seventh-grade year. Again, I entered. These were the days when there was just a bare floor for floor exercise, no padding on the beam, and no flexibility in the uneven bars. Made of wood with a thin piece of metal down the center, bars were prone to snapping in half. Meets were excruciatingly long, judging slow, and preliminary and final rounds held on the same day. It was not unusual for a final competitor to land her beam dismount at eleven o'clock at night. But I was thrilled to be there. My adrenaline made me giddy, and I had to keep moving in the warm-up room just to calm my energy.

Sitting in the stands, keeping scores on her tablet and cheering me on, was my mother. She had staked out a spot on the bleachers and set up a way station for me. When I needed a respite from warming up, going over my routines, performing, and scoring, I went to find her, refuel with food and drink, confiscate a Band-Aid or a Kleenex, and go away again. She glowed with fresh enthusiasm and determination. At the time, I didn't know that she was a whiz at mathematics. She studied the judge's scoring, caught on quickly to the numbers, and kept track of how I was doing all through the day-long meet.

By the time darkness fell, I had not only made it into the final round, I had won my first gold medal. The silky blue ribbon sliding over my head was made all the more marvelous by my mother's fervent applause and bright smile beaming from the stands. Even from this far away the tears on Barbara Ann's face glittered in the bright lights.

I held still, sharing my victory with my mother and sister for as long as I could, until finally, the judge gently tapped my arm and motioned me to the floor.

Chapter 17

Cracker Jacks

Toward spring when I was thirteen, Barbara Ann came into my room and pretended we were ordinary girls. She sashayed over to my bed in pink pedal pushers, hair bound in a riot of curlers and skin flushed from Calgon and steam.

"Stop reading," she said, perching her hips on the mattress edge. "*The Sound of Music's* at two o'clock."

"So?" I flipped the page. I was deep into *Jane Eyre,* with Mr. Rochester draped on my shoulder as he hobbled, swollen-ankled, back to his horse, the two of us drenched in fog and promise.

"So, Mama said she'd drop us off."

A small, astonished yip came from my throat and I clapped my book closed. It was 1965, and in our small town of Morrison, Colorado, *The Sound of Music* was on everyone's lips. My friend Natalie had rushed out to opening night and the next day she'd trilled "Do, a deer . . ." nearly perfectly to me over the phone. But that was as close as I'd ever dreamed of getting to the film. Julie Andrews was playing a nun, a heathen. "Catholic" was still a strange and hushed word in my home, vaguely sinful, carrying ghosts of idolatry and odd rituals. I knew I wasn't supposed to desire or delight in the happy melody of a nun.

Barbara Ann stood and strolled to my closet, sliding the door aside and pondering my wardrobe. At fifteen, she was leggy and fully breasted in a way I'd never be, and already savvy to how rules might bend and sway. I couldn't fathom how she'd gotten our mother to agree.

"Roddy's coming," she said, casually.

"What?" I inhaled. "What?"

I didn't want to sound like a dog, barking *what what what*, but I felt like one, instinctive and agitated. I stared at the back of her head.

Barbara Ann flipped through culottes and home-sewn blouses, wire hooks *screak-screaking* as she zipped past outfits that wouldn't do. As if on cue, a raucous sound burst into the hallway and headed for my door. Roddy was on the run again, chasing after his ladybug toy, its whirring wheels and flashing eyeballs thomping along the wall. At eight years old, Roddy had no friends and spent hours scooting after his robots, quivering with excitement and flapping his hands, his corduroyed legs rigid at the knees, trembling, as if he were an open, buzzing current.

"Do you want to go or not?" Barbara Ann said, cocking her hip.

My heart raveled with yeses and nos. As a member of a family with someone not quite right, someone strange in the eyes of the world, I didn't know the right answer. My little brother no longer passed for "normal," not even from far away. Though he mostly stayed calm at home, dressed himself, brushed his teeth, and ate like a gentleman, outside our family home he often short circuited. The world was wired with triggers that set him off: lights changing, bodies bumping, horns howling, eyes watching. Each one flipped a time-delay charge beneath his skin, crackling his nerves until he worked up to a moment of implosion, when he'd disintegrate into a fit of flapping, twitching, and frightened barks. What was wrong with him had a string of names, words my parents had collected from different doctors and articles over the last few years, and which felt cottony and crowded in my mouth: autism, aphasia, perceptually handicapped. Only my family seemed to know these words. Whenever we stepped out of our home, only one word followed us, sticking to our heels like a mangy cur. *Retarded.* I didn't think of my brother as some sort of moron, but I knew the rest of the world did. As a young child I was embarrassed for him and for my parents, but not for me. I had been too busy running faster, climbing higher, spelling perfectly, and pleasing my teachers. But now that I was soon to turn thirteen, I felt a strange shift happening, a greater desire to fit in, a heightened fear of spectacle.

Barbara Ann *humfed* into the closet. "We'll be fine," she said, thrusting a dotted Swiss blouse and a pair of navy culottes toward me. "Roddy can sit between us. It'll be dark in there."

I so wanted to believe her: that I could be like my friends, like any other teenager. I yearned to feel more of life, to understand how I belonged. My thoughts slipped to the boy I'd fallen in love with, Wyn Anderson, who only days ago had flashed me a smile in school, letting drop that he was heading to the Cooper Cinerama that weekend. I thought of how my cheeks had turned hot and my stomach jambly and how I'd moved in a rubbery way down the corridor to home economics class. Word had traveled through currents around the lunchroom that he'd been asking for my last name.

A rosy feeling bloomed in my chest as I pulled my blouse off the hanger—a kind of courage. Barbara Ann was right: we'd be fine. The odds were in our favor. Anything that excited Roddy would be nowhere near him—no wind, no washing machines, no battery-operated ladybugs with flashy eyeballs that worked him into a froth.

"Besides," she added in my doorway, "it's a musical. Roddy loves rhythm."

Swiftly, I rummaged in my piggy bank and plucked up my comb, lip gloss, and Kleenex. For a moment, I paused at my doorway, breathing in little puffs, and then veered off to the kitchen, where I yanked out the Nabisco Grahams, Roddy's favorite. Wrapping a fistful in waxed paper, I tucked the bundle into my pocketbook and dashed out to the car, dipping under the garage door just as it trundled closed.

For fifty-five minutes, sagebrush and craggy hogbacks blurred past my car window before blending into thick traffic on South Colorado Boulevard. Suddenly, we were pulling into the sweeping entrance of the Cooper Super Cinerama. Fashionably, my curlers (necessary for tomorrow's church) were tucked beneath my blue paisley scarf, a tip from Barbara Ann, who'd swiftly allayed my fears that we both looked like hot air balloons.

"No, we look like we're getting ready to go out tonight," she'd countered.

Thrilled, I stepped out onto the curb. *I deserve to be here, at the Cooper, like everybody else*, I thought.

"Take Roddy's hand," Mama shouted out the window. "Keep an eye on him. Make sure he sits between you."

Roddy scooted out and stood furtively beside me. He wore a plaid, collared shirt, tucked into belted shorts, and his pale legs vanished into brown socks and Hush Puppy shoes. He was just tall enough to reach my chin and his cowlick brushed my nose. I took his hand. The crowd pulled us forward like a swift running current. Within seconds, the three of us were swept through the glass entrance and deposited into the bustle of the lobby.

Barbara Ann pointed to a bench, pressed up against the wall, adjacent to the ladies' room.

"Over there," she ordered.

On high alert, we somehow knew our jobs. I herded Roddy to a spot on the bench and looked up to see Barbara Ann dive into the waves of people. She called over her shoulder, "I'll get us tickets!" and instantly was swallowed up and gone.

A zing of worry circled my stomach, but I batted it away. The hot, tangy smell of buttered popcorn, tangled with sweet stabs of Butterfinger bars, Jujubes, and black licorice, permeated my nose. The room was charged with energy. Kids my age and older swarmed in clutches of threes and fours, chattering and glancing about the room. I was inside a new world, one thrillingly askew, where anything might happen. Surely, Wyn was here. I knew it. I could feel him.

Roddy twitched, so slight, like the flick of an ear. I murmured, soft-voiced. "It's okay. She's coming back."

"Yaas, Mossie," he said, darkly. His name for me, like many of his words, left out letters that troubled his tongue, like *r* and soft *g*. I was supposed to correct him when he did this, but right then I didn't care about house rules.

"Barbara Ann's getting you some Cracker Jacks," I whispered.

Roddy's shoulders bunched around his ears. He pulled on his lip.

"Yaas, Mossie," he muttered.

"And a Fresca, too."

"Fresca, too," he repeated, as if he hadn't really heard.

"Yes, Fresca."

"Fresca."

Little sparks of anxiety tickled my chest: Roddy's echo was never a good sign; any moment now he might start shouting. Searching for Barbara Ann, I scanned the crowd, but her pink-scarfed head was nowhere to be seen. Through the jumble of bodies, a blonde-headed blur of curly hair and a turned-up nose caught my eye. *Wyn?*

I crouched, not at all sure I wanted him to see me. Heart fluttering, I rose stealthily, stepping backward up onto the bench seat. The sea of heads swelled and swayed, forcing me up on tiptoe, and, in small bursts of desire to see and not see, I hopped up and down on the bench. From the far side of the room, I must have appeared like an agitated fish, leaping above the crowd for a better look and plunging down each time I glimpsed a yellow-headed boy. Once, I dropped so fiercely into a squat, the button of my pedal pushers popped and spun off across the carpet.

I didn't want to bob this way. I wanted to stand still, long enough for Wyn to spot me and flash another smile, to come over and say hi in front of everyone; but I couldn't. If he came closer, he'd know who I really was: not the girl who'd caught his fancy, but the other one, who lived in an unlucky family with a confounding boy. No one I knew harbored this secret, none of my friends at school. On my best days I thought this meant I was inside some tragic story, like Jane Eyre, who made her way forward despite odd family circumstance. But more often, it simply meant I was flawed, deep down, in a place that felt black and bottomless. Floating there was something I believed and had never spoken of to anyone: God had smitten my family.

"Cracker Jacks!" Roddy shouted.

Buckling, I sat down, hard.

"Yes, shhhh, yes, she's bringing some. Don't worry."

"Don't worry, Mossie!"

"Shh-shh-shh, yes. I mean no. It's okay."

Heads swung our way. I yanked out the emergency Grahams and pushed one into Roddy's palm. He snatched it and started munching in dinky, angry bites. Desperately, I looked around, and, suddenly, there was Barbara Ann careening toward us, weighted down with Frescas in both hands, Cracker Jacks pressed under one armpit, and three peppermint-striped straws sticking out from her mouth like blow darts.

"Where have you been?" I bounded to my feet.

With a lidded look, she freed up her mouth and handed Roddy his Cracker Jacks.

"Getting the tickets," she said, thrusting a bag of Sugar Daddies into my hand. "Here."

"Open it!" Roddy shouted.

I must have flinched.

"Stay calm, for heaven's sake," Barbara Ann said, frowning.

"Wyn's here," I whispered, cupping my mouth.

"Uh-oh," she said, instantly rearranging the loot and reaching for Roddy's fingers. "Let's get inside where it's dark."

We fell into line: Barbara Ann in the lead, Roddy shuffling in between, and me bringing up the rear. Scooting into our seats, we bookended Roddy on either side. I yanked open his Cracker Jacks, held his wrist, and poured some into his palm; Barbara Ann punched a straw through the ice cubes and folded its bendy neck to his mouth until certain he'd taken a sip. For several minutes, we supplied him as his head dipped from straw to sticky corn. At last, the lights dimmed, enveloping us in darkness.

Slithering down, I blew out my lips. My spine loosened, bone by bone, and a cascade of knots released down my legs. No one would see us now. Balancing the box so Roddy could reach inside, I gratefully turned my eyes to the screen.

Within seconds, I was swept into the sky, soaring high over the peaks of Salzburg, and then, with a gentle dive, descending on the camera's wings to a bare hilltop and a tiny figure, twirling and hatless, who didn't look big enough for the open-throated notes she was flinging into the air.

The hills are alive . . .

Julie Andrews and the sheer joy of her voice stilled me. I sat spellbound, my Sugar Babies suspended at my throat, half torn open. Maria swept me along in a breathless tide of freedom and possibility: a nun tearing around on a mountain top without permission, someone who couldn't bear the rules, the closed rooms or silence of the abbey, so like my house. So like me, she didn't fit her life.

I could have closed my eyes in that moment and needed nothing more, but there was more: the Von Trapp children high stepped to the pitched bleats of their father's marching whistle. Within seconds, Louisa was me, blonde and thirteen, and Liesl, sixteen and dark, was Barbara Ann, and also me, since she was falling in love.

For several minutes, I lost track of everything around me, even the wrapper crinkling in my palm and the bite and pop of sugar on my teeth. Ominously, the Nazis were moving in. So absorbed was I in the dissonant, frightening horns and deep pounding kettle drums that I forgot Roddy was sitting right next to me, absorbing the same agitated rhythm. In the next instant, he exploded and I let out a thin, high squeal as he vaulted up and out of his seat, whirling his head and flapping his hands, lurching to and fro as if he were a bucking bronco.

Tearing my face from the screen, I shot Barbara Ann a horrified look and we both and bounded into action, snatching at Roddy's arms and hands. His limbs, whipping around like ropes, slapped my cheek and lip, *whap whap*, sending me sideways.

"Ow!" burst from the chair in front of us, and from all sides came a hissing like missiles through the darkness, "Shhhhh!"

I must have appeared as fitful and feral as my brother. Like a wild forest child unleashed from a pen, or, at the very least, an orphan in need of parents who'd do the right thing and yank me out to the lobby for a good thrashing. But I flailed on, even as I believed that, somewhere in the darkness, Wyn was staring open-mouthed at my large-headed flapping shadow. I had no choice. I was caught in a situation far beyond my control. Abandoning Barbara Ann and Roddy was unthinkable.

I don't know how long the three of us flailed. It took my sister, taller and stronger, to bring Roddy down into his seat. She caught him in a kind of wrestling hold, folding and clamping him into his chair. She and I rasped in unison, "Stop. Stop it now or no more movie!"

Seconds passed, my pulse pounding as my fingers clutched Roddy's arm. Through his shirt sleeve I felt him soften, but I held on anyway, scrunching down, pressing my spine against the seat, craning my neck so I might catch Barbara Ann's eye. Two of my curlers dislodged, and I yanked them out with my free hand, shuddering as the damp curls fingered my neck.

What now? I mouthed, but Barbara Ann wasn't looking my way.

Through the dim light, I saw her fingers over her mouth. Like me, she'd slid into her seat, her scarf off-kilter. Her fists were bunched to her mouth as if she were trapping something; her shoulders shuddered. When she turned to glance briefly at me, tears glistened on her cheeks.

A thick syrupy pain rose in my chest. I couldn't bear to see her undone. I knew it meant we'd failed at our one chance to be normal. A noise escaped from her through the darkness, like a sob pushing out between her fingers. I squinted, searching for her face. Then I spotted, in the folded divot of her brow and the crimped corners of her eyes, something that astonished me: mirth!

My hands clapped hard on my mouth as I dove forward, plunging my head down between my knees. Sputtering, I fought back waves of laughter roaring up from my shoes. It came in pounding swaths, relentless and hard, burning my stomach and escaping from my clamped mouth in a wheezy wailing. I sounded like a moaning dog. My nose ran all over my hands. Sugar Babies bounced around my shoes. I wasn't supposed to laugh this way, but I couldn't stop. I didn't want to. Something had cracked open my ribcage, and the pressure inside, held for so long, was bursting with all the force of the earth, blessedly powerful and out of my hands.

How long I heaved, I don't remember, resting between bouts of laughter and then plunging again, wheezing and coughing. Vaguely, I knew Barbara Ann was but three feet away, doing exactly the same thing, and somewhere above me, muffled and far away, I heard the bright notes of birds.

I wouldn't fully understand for two more decades why I hadn't dared look up and take in the final moments of the Von Trapps' happy ending, choosing instead to stay where I was, folded in half, peering at Roddy's socks and Hush-Puppied feet, his pale unmarked shins stilled and relaxed, a confetti of Cracker Jacks littered about his toes. With each new swell of hilarity, rising and receding in my belly, I felt a deeper and fuller sense of relief. I knew finally what I'd known all along. I was not going to pull this off—pretending I could be like everyone else. A door had swung open on invisible hinges and, for the first time, I saw what was inside. I wasn't like other teenagers. I never would be. My life wasn't going to happen that way.

At last, feet and legs began moving all around me, taking people out of the row and up the aisle to the lobby. Lifting my head from my knees, I squinted. Houselights and glances seared the room. I saw Barbara Ann two seats away, gazing about, shoulders resting against the seatback. One curler was missing from the side of her head, making her look deformed, as if a divot was missing from her skull. I touched my own head, patting a half-moon one way and then another, my fingers dipping into depressions where I, too, had holes.

Far down in front, thick waves of stage curtains began to close, splashing at the midline, a brief flouncing of hem. The theater was nearly empty. Beside me, Roddy upended his Cracker Jacks box and shook it softly.

"Toy in there," he said.

Chapter 18

Tears

When I was sixteen, my family settled into a kind of normalcy. Like most families hit with tribulation, mine got on with life. Between my winning in gymnastics and making straight As, Barbara Ann getting into college, Roddy learning how to count to 100, and my father's salary steady enough for a big house in the Colorado foothills, my mother occasionally smiled. I did not know we had more ahead of us.

On one particular Friday in October, the afternoon was crisp and cut with fall light, conditions that made me giddy. My friend Sherry and I were goofing around in my backyard, taking liberties and indulging in disrespect. We wore short, flared cheerleading skirts, white blouses with puffed sleeves, and matching gold vests. Sewed on our backs were dark green *BC*s for Bear Creek, and spilling down the thighs of our skirts, our names, embossed in green, thrashed as we kicked and lunged.

I considered cheerleading a frivolous activity, but like most girls of my active nature, I seized whatever sanctioned outlets I could to avoid sitting in the bleachers. As a cheerleader, I could flip and jump and shout, and no one would stop me or tell me to sit down and cross my legs. It was better than nothing—better than sitting on my duff in the stands, bored and barking like a goose. We had the sorriest football team in Jefferson County but I had a job to do: scream on, no matter what the score or how utter the failure.

"Blah blah, sis boom blah—we missed the goal—ha ha ha!"

I flapped my crepe paper shakers and kicked like a chorus girl, madly, with too much enthusiasm. Sherry pranced beside me, pumping her arms, up and down, in and out, furiously marching her feet. Tonight's game was less than two hours away and we both knew it was hopeless: we were going to lose. We'd been losing for weeks.

"Never score, we're not sore, we just stink and stink some more," Sherry croaked.

I dove into a forward roll and she followed, both of us landing on the grass, side by side, sitting with our legs stretched out in front. Instantly, we started walking on our buttocks. I couldn't bear it—I spit and burst into laughter, flopping into her, and we both crumpled onto the grass, our shakers flaying green and gold.

"All right you two," my mother chided through the patio door, "act like ladies and get going. It's five o'clock." The screen veiled her face but I could tell she was smiling. A smaller shadow hovered beside her. Through the sliding door, two small palms appeared, pressed to the glass: Roddy's hands.

Sherry stuffed her shakers into her mouth, muffling, "Oh no, what if we miss the game?"

The sight of us reflected in the patio glass, hair askew, vests twisted, doubled me again, and I folded over, nose near my knees, wheezing.

Sherry and I had been comrades since fifth grade, since Mrs. Larson's god-awful class. We had both come of age bouncing on trampolines and hurling down tumbling mats, and our bodies had blossomed similarly, with small buds for breasts and fitful on-and-off rhythms to our monthly bleedings. Our friendship was a protector, a small bubble of safety. Both of us were in many ways innocent, terrified of the cool kids who smoked dope, who *went all the way*. We on the other hand went to church and still obeyed our parents, or at least tried to hide our mild misdeeds from them, mostly without success. With Sherry, I didn't have to put up a cool front or pretend I knew how to flirt with boys. We shared our most private thoughts; we giggled at passé jokes, burst into hysterics, wet our pants, and made fun of life before we went back to being serious and pretending that we cared about football.

I got up, brushing grass off my skirt. Sherry whisked my back, sweeping away tiny sticks and ants, and then turned so I could do the same for her.

"Uh-oh, dirt on your behind," I said, soberly. She didn't turn, but held her hands fixed against her skirt and swished her bottom back and forth.

I knew things about friendship. You could not create it by yourself. You had to find another, and then the two of you had to do important things, like be brave, spend time together, have each other over to your homes. Share your life. Deep down, I knew what it was to lose a friend: I had lost Lily to Texas and knew that when a friendship ends you lose a bit of yourself.

At some level, all of this lived within me, though none of it rose to the surface; it didn't have to. Friends were like breathing for me: vital and ever present. I was never without them. I collected them, not by the dozens—never in large numbers—but always by the handful. And among those, one was always a close, enduring soul mate.

"I'll drive," I offered, popping the Belvedere's trunk. We laid our shakers on the floor, smoothing the disheveled strands, and then hopped in. I started the engine and checked myself in the rearview mirror. Egad, I looked a mess.

"Hang on, I need my brush," I snorted, hopping back out.

The light was falling and I was anxious now. Goofing aside, we couldn't be late to the game; it would mean a demerit and a mark on our good names. I touched the kitchen door knob and stepped inside, banking left to run down the hall to the bathroom.

Halfway there, I halted. A deep mournful cry seared my ears, coming from somewhere in the house. Moving down the hall, I crept toward the sound, to my parents' bedroom, and hesitated at the door. It was partially open, wide enough for me to spot my mother inside, sitting on the bed. Her arm encircled Roddy's back and she held her mouth close to his ear. His head hung forward in his hands, and his legs collapsed inward, knock-kneed.

At twelve years old, Roddy nearly matched her size, but he was crumpled like a child into her arms. She rocked him and murmured, "I know, honey. I know."

Roddy's cry was a sound I had never heard from him: a mixture of disbelief, startle, and pain. As if he'd seen a ghost of someone he had cherished and would never see again. It held no envy or outrage, but something else, some other emotion.

"I want a Sherry friend," he said. His voice trembled, muffled in my mother's dress.

I covered my mouth. The sound of my brother's sob generated a pain I had no words for. It buckled me. I held onto the doorframe, unable to move.

It came again, his broken voice. "I want a Sherry friend, Mama." His head buried in my mother's lap, his forefinger waved at the window where, outside, Sherry waited in the car.

His words raked over me. A deep and shuddering loss moved the air. I leaned forward and braced both hands on my knees, flashing to the scene moments before, witnessing it from Roddy's eyes, through the glass: me and Sherry flailing like happy fools, undone by laughter and delight.

For an interminable time, I hung there, sensing that I couldn't go in. The intrusion would wound him again, the sight of me and what I had, what I would always have. I didn't step into the room. I eased the door closed and turned back down the hallway, slipping out to the garage and the waiting car.

Sherry had one foot up on the dashboard and was tightening her laces. "I bet the traffic's awful," she said, amiably.

I didn't answer. As I backed the car down the driveway, she regarded me. She knew me better than anyone.

"I have a brush, you know. You can use mine," she offered.

"Oh." I sounded sickened, grateful to have to watch the road. I kept my eyes averted.

With Sherry, I had shared my hopes and dreams and my innermost thoughts, but I couldn't tell her what I had just seen: that our friendship was an injury. I couldn't ask her to hold that. Saying certain things out loud gave wings to the words. The only way I could fathom holding this wound of my brother's was to push it back under my ribcage.

"Are you okay?" Sherry whispered.

I nodded, casting a grateful glance her way. "Headache," I said, offering her the only reason I knew we could both accept.

In all of the years I had shared with Roddy, I had not known this about him: that he saw this part of my life and could perceive something as abstract and indescribable and essential as friendship; that he could know he needed it and that he was without it. Even though he had me, and Barbara Ann, and my mother and father, he recognized something else in Sherry and me, a different kind of love and safety.

Now, as Sherry clicked on the radio and we inched in traffic, I knew he was still crying. My throat stung; I blinked hard, struggling to see the road. For the first time, my brother's loss shifted from something outside of me, something he had and that I could make better, to something inside of me, something I tasted and swallowed and held in my stomach. I didn't know that this moment in October 1968 would never leave me; I would carry the memory of my brother's cry the rest of my life, and each time it arose, it would have the power to buckle me.

What I did know as I drove down Sheridan Avenue was that I had witnessed an ardent cruelty—a God who gives a boy enough understanding to know what he is missing, to see and feel what he can't have, and who denies that boy this simple happiness. For the longest time, I had thought my friends were enough for Roddy—that by including him in our play and games, or joining him at his marble chute, I had provided him with friendship. But I had only given him a sister's love. He wanted his own friend—a best friend. More than a person, he wanted the essence of friendship, the special thing that comes from resonating with another.

More than any other disappointment in his life, this one would break my brother. He would turn ever more inward, so thoroughly that he would never cry again.

In the stadium parking lot, I got out under the lights. The thought of running back and forth on a field with Sherry, chasing a score, bouncing up and down, flailing mops of crepe paper, struck me as heartless, all the more so, given what I knew: that I was privileged. I had woken up that morning inside my brain, inside my fated mix of genes, none of which I had earned, and all of which granted me this special thing, this ability to make and have a friend.

Sherry tossed me my shakers and I caught them, one by one, grasping their soft silliness to my chest. Years from then, my mother would tell me that this was the day my brother broke inside and turned inward in a way she had never seen before. He lost his wide-eyed assumptions that he was like everyone else in his life, and especially his sister. Until that moment, only people on the outside had hurt him: the taunting bullies in the school parking lot, the staring kids in restaurants. This time, his deep wound did not come from a pack of heartless boys; it came from me. In the near distance, the band boomed alive, announcing the start of the game. Hurriedly, I took off toward the field, running, shakers held high in one hand and with the other, wiping my eyes.

Chapter 19

Trapeze

By the time I turned sixteen, training for competition ruled my waking life. At dawn, I arose, showered, and drove myself to the gym in the dark, fitting in ninety minutes of practice before splashing my face with water and running to class. After school, I returned to the gym and lost track of time. My mother would have to appear in the gym's double doorway, gesturing to her watch and motioning me to come on so we could get Roddy to his tutoring lesson across town. Smeared in chalk and sweat, hands and ankles throbbing, I would jump down from the high bar or beam or trampoline, landing with a reluctant two-footed thump on the ground.

At the beginning of my senior year, I learned that my high school, Bear Creek, would host the 1970 Colorado girls' state gymnastic championship. At long last, I was to compete with my team on our home turf, for all to see.

I couldn't admit even to myself that I was terrified. A swath of silver and gold medallions dangling from brilliant blue ribbons hung on my bedroom wall; the *Rocky Mountain News* had announced I was destined for the Olympics, and the *Denver Post* ran my photo after I captured the state championship title two years in a row. Despite all this, I was jittery. I had grown used to performing in faraway gyms where my mother and Barbara Ann were the only spectators I knew. Even my father wasn't there; he couldn't be: someone had to watch over my brother. I had become comfortable performing in the half-light, where the stakes were low and consequences mild. For the first time, I would be center stage, with curtains whipped back and all lights ablaze.

A few weeks before the big event, I began to short-circuit. I had mastered and added a new stunt to my uneven-bar routine—a hand-stand-pirouette on the high bar. Without warning, during practice, gravity reached up from the floor, clamped onto my limbs, and yanked me down. Time after time, I jumped upside down, turned on the top bar, and gripped my hands like talons around the wood, only to rip off at the bottom of my downswing and slam into a hard, tangled heap on the mat.

The Wednesday before the meet, I pushed myself up from another crumpled landing and drew in a tight breath.

"You okay?" Pat, my coach, popped her head out of her office door. The gym was empty and we were well past the dinner hour, but she had stayed on, agreeing to finish up some paperwork as I battled on for a few more tries. She had been coaching me for five years now, long enough to know I had a need to win and would push myself to the brink.

I didn't answer. My bones were fine and soft tissues attached, nothing twisted or wrenched, but something had lit fire to my left hand. Pat frowned and stepped through the office door toward me.

I turned my palm upward, and there, in the center, was a fresh rip the size of a quarter glowing like a hot coal. Missing were several layers of skin and a hard-won callus, which must be hanging off the bar somewhere above me. Beads of blood oozed up through the only skin layer left intact.

At any other time of the season, I would have scoffed at this injury, merely swabbing it with ointment and taking a few days off. Skin tears like this were a part of my swinging life. Usually, though, they happened early in the fall, when my palms were soft and unseasoned, and there was still plenty of time to heal before the first competition.

In that moment, I stared at my bright raw hand and knew I was in trouble.

"Go home," said Pat. "I mean it. I don't want to see you until Saturday."

For the next forty-eight hours, I moved inside a blur of dread and panic. A late spring snowstorm turned the roads and hills around my house hard and icy, then greasy with mud. Wrapping in layers, I went jogging anyway. Twice a day, I re-swabbed my hand with ointment and smothered it in gauze, then grimly went through tedious sets of sit-ups and leg lifts. My brain ran through my routines in an exhaustive, mindless loop. Both nights I jumped awake, startled and confused in the darkness of my room.

The thought that I might spare myself and simply forfeit this meet never entered my mind. A tangle of reasons intertwined to make this so. I had both my ancestors' hardscrabble genes and my father's competitive, single-minded drive; I believed in the unspoken rule of athletes that whining made you a loser—the only injury that would have kept me from competing was a broken bone; and lastly, who would I be if not a champion? I had come of age as a winner in my family and also in my mind. It was my path to happiness and the way I helped my family. I was no longer sure how to be anything or anyone else.

When Saturday dawned, I slogged into the gym and dropped my sports bag onto the bleachers. The vast room was clean and gleaming, the mats washed and the equipment carefully arranged, with judging chairs and scoring cards placed exactly so. People were trickling in.

Unwrapping my bandage, I stared at the situation. Exposed was a pale layer of newly formed skin stretched over a dark pink underbelly. Appearing at my shoulder, Pat peered down at my palm and we both stood there for several moments.

"Here's the good news," she said, finally. Her arms were full of score cards and clipboards for the judges. "Bars are your last event."

Halfway through warm-ups the stands were already packed and the doorways clogged with people. Shaky and muddled, I marked through my routines as best I could, favoring my palm and skipping warm-ups on the uneven bars. Hard-wrapped in a protective bandage of gauze and white athletic tape, my mummified hand swung like a club around my body. For the first time since I had scaled my first cottonwood tree, I felt like a clumsy, flightless human.

Mercifully, my first event was vaulting, which I took as a sign that somehow luck was on my side. It was an all-leg event, requiring only a quick tap of the hands on the way by. To me, vaulting was almost playful, the equivalent of bounding off a diving board and floating free for a few milliseconds before gravity took hold. A handspring Yamashita was, in those days, a marvel in gymnastic circles, and I had a good one.

Focusing adrenaline into my thighs, I shot down the runway and punched the springboard, soaring upside down. As I popped my hands off the horse I cringed, the sliver of pain shooting from my palm to my brain, and as I jack-knifed up to a V-sit in the air the world suddenly warped into a dangerous place. I was way off, my body rotating too fast and far, the floor zooming up to meet my face. My toes barely skimmed the ground as I ducked my head and rolled, bouncing my tailbone against the floor as the force hurled me off the end of the landing mat.

A collective gasp whipped around the gym and the audience fell quiet. In the hushed silence, I collected my legs under me and stood up, shaken. My eyes found my mother's face in the crowd: she was ashen, her hands cupped to her mouth. I had never crashed in competition. If I faltered, my mistakes were always slight and easily absorbed, amounting to little more than fraction of a deduction in my score. But this was altogether different; I couldn't cover up this colossal botch.

In the next few seconds of silence, an old part of me kicked in—the part that knew what to do in the midst of utter calamity. Facing the head judge, I presented to her and smiled, then rolled my eyes, as if this fiasco was nothing to me and I had crash-landed simply to add flare to these proceedings.

The judge grinned. Laughter bubbled up from the audience, and applause broke out as I exhaled with relief and trotted back to the bench. I had salvaged some dignity. Still, my hand throbbed as if it had been sliced and stitched back together with a nail. Three more events lay ahead, including uneven bars, the most punishing one to my hands and the most likely to injure me seriously if I faltered.

Passing up the cluster of my teammates, I climbed up to the second tier of bleachers where my mother and Barbara Ann were settled. For seven years my mother had parked herself on hard seats just like this all over the county, doing the math, adding up my winning scores.

"Okay, hon," she said, making space between her and Barbara Ann. "What can I get you? I have water and juice."

People were packed into the seats all around and there wasn't much room. My mother handed me a cup of liquid, and Barbara Ann, with teary eyes, helped re-bandage my hand with ointment and an extra layer of gauze. My mother turned and agreed with someone behind us, "No, she's no quitter. That's for sure."

This respite was enough to help me face the next two events. I descended the bleachers and, though I was far from my best on balance beam and floor exercise, I managed to limp through and keep my scores in the high middle range. Normally, I'd be checking in with my mother to see how my scores stood overall, but part of me didn't want to know. Bleary-eyed, I stared at the scoreboard and heard my coach call me over just before uneven bars.

"All you have to do is get through this routine and you'll still have a shot at winning all-around," she said, handing me a block of chalk. "Don't be Superwoman; skip the handstand; no twist on the dismount. Go."

Hands and thighs smothered in chalk, I faced the uneven bars and felt space stretch out in front of me. The fact that I might not be able to stand the pain and hang on meant I would let my teammates down and, worse, I would let my family down. I could not bear to see my mother deflated.

The audience fell quiet as I punched the board and sailed over the low bar, reaching for the high bar and the fire that would ignite in my hand. The instant I gripped, pain seared through me, and I sucked in my breath. This wasn't good; I had to breathe or I wouldn't make it to the end. I released my hands, dropping to the low bar, exhaling as

I gripped and clutched. Somewhere halfway through this swing and before the next, I leaned in toward the pain, long enough for my body to remember itself, to assume a deeper flood of hormones. In the next few seconds the pain sighed, enough to turn my brain to the rhythm of swing and release, loft and loop. When the moment came for the handstand, I did not hesitate but bounded with both feet off the low bar, drove them to the sky into the handstand and switched my grip at the top for the downswing.

There is a moment every athlete, dancer, and artist knows, when all of a sudden, your ability is in your own hands—it's yours and no one else's. Later, a friend would tell me that the Catholics call this *charism*—when the spirit within you *becomes* you.

As I whooshed under the bar, I no longer felt I was on my way down, but on my way through to the next limb, softly catching and rebounding. My body swung past the floor, my pelvis stretched into the low bar, folded around it, and popped off into my full twisting Hecht dismount on the other side.

For a few split seconds I hovered in the air, feathered and weightless. The floor was miles below me, my feet exactly where they should be. I had gained back my loft and all of my parts and limbs were flying together. This time, when I touched down, the joy and applause from the audience belonged to me.

Chapter 20

Chant from Another World

One late spring afternoon when I was seventeen, in my last semester of high school, I pushed back from my bedroom desk, dazed from four hours of homework. I had at least another hour before I could quit, but first, I had to quiet my body. My stomach had been roaring for the last hour, daring me to feed it. Snacks for me rarely involved anything remotely solid. I was bent on staying thin for college competition, meaning that only a sugarless can of TAB would do, slowly sipped until dinnertime, and if that didn't depress my appetite, I had a drawer full of sugarless Trident.

Our house in Willowbrook was designed in such a way that I could stand at one end of the bedroom wing and see all the way to the other end of the house. The instant I stepped into the hallway, I spotted my mother several yards away on the long stretch of stone tiles running to the kitchen. She was utterly still, her gaze fixated on something outside the sliding glass doors, her expression an odd mixture—not of alarm and agitation, but a kind of wistfulness and detached wonderment.

"What is it? What's out there?" I called out, quickening my pace. I imagined some impossible wonder, like a polar bear or wildebeest, moseying across our back yard.

She didn't respond or seem to have any notion I was there. I kept coming, growing more puzzled and alarmed with every step. As I reached the floor-length drapes, I caught and pulled them back, craning my neck to follow her gaze.

There, at the edge of the patio, in full sunlight, was my fourteen-year-old brother. His torso lurched to and fro as he rocked from foot to foot, knees locked and legs rigid, both hands beating the air, his brown hair rustling softly about his face. I couldn't hear through the glass but knew well enough that he was whispering and whistling in a kind of wild mimicry of the wind.

To one of our scant neighbors, my brother would seem to be having a seizure, an epileptic fit of some sort. But, in fact, Roddy was flying high. He was in windy ecstasy, and if given the choice, he'd stay right where he was for the rest of his life.

"Mother, why don't you stop him?" I asked, appalled.

There was a tacit agreement in my family that we wouldn't let Roddy buzz on like this—partly because the longer he went on the harder it was to get him calmed again, and partly because he might accidentally trip over a chaise longue and whack his skull on a weight-bearing pole. Immersed in one of his highs he was utterly oblivious to any solid object or person nearby. The instinct to step in and stop him, to protect him from himself, was embedded in my bones.

In all honesty, another reason spurred me to step in and stop him—something deeper and more complex. I didn't know at the time, and wouldn't until I separated from home, that his habits unnerved me. Though I had come of age with my brother's spastic reveries, still, his obsessive twitching in my peripheral vision never failed to alarm me. Fitful messages darted straight to my amygdala and relayed that all was not well, something needed to be attended to, pills had to be taken, reasoning restored. He was acting as if he were suffering a psychotic break or a dangerously bad trip. It was the kind behavior wired to raise red flags and signal EMTs.

Still, I hesitated with my hand on the door handle. My mother's odd behavior was more disturbing to me than my brother's. I had never seen her observe Roddy this way, unaffected by his behavior, as if she were his doctor or therapist, rather than his mother. In some deep place it chilled me. I wanted to snap, *What are you looking at?* But sensing some new surrender in her, I kept silent. Instead, I turned to see what she was seeing.

From here, the scene appeared like a far-off dream. Roddy leaped and moved in ways I couldn't fathom. As much as I had trained to flip and fly, controlling my spin and plugging into the forces of physics and gravity, I moved like a being with mass and blood. I could not move like Roddy, who was more like an element, like a thousand threads of electricity.

Not that I hadn't tried. Before Barbara Ann had left for college, I had walked into her room expecting to find her sorting and stacking laundry, but, instead, caught her flailing about.

"What are you doing?" I screeched with delight, relieved as always for a reason to laugh in our dour household. She looked wild and ridiculous.

"I'm trying to be Rod," she said, matter-of-factly.

"But what on earth for?"

"Why not? Join me."

I did. Scooching the bureau to make room, I launched into my best effort, whacking my knuckles on the corner of the bureau and knocking the lamp. Thirty seconds in, my skull cracked against Barbara Ann's and we both sank to the floor, holding our heads and whispering *ow, ow, ow.* It came to me that Roddy never injured himself like this; he flailed in any space, closed or open, indoors and outdoors, without collision.

Now, on this side of the patio glass, I pondered the inner life of this boy who was my brother, rocking, flapping, repeating whispery shreds of *e-e-e-e-e.* If I were inside him, would I be in the midst of a glorious hallucination? Scores of young people were altering their brains right then, in 1970, spurred on by Timothy Leary and Allen Ginsberg— brash upstarts who preached tripping as a creative act, a doorway to a higher consciousness. At seventeen, I was trying to make sense of this, the idea that my brain, any brain, held altered rooms of reality. One only had to find the key. Was this what my brother had: an infinite ring of keys?

Once, as a child, I had played a popular game designed to alter the brain. Surrounded by fifth-grade girls in the restroom where we couldn't be seen, I blew my lungs into large balloons, exhaled hard, inhaled again, and held my breath, bearing down. Greta, a robust girl who was the first of us to develop breasts, clutched me around my stomach and cinched my organs. The world spun magnificently, a delirious and delicious rush that flooded my limbs and choked off my consciousness. Thousands of bubbles shivered under my skin, quivered up my nose, flooded my brain. A frothy joy buoyed me as I floated to the ground. Awakening on the floor, I saw faces above me. The air was full of whispering and awe. I wanted to do it again.

Now, I felt an urgency to stop it all. Timothy Leary frightened me. I thought of the brain as a precious, vulnerable thing, prone to damage. Sliding the door open, I stepped out into the spring air just as my brother emitted a round of hissing sounds. His whisperings were like a chant from another world, a foreign code of frequency, short-circuiting circuitry—a way of being in another dimension only he understood.

"Rod." I said again, reaching for his arm, "Rod!"

My touch made him flinch, enough to break him from his spell. Instantly, he came to rest, as if I'd pulled a wire and disintegrated his current. For a slit of time, my fingers tingled like tuning forks and, as their resonation died, I felt a wisp of loss. How could I have known there would come a day when I would miss the passion of his wild gyrations? When not even the wind would excite him?

"Come on now," I said in a feather-light voice. "Let's go in and have a Coke. Would you like that?"

As I turned Rod toward the door, my mother's catatonic gaze met mine. Something in the measure of her lips, her complacent smile, spelled out submittal, a kind of giving in, edged with loneliness. She was still a young woman at thirty-nine, petite and attractive, with lushly dark hair and refined, wrinkleless features. But she was also a mother of two daughters who were leaving her, whisking off to college for an intellectual life that had been interrupted for her and had died when she married. Barbara Ann had disappeared to Colorado

State College two years before, and within a few months I, too, would abandon this house, hop on a plane, and fly two thousand miles to the University of Massachusetts: my new life, fueled by ambition and goals and buoyed by a scholarship. My mother, on the other hand, was looking at long stretches of days in a secluded prairie home with her son, who was not going on, who would not apply to college, find a mate, or start a family.

I felt my mother acquiescing, and suddenly, I knew why she had birthed another baby. My younger sister Camela (Cami), born two years before—as Barbara Ann went out the door—had supposedly come as a surprise. Now I wondered. I couldn't know that, shortly, my mother would become pregnant yet again and I'd answer the phone in my college town apartment to learn that she had delivered a baby boy. My new brother, James Owens, would bring her a happiness she hadn't felt since her wedding day. His birth would be the reason she finally dried her tears.

On the patio, I gently but firmly steered Rod to the door. Like the sibling I was, I had an overdeveloped sensitivity to staring eyes, and right then, some inkling made me glance back over my shoulder. Sure enough, up the hill, where a large house jutted out over the rocks, a pair of large-lensed black eyes stared down at me. In the glare of the sunlight I couldn't see who held those binoculars, but I knew nevertheless. The Armistead boy, a teenager my age, stood poised before his family's massive picture window and, assuming he was hidden, was taking in the show.

"I'll be there in a minute, Mom," I said.

When I was sure she and my brother were inside, I backtracked to the edge of the patio, right where Rod had been flying a few minutes before. Grounded on that spot, I stood and stared pointedly at the Armisteads' picture window. Slowly, the binoculars sank to the boy's side, and for a moment his silhouetted figure remained, furtive, uncertain.

Mellifluously, I floated my arm as high as it would stretch, counted to three, and, like a switch blade, flipped out my third finger.

Asshole, I mouthed, dredging up that old, venerable term.

His silhouette disappeared.

In all of my years, I hadn't wanted to escape as much as I did that afternoon, to step away and leave it all behind. My parents had held our family together and, in some ways, our struggle appeared to be a success story, and yet I felt an undertow, a persistent pull on my ankles that exhausted me. I didn't know this was an ache for my mother and that I shared it with other siblings of disabled children. I only knew that Barbara Ann was gone and in her place was a new baby sister, whom I changed, burped, and walked to sleep. I felt the weight of it all, the coping with things none of my friends had on their hands—and, most relentlessly, the staring, ogling world.

Chapter 21

Dive

On a warm fall day in 1970, I said goodbye to my family and boarded an airplane bound for New England. I was eighteen, and the idea that I no longer had to answer to Baptist rules, or my brother's needs, or my mother's underlying sorrow, intoxicated me. My mother stood on the patio, holding Cami on her hip and half-shadowing Roddy, who lurked behind her, pulling on his lip. If I hadn't been so bent on escape, I might have noticed the pink rims of my mother's eyes and the Kleenex in her hand. She waved as my father and I backed down the driveway, circling her arm around Roddy and pulling him close. As we turned, Roddy fluttered his soft hands, but I couldn't tell whether he was waving goodbye or simply excited by the wind. Either way, he disappeared.

Nothing could dampen my giddiness at being on my own, not even the nauseating bumpy plane flight or the loss of my luggage or the implacable weather. When I stepped into the gym at the University of Massachusetts a few days later, I looked like a drowned goat. The unforgiving downpour outside, coupled with pitiless gusts of wind, had mangled my umbrella halfway across the campus green. My suede jacket, a going-away gift from my parents and the most expensive piece of clothing I had ever owned, was darkly splattered and ruined.

My boots were badly chosen, more for style and their matching buck-skin color, not for the real work of keeping my feet dry. Most of my luggage had not arrived, lost somewhere in the twenty-five-hundred miles between Denver and Hartford, leaving me with nothing clean or dry to change into.

Still, here I was. The sight of the gym, with its familiar maze of mats and rings and bars hazed in chalk, thrilled me. I stood just inside the door, disheveled, dripping, suddenly relieved I hadn't brought a leotard. A long-legged gymnast up on the beam was executing what was considered a marvel in those days: two front walkovers on the four-inch-wide surface as if she were on the floor. Closer to me, on the bars, another gymnast threw a flip between bars I had never been able to master. If this wasn't enough to rattle my confidence, the room was full of males as well as females—a new thing for me. Despite the fact that I had spent half of my life barelegged and swinging on gymnastic bars, I had never shed my shyness. For all of my yearning for independence, I was an introverted girl who preferred watching from the edge of the room before stepping into the limelight. Until that point, my athletic life had been separate from males. Now I realized I'd be sweating, grunting, and crashing alongside them every day.

"Margaret?" A buxom, big-hipped woman in a warm up suit came toward me—my new coach. Her size alarmed me. I had accepted the university sight unseen and instantly wondered if I'd made a mistake.

"Margie," I answered.

Motion ceased on the nearby beam and uneven bars and all eyes turned to me, curious.

"Come on, get dressed!" called out one female gymnast over by the chalk stand. Later, I'd come to know she and I were the two promising freshmen who had been granted partial scholarships. She was brazenly bare-legged, flushed with adrenalin, eyes glittering with excitement.

Excuses boiled up in my throat: "Well, I can't right now, I'm looking for my luggage." And then I ran.

The sheer intimacy of that small space, packed with bodies of all genders and talents equal or better than mine, unnerved me. All of my weaknesses were about to be exposed: my tight flexibility (a constant enemy), my propensity to bend my knees every time I *kipped* from low to high bar, my unshakable fear of the balance beam that plagued me with recurring dreams of foot slippage and crotch landings. I had managed to hide these foibles or, more truthfully, I had gotten away with them as a reigning state champion back in the Rockies. Here, I wasn't so special.

Chilled and wet, I stumbled into the dormitory lobby, shaking water from my hair, and nearly tripped over an enormous black army trunk. Instantly, I knew it was my father's, the one I had jammed full of everything I owned and needed, which I thought was lost forever. Relief flooded over me. I grabbed its leather handle and hauled it into the elevator up to the second floor, then dragged it down the hall to my room. Skipping dinner, I chose instead to put away my things, making careful stacks in the closet drawers, shaking out my bedspread, arranging cosmetics, and sponging up the leaked Merle Norman cleanser from my cosmetic bag. I didn't know I was doing more than unpacking: I was nesting, setting up a home in which I could retreat and center myself, one without clutter and chaos. This was how I had always grounded myself at home, keeping my bedroom clean and impeccable and shutting the door.

The next day, the rain retreated long enough for me to smell the earth and trees, and to notice a bright red thread lining the lips of leaves. I pulled myself together, put on a new purple leotard and white sweat suit, and marched myself to the gym. My plan was to stay loose and casual, warm up, and throw a few tricks on each event—nothing risky. Despite efforts to keep my fitness up over the summer, I was weak and stiff and didn't trust my body. Not until I joined the tumbling line did I sense any of my old confidence coming back. The men and women tumbled together, partly out of necessity, since there was only one floor exercise mat. To my relief, everyone wanted a spotter, even the men: no one was throwing tricks alone this early in the season. It was the one time I had access to the best spotter in the gym: the men's assistant coach, a graduate student named Matthew. He was unsmiling and terse with his feedback, correcting me on my back handspring, and I came away feeling a bit green and silly, but I took what he said to heart and after my next turn he said, "Better."

That evening I returned from the cafeteria and crawled into bed, unable to move. My tonsils were on fire and my whole body ached with fever. I fell into a shivering, fitful sleep. For the next five days, I stayed beneath the covers as my roommate brought me antibiotics from the clinic and tiptoed in and out of the room between classes. Vaguely, I heard her whisper that she was going away for the weekend. I lost track of time and didn't care about anything; the twisted sheets stank from sweat and cloistered mats of hair, and my raw throat flamed each time I swallowed. Tonsillitis had felled me several times in my life, hospitalizing me when I was five and religiously returning every few years. But this was the first time I'd had to suffer it alone. I came to in the middle of darkness with tears in my eyes, wishing for my mother who, if she were here, would be pressing cold cloths on my forehead head and around the back of my neck, and bringing me popsicles and ginger ale ice cubes. Finally, on the fifth day, my fever broke and a ringing rattled through my tender brain. Rolling to my side, I slapped for the phone.

"Hello?" I croaked, hoping it was Barbara Ann or my mother, anyone who might lend me solace.

"You'll never win the Olympics this way," a male voice answered, sardonically. Through my fog, I dimly thought this might be a crank call.

"Excuse me?" I said, annoyed. Speaking took all of my effort.

"Let's put it this way: Are you planning on showing up to the gym one of these days? Or maybe you're not like the rest of us; you don't have to practice."

The voice—its droll, unsmiling tone—came to me. It was Matthew, the men's assistant coach. I cringed, feeling chastised and guilty. Here I was, one week into my new life and already looking like a flake. Though I wasn't faking this illness, part of me knew I had been relieved when it hit me. I didn't have to show up or perform.

"I have tonsillitis," I said, defensively, though this was no longer true: my fever was gone. He said nothing back, and after a few more seconds of dead air I added, indignantly, "I'm not lying."

"So what? You want soup? Borscht? Matzo ball?"

In spite of my lethargy, I laughed. I had never heard the word matzo ball, much less heard it pronounced in the cadence of a Jewish yenta. I didn't know either existed and wouldn't know until much later that Matthew was, in fact, Jewish. Because of his six-foot frame, dark straight hair, and Roman nose, I had mistaken him for Italian. I wasn't sure if he was joking but when he spoke again I detected a smile. He told me to get some sleep and come into the gym the next afternoon, just to stretch and stay limber—nothing vigorous: time was ticking.

I hung up the phone and rolled back onto my sweaty pillow, flabbergasted. He had noticed my absence. The one day I had spent in the gym, he had tersely corrected me and hadn't once said my name. Now, I felt a twinge of courage. Perhaps he'd seen some promise in me, somehow, in this vast sprawling herd of freshmen.

The next morning, I got out of bed and toddled to the bathroom at the end of the hall, standing under a hot shower and washing the remnants of illness from my hair and skin. At half-past three, I slipped into soft, pliable clothes (leotard, leggings, sweat pants) and walked to the gym. I did as Matthew had suggested, stretching through a slow warm-up and walking through some dance moves on floor and beam. As I breathed and stretched, I felt a twinge of belonging.

Over the next weeks I came to know my teammates, all of whom hailed from different parts of the world: Isabelle from Cuba, fluid and flexible, a liquid beauty on balance beam; Bea from Washington, D.C., strong as an ox on uneven bars; Ellie from New Jersey, explosive on floor exercise. They all had strengths and weaknesses, and I found my own fit right in. Beam was still my nemesis but I held my own on the other three events. We bonded swiftly as athletes do, encouraging each other, spurred on by our equal intensity and desire and our complementary talents. Bea was especially funny and wise; I liked her immensely.

By the end of September the gym had become my new home. Every day, for four straight hours, I worked fiendishly hard, falling down, getting up, trying again, suffering through leg lifts, pull-ups, stomach crunches, and then jogging back to the dorm. Utterly exhausted, I skipped the dining hall, a practice that would become a habit, and fell into a deep sleep.

Not long into October, I summoned my courage and asked Matthew to stay after practice for an extra twenty minutes to coach me on my full-twisting back layout. Rapidly, I had come to trust him with my safety and I felt most confident when he was there. His spare, no-nonsense coaching suited me: he said little, didn't sugarcoat, and expected me to listen. I was determined to learn the trick and, though tired and winded, I didn't want to leave the gym without trying it alone.

Lofting skyward and backward, I dropped my shoulder into the twist, and knew instantly that I was off, sluggishly corkscrewing through the air. Bracing his feet on the frame of the trampoline, Matthew reached under the hurling meteor of my body. The two of us, entangled, crashed on the metal teeth of the springs, his pant leg ripping at the knee, my thigh lacerating as it scraped the coils.

"We have to stop meeting like this," he quipped as we unraveled our limbs.

I scoffed. He often ribbed who he was working with, diffusing frustration and disappointment with teasing and humor. This made him a good coach. But he had never done this with me. A small part of me sensed a nuance: a flirtation, a pinch of provocation. I couldn't be sure; he was a reserved person, ironic, amusingly sarcastic with everyone. Nevertheless, a tiny glint of pleasure twirled in my stomach.

The next thing I knew, the Thanksgiving pre-season meet was upon me. I didn't feel ready, partly because I was throwing all new routines and partly because I carried an extra five pounds from the dorm room peanut-butter-cracker parties. To top it off, I accepted an invitation to travel to Boston with my roommate for Thanksgiving dinner and the next day, as I arrived at the competition, I was heavy with turkey and pie. Dutifully, I managed to finish my new floor exercise and beam routines and come away with respectable scores, but I knew it wasn't a good first showing. As soon as the last event was over, I was eager to get out of the gym and put the meet behind me. Slipping on my warm-up suit, I signaled to my roommate in the stands for a ride back to her house and, at the same moment, heard a voice behind me.

"Chinese?"

Sure enough, it was Matthew, as terse as ever.

"No," I said. "I'm American."

This time, he scoffed, and for the first time I saw him smile.

"A few of us are heading to Chef Chang's. You should come," he said.

"I don't have a ride," I said, blushing. Suddenly, I felt very young and awkward.

"I do," he said, gesturing to the exit.

Sitting in the booth across from Matthew, crammed in on all sides with fellow gymnasts, I confessed I had never had Chinese food. This was a first for me, and a far cry from the biscuits and gravy I'd grown up on. He showed me how to use chopsticks and teased me mercilessly as shrimp and snow peas twanged across the table. When my sweet and sour chicken bounced off his face, leaving a touch of red on his cheek, he whipped his head right and left, looking for who might have zinged him. I laughed. We all laughed. He had me.

The first season of competition overtook me, and simultaneously, I slammed into love. As our fledgling team climbing up higher in the scoring with every successive meet, I returned from classes, workouts, and competitions nearly every night to Matthew's Holyoke apartment. I stopped by my dorm room so infrequently and sporadically, and then only to fetch clean clothes, that my exasperated roommate moved out to a triple-bed down the hall. By Christmastime, I had petitioned to move off campus and I left the dorm behind. I felt stronger and happier than I'd ever been. Not only was I recklessly in love, but I was mastering new techniques and was conquering tricks that had always eluded me. For the first time, I felt utterly freed from the shadows of sorrow that had haunted my childhood and my family. At the time, I told myself that distance and the cost of flying prevented me from going back to Colorado that year. But in truth, I didn't miss home and I was in the process of cutting myself away from an old unhappy life. Other than a short and hasty trip home for Christmas, the only time I flew back to visit was in April, for Barbara Ann's wedding. I went alone, without Matthew. I didn't want to share him or to muck up my new life.

Barbara Ann was busy doing what I was doing: running away. Though only nineteen, she and her good-looking, somewhat-wild boyfriend were getting married in Lakeridge Baptist Church amid pink and white roses, and bridesmaids (me included) dressed in pink empire, floor-length dresses. Ruddy was the ring bearer. He did a fine job promenading down the aisle, the pillow of rings (slightly listing to one side) held before him. Remembering what to do, he waited obediently at the altar while the rings were freed from the pillow ribbon, and then he stepped up onto the dais beside me. His eyes darted off to the side and his body stood off center, too close to me, but nonetheless, he remained patient and still, pleased to be part of these strange proceedings. I didn't know at the time that Barbara Ann had a child in her womb; nor did I know this was also true for my mother.

In swift order I returned to Amherst, my studies, and Matthew's bed. I sped through the semester. As June arrived, I suddenly realized that all of my teammates were leaving for the summer, back to their respective states up and down the coast. I couldn't understand their hurry. I was expected home, in Colorado, but I found this unthinkable. Three months away from Matthew would be tortuous, and, even worse, I dreaded the thought of going back to everything I had flown away from. I dawdled and made excuses with my parents that I had to stay a few weeks for a make-up exam.

Happily, Matthew was as miserable as I was. He cooked up a job for me on the UMass campus as his graduate assistant, typing up an official agreement on University letterhead. Next, I lied, boldfaced, to my parents, concocting a fake apartment address. These were the days when openly sleeping together out of wedlock was verboten; even though couples practiced it all across campus and in surrounding towns, no one admitted as much to their parents. Supposedly, I was rooming with Carla, who was also living with her boyfriend in another apartment and lying to her parents. I informed my mother I would be coming home for a short visit but had to be back in Amherst to move in with Carla and start my job by the first of July.

All went so smoothly I began to relax. My parents read the letter carefully, and if they had any misgivings they didn't tell me. During my ten-day stay in Colorado, I passed the time by sewing a new dress, a red print I picked out for Matthew. As my mother ran errands in the afternoon and bustled about fixing dinner, I sat with Roddy and Cami in the downstairs den, restless, plying the marble shoot with noisy orbs and stacking letter blocks. Roddy was happy to have me beside him, and I was happy to be leaving soon.

After what felt like an eternity, I finally boarded and strapped into my seat on a Continental Airlines jet, readying for take-off from Denver airport. In mere hours, I'd be back with Matthew and our new life together, and I was light-hearted with anticipation and pleasure. I wore my new flattering red dress, which flounced softly at the hemline and dipped low enough at the neckline to subtly show the lace bra underneath—another falsehood: on campus I went without a bra no matter what I was wearing. Only in the gym and in front of my parents did I harness my breasts.

Now, sitting on the runway, I longed to shed my bra and vowed I would do so the minute we got into the air. *Come on*, I thought. *What are we waiting for?* A stewardess appeared with a load of magazines in plastic covers and I chose *Ms.*, flipping through the pages to distract myself. After another few minutes, each one stretching before me like an hour, I lifted my eyes and gasped. There, coming down the aisle, was my father, grim faced. He looked as if he was going to strike me.

"Get up," he said, his tone ugly. "You're coming home."

My stomach roiled. I stared at him. "Why? What's wrong?"

He didn't answer and, expressionless, waited as I unstrapped my seat belt and gathered my things. I stood up and stepped into the aisle, queasy and weak-kneed. The cabin was deadly quiet as I made my way down the aisle and to the exit. Somehow, my father had found me out in time to stop the plane.

On the way home, he didn't answer my pleas for explanation, and by the time we arrived back home, I was a mess of nerves, chagrin, and indignation. Without a word, my mother handed me a letter as I came through the front door. It was a late birthday card from Carla, my so-called roommate. Inadvertently, she had put the wrong return address, the one that was her true address, not the one she and I were supposedly going to share. My parents threatened to take away my tuition and pull me out of college. I had a partial scholarship but it was not enough to cover my tuition and expenses; they had the power to keep me from school. They were trying to protect me, to keep me from ending up pregnant and abandoned, but they were treating me as if I hadn't already turned into a woman, as if I hadn't separated and left my childhood behind.

Ironically, my parents believed that keeping me from a college education would keep me from an early pregnancy, when the opposite was more likely. Not to mention that I'd be stuck going nowhere. I didn't know at the time that I was living the plight of women in the 1970s—pushing hard against my family's mixed messages to study hard, go to college, make good grades, but only to honor your father's good name and also to capture a husband. Not for your own aspirations. Don't expect to own your own destiny.

I didn't bend. Like the young women of that era, I straddled the chasm of sexism and feminism, the old and the new, and did what I had to do. I lied. I stuck to my story, insisting Carla had made a mistake: that in fact the address on the envelope was her old address, not our new one—an honest mistake. Carla rallied and agreed to talk to my parents on the phone, confirming her mistake. A week later, I boarded the plane again, and this time, I got off the ground. Climbing above the clouds and crossing the continent had never been so pleasurable, the flight so marvelous. I vowed never to get caught out again.

Before the summer was over, I did the one thing I knew would guarantee I never had to go home: I got engaged. Part of me sensed this was a bad idea, swapping my dependence on my parents for dependence on a husband. Not that Matthew and I weren't in love; we were, quite madly so. But in truth, I was not ready to marry. Though

I wouldn't admit it to myself, I needed to breathe, to feel what it was like to answer only to me. But I was too young to realize this at the time. Since my mother had been married at eighteen, and Barbara Ann at nineteen, I told myself twenty was plenty old enough. But I was wrong.

A few months before my wedding date, I was itching to get out of the small town of Amherst in the hot summer months, a deadly quiet town whenever the university closed down. Through the gymnastic grapevine I learned of a teaching job at a booming gymnastics camp in State College, Pennsylvania. I jumped at it, my first real salary; as a young liberated woman I was anxious to make my own way. Though the job meant I'd leave Matthew behind in Massachusetts for the summer, the alternative was to tediously assist him with office tasks as he worked on his graduate dissertation. Not only was the work excruciatingly boring, it meant I was under Matthew's wing. He was already my coach and would soon be my husband; I didn't want him to be my boss. Had I been able to see my younger self, I would have realized I was already chafing against the confines of a traditional relationship. At twenty, given my nature, my Southern Baptist upbringing, and my tamped-down childhood, I was primed to resist any thwart to my freedom.

The camp, on the other hand, supplied me with a paragon of free spirit. The gymnasium, a converted rustic barn in the middle of an Amish farm field, was a few hundred feet from a swimming pool, bordered on one side by three trampolines sunken in the ground. Cabins dotted the path from barn to pool, full of starry-eyed young gymnasts. Classes for children ran all morning and afternoon, and. in addition to teaching non-stop, I supervised one of the cabins and spent all day Sunday greeting incoming campers, touring them around the grounds, and helping them settle into their cabins.

By evening I was exhausted, but the hours between dinner and darkness were the most exciting of the day: the barn and all of its equipment turned into a playground for staff, no campers allowed. We put on our knee wraps, hand guards, and the barest shreds of clothing, and wowed each other with impossible moves. Lubricated by adrenalin and the hot night air, we egged each other on, bent on outdoing one another, not just with skill but also with daring. Our bodies were such well-oiled machines that we felt invincible, capable of challenging the forces of physics and coming out unscathed.

On one of those evenings, three weeks into the camp's first session, I found myself scaling a tower of mats up to the barn ceiling. The thick heat of summer wrapped around me and sweat clung to my skin. I was twenty feet up, having just accepted a dare to dive off the cross beam into a crash pad below. Several others had already taken this plunge, all males, one of them crazy enough to have climbed even higher until he reached the rafters. But only one female had attempted it so far. A few moments before, my teammate, Ellie, had balked up on the beam, reversed her steps, and climbed back down. Now it was my turn.

The cross beam was a rustic wood, barely milled, shellacked to keep from splintering. I stepped onto the slender surface and felt my way to the center where I stood and pondered the situation. *This is nuts*, I thought, observing what everyone else in the room already knew.

I was too high up to simply lean forward and dive straight toward the mat, ducking into a roll at the bottom. The momentum of the fall would break my neck. Instead, I would have to push off and stiffen my body up and out into a swan dive, then tip like a wooden plank, rotating just enough during the fall to land, flat-backed, on the mat. That was the only way I could protect my spine. If I miscalculated, I could snap a vertebra.

The barn fell quiet, the room taking on a curious, amused air. A cluster of sweaty faces looked up at me, expectant. One of them was Matthew's. He had missed me enough to make the long trip down and stay the weekend, the first of several times he would come to visit me. Now he was enjoying this thoroughly; the thrill of it, the audacity. He made no move to stop me. He knew me well enough. If he said anything, I wouldn't heed him. I felt an urgency to go through with this, to step into the bravado of men. It was the Seventies, and women were pounding down doors, proving their mettle. We were not at the point where we could be females in this male domain; we had to be male, to play by their rules, to come up or down to their level. Ellie had already chickened out; my doing the same thing would prove that the world and my parents were right: that deep down, women were inferior.

Okay then, I said to myself. *This is going to happen.* Turning inward, I felt the length of my spine, from my skull down to my tailbone. I pictured myself airborne, felt how it would feel to drive my heels up behind my head just enough and slowly tip one hundred and eighty degrees to a dead man's landing.

Exhale, inhale, slight give in the knees. Push off.

Suddenly, I was airborne, without any way to stop myself. I snapped both arms out like a pair of wings, tightened every strip of bone and muscle, fused my vertebrae, pointed my feet, drove my heels up behind my head and rotated, ever so slightly, closing both eyes, suspended in one glorious, aerodynamic free fall.

Wham! My heels, thighs, shoulder blades, and skull slapped the mat at the same exact moment. The room erupted into shouts and applause. I opened my eyes. Matthew's face was right above me, his eyes full of relief, his handsome mouth flashing a pleased and possessive smile. I clasped his offered hand and leaped up beside him, and for a few moments we stood together, absorbing the lights, the ionized air, the hot headiness of our supple youth. Everything lay before us.

Chapter 22

Falling

In my third year of college competition, I suddenly began freezing, midair. Kinesthetically I was lost, torquing and flying blindly, bailing and crashing without knowing why. I no longer knew up from down and failed to sense the ground until it came rushing up to meet me. I slammed into it over and over, each time as stunned as ever.

"For the love of Pete, if you can't follow through, scratch. Go sit on the bench and let somebody take your place!" Matthew hissed at me during the warm-ups for a high-stakes meet against the French Olympic team. He had just seen me balk in a full-twisting back flip and had lunged in to grab my flailing body. As soon as he put me on my feet, he said, "Get off the floor."

His tone felt hot, like smelted metal on my face. He had never spoken to me in that way but I didn't protest. Hesitation in the sport of gymnastics can be deadly, not only for yourself but also for your spotter. I hung my head and said nothing as we stood behind the bleachers and he dressed me down. We were both embarrassed for me. I was no longer a novice but I was behaving like one. I had prided myself on being the cool performer, the one who hit routines nine times out of ten and executed the difficulty with form and grace. That was the gymnast my husband knew and admired and had fallen in love with—not this one, this unpredictable flake.

In the year leading up to that meet, I had developed the worst type of injury, a chronic one—the type that never heals. My inflamed left shoulder socket was likely due to how I'd been formed before birth, a tendon sheath that was tighter on that side. My tendon fired back and forth like a piston through that squeezed opening, heating and swelling like a boiled sausage. It wasn't built for the relentless yank and pull of the uneven bars, or the repetition required to master a new trick or strengthen the body. All that friction triggered nodules, little calluses, sprouting along the insides of the sheath, turning the surface into sandpaper.

I knew very little about how pain worked deep inside the brain. In my early days of competition, I had broken a toe, sprained both ankles, hard, and once been casted and fitted with crutches. But none of those injuries had stayed with me. I healed, tossed the crutches aside, and went back to training as if my joints and sinews were springy and new.

Now, I couldn't escape the pain. It had settled in my body like an organ, an ever-present mass that lived in my shoulder, sprouting tentacles that reached deeply into my brain and caused me to lose my bearings. Later, I would learn how the nervous system reacts to chronic injury and what the brain does to protect the body. It dials up the heat, sending out hotter and hotter signals so the body will be forced to stop and heal, until even the strongest of wills cannot override the pain.

The summer before, my shoulder had shouted in protest. I awoke to a searing heat in my left arm. Matthew and I were living in a cabin on the Woodward Gymnastics Camp grounds; he was the camp director, and I, the girls' program director. My shoulder had been bothering me off and on, a throbbing ache that worsened as I lifted and pushed campers through back handsprings and caught them as they flew off trampoline in wrong directions. I had begun to live on anti-inflammatories, taking them like vitamins, and in the evenings, I retreated into our cabin and iced my shoulder as Matthew directed the night events of the camp. Naively, I assumed I could keep going on this way.

But that morning, in the cramped cabin loft, I shifted on the futon and gasped. A hot-white current shot from my shoulder socket in every direction, crackling down my arm and up into my throat.

Matthew stirred beside me. "What is it?" he said, wearily, sitting up. We had both grown tired of this persistent pain of mine and the despondency that came with it.

"A knife," I said, wincing, holding my arm against my ribs, "in my shoulder."

The pitch of my voice, its bare rasp, must have told him this was urgent. Hastily, he slipped on sweat pants and told me to stay still; in a moment he was on the phone, arranging substitutes for my morning classes and an appointment with the doctor.

That afternoon, the doctor informed me I was having an acute attack of tendinitis, a so called frozen shoulder. The doctor shot me full of cortisone and put me in a sling, ordering me to keep my arm still at all times. No spotting and absolutely no working out. Immobility was the best and only solution.

In the months that followed that first attack, I lurched from remedy to remedy, searching for a way to keep training and competing. Shortly after college classes started up again, I had driven with Matthew to a clinic in Springfield and stretched out on a table, allowing a healer from China to insert needles into both of my shoulders, arms, and hands. Pinned to the table, I held still as he waved smoking herbs about my face. In those days, acupuncture was seen as hocus-pocus—an exotic phenomenon unsanctioned by the American Medical Association and not covered by college insurance. But I was willing to do or try anything. I was reaching my peak as an athlete and had only about a year and a half left in me. My youthful talent as a freshman was now fine-tuned and I felt in my bones that I was capable of winning nationals. I was coming into my own and I cared for my team. They were counting on me.

On the way home from the acupuncturist, groggy from herbs, I fought to keep my eyes open and, once home, I fell into a deep sleep.

Miraculously, within a few days, I could lift my arm above my head without a trace of pain, something I had not been able to do for months. Astonished and euphoric, I went right back to the gym. I didn't understand that my injury was telling me to rest—that even though this treatment brought me relief it did not mean I was fixed. I couldn't hear that it was time for me to step away from winning. Violating my part of the healing bargain, I dove back into training.

All of this added up to this moment: me standing behind the bleachers with a tattered shoulder and a fed-up husband.

"Be there in a minute," Matthew called out to one of my teammates, who had stuck her head around the bleachers, wondering what on earth we were doing back there. I imagined them all looking for us, or at least looking for Matthew, whom they could still depend upon.

He turned back to me. I looked down; my eyes stung. I didn't have anything to say for myself and I had no idea how to recover my dignity. Two more teammates' faces peered around the end of the bleachers. Matthew and I never held private conferences, never breached the professional line. Neither of us had ever brought our marriage into the gym.

"Stay here and get a hold of yourself," he said.

I watched him walk away, his tall, broad-shouldered figure handsome in a dark blue sweat suit, long legs striding with confidence. As frustrated as he was with me, Matthew didn't want me to quit. I knew this; he wanted me to go back to who I'd been. Recently, I had tried to sit out this last prestigious meet against the French Olympians, but he had talked me out of it.

"Nah, you don't really want to do that," he had said, expertly stripping the white athletic tape and wrapping it around my ankle. I had just finished a twenty-minute whirlpool treatment for sore cartilage in both knees and was sitting on the physio table with an ice pack on my shoulder. Anyone coming into the room would have thought I'd been in a car accident.

"Matthew, I'm tired."

"Of what?" His tone softened slightly.

"Hurting," I said.

Silently, he smoothed the tape edges against my skin. He kept his eyes down, offering me, instead, his strong aquiline nose and fine high cheek bones, his thick dark hair. He put the tape back into the drawer. I sensed he was struggling as much as I was with this conundrum. This was the moment when I needed him to be my husband—to care for me more than the win.

"Back off routines for the next few days," he said, finally. "Do your strength work and step up the running. Get a lot of physio, hot packs, and ultrasound. Pace yourself. You'll be ready to compete."

A dark tiny shadow moved through me: the thought that we might not make it. I looked down, forlorn, unconvinced, except for the sliver of me still listening.

"The team needs you, Co," he said, evoking the nickname he had given me.

This swayed me. In truth, the team needed every one of us if we were going to win. We were not a big team, not like Springfield or Southern Illinois with a depth of fifteen to twenty ready gymnasts. We were only four all-around competitors with a handful of others backing us up on each event. My team couldn't afford to lose my score.

Now, huddled behind the bleachers, teary and smarting, I bent forward into a deep stretch, burying my face into my knees for several minutes, until my eyes stopped stinging. Then, slowly, I straightened up and began to crawl through the scaffolding under the bleachers to get to the opposite wall and the exit door. Small wonder Matthew had begun to turn his hopes away from me, shifting his attention to the healthier, younger freshmen, working with them extra hours, pushing them through vigorous strength work. His waning interest in me and my injuries was not lost on me. I felt helpless against this, betrayed by my body, disabled, envious of others who did not have my pain.

It wasn't so much that I needed to win another medal; I was no longer competing for that. It was the familiarity of my body in the air, the liquidity of swinging, the exhilaration of blind sight—knowing where the floor was when I couldn't see it, switching to deeper sensations for navigation and landing. It was a language I knew and spoke effortlessly with my teammates and my husband. Subconsciously, I knew my team was my family, my tribe—my talented, smart, funny, passionate, bonded family. Not only did we spend inordinate hours in the gym together, we ribbed and cajoled each other out of bad moods, took care of each other's disappointments, cheered each other on, shared our fears, hung out together, laughed ourselves sick: all the things I had longed for in my real family. Finally, I had a small circle of siblings who knew and needed me, who gave me the closeness and harmony I had longed for as a child. I couldn't bear to live without them.

Emerging from the scaffolding, I scooted to the exit door and down the stairs to the locker room. Bending over the sink, I splashed icy water on my eyelids. The door creaked and in came a middle-aged woman, no doubt someone's mother. She smiled, but her expression quickly melted into concern and pity as she looked at my face. I ducked my head back into the sink and splashed until I heard the stall door click closed. Then, I looked into the mirror to see what she had seen.

There, gazing back, was a red-eyed, gray-skinned, exhausted young woman. Her tightly bunned hair was bleached and brittle, and the tendons in her neck and bones of her sternum pushed out through her skin.

A stone of uneasiness dropped and sent rings rippling to the outer edges of my stomach. I knew something was wrong: my determination and stoicism were no longer helping me. I was agreeing to things I did not want to do, as if I had no choice. The thought of scratching from the competition and sitting on the sidelines taunted me like a seduction: a luscious and dishonorable desire. I was done for, my body woefully compromised, but I didn't have the bravery to bow out, to feel myself beached on the sidelines. The thought opened a vast hole in my chest. In the darkness of that hole lurked my childhood: the loneliness of being a spectator, sidelined and helpless—waiting out my brother's fits, my mother's rages. My gymnastics had eased my mother's mourning, as well as my own, and had given me an escape route to another life. Now I had this new family, a passion and talent, a way to shine. I had the joy and anticipation of greater heights, of flying to a higher horizon. And I had a deep-seated fear that I could fall and lose it all, just as my mother had so many years ago.

Above me, through the ceiling of the locker room, the stands rumbled as everyone stood for *The Star-Spangled Banner*. The burn in my left shoulder pumped down my arm and into my hand, like a deep and fast-running pulse. With my one good arm, I opened the door.

Part III

Fortuity

Chapter 23

Coppertone

My mother's coffee pot was an ancient Sunbeam, the kind that wields heavy in the hand and percolates the grounds to a watery gruel. Lord above, how I longed for a French press and a bag of dark-roasted beans. Pouring myself a cup, I moved through the back door into the Florida sun. It was a sultry morning and I was stepping into it gingerly, much as I had the three mornings before—with a stolen hour on the patio deck of my parents' pool, a breakfast of caffeine, and a slender volume of Marie Howe's poetry, her words a portable cave into which I could vanish.

I was twenty-three and not entirely sure why I was there, however briefly, in Orlando, the sprawling, tawdry town my parents now called home. They had moved from Colorado, where I'd grown up, to a part of the country that felt utterly alien to me. I found the blistering heat and spongy terrain, enlivened by June bugs the size of pocket knives, peculiar and slightly horrifying. Yet, there I was.

"Honey, I'm off," my mother trilled, startling me. She poked her head through the back door, sweeping her eyes once around, searching the jumble of chaise lounges and worn lawn chairs, and then casting farther, out to where I stood, close to the lip of the pool. "Need anything before I go?"

Her voice was tender, laced with a girlish gaiety. In honor of my surprise visit, she was fetching Rod home for an overnight, picking him up from his group house where he lived with three other autistic young men and where he was supervised by a high-turnover staff—a constant worry for my parents. She was pleased to have me there, though a tad puzzled. She'd been careful not to ask many questions and I hadn't offered clues as to why I'd arrived. I was her independent child who stayed away for long stretches without calling home, who had married outside the Southern Baptist fold—to a Jew, no less.

"I'm fine." I pecked my cup with a fingernail. "This'll do me."

She studied me, one hand holding the door ajar. I watched her retreat into watchful silence and wondered how she saw me, the daughter who had strayed and would stray again. Some years from now she would tell me I had been her easiest child, sunny and busy, winning blue ribbons, heels never touching the ground.

"Did you eat anything? You ought to eat something." Her chin tilted, as if she were about to say "You're skin and bones."

"I'll make myself some toast," I said. "In a bit."

She paused, two beats. She knew I was hedging.

"All right then," she said. "Back in a jiffy."

I cupped one hand around the back of my neck: the way I wanted to be comforted. For as long as I could remember, my mother had been a woman of fractured attentions, pulled by a long line of needs and wants. First, and always, my father; then, especially, Roddy; then, my two much-younger siblings—Cami and James, late-in-life babies who'd arrived fifteen years after me and who in a few hours would clamber off the bus from elementary school, demanding things of my mother in ways I never had. My hope that I might find something different, that I would claim a moment of my mother's attention now that I was an adult, proved how disoriented I was.

A week ago, a flurry of arrangements had put me in my car, tattered map beside me, sandals and sunscreen stuffed in a duffle. I had been gripped by an urgent need to flee the March winds of New England, where every breath was cut with cold and snow hung in gray jowls from the wheel beds of my car. If I had reflected for even a moment

I would have known I was fleeing emptiness, partly from my shelved life as a national championship gymnast, and partly from my marriage, which was faltering, though I didn't fully believe this yet. I was too young to know there are forces in life stronger than me, deeper than my own will. I believed I would navigate back to my husband. All I needed was a respite, I'd assured him. A brief reprieve. I had taken a hasty leave from my part-time job at a bookstore and had driven nearly nonstop down the long scrambled coast of the Eastern seaboard.

Now, I stood on my parents' patio in lonely despair, hardly touching my coffee. The heat from the concrete deck penetrated the soles of my feet and flickered up my legs. Shifting my cup to one hand, I clutched the flimsy metal arm of the lounge chair and spun it so I could face the sun. Easing onto the battered webbing, I sighed from the dry ache in my joints, like an old retired greyhound.

For a small moment I felt relief. Splashes of sun washed my thighs and penetrated the threads of my suit. I was dressed scantily, in a maroon swimsuit cut high on the leg, which bared part of my pelvis and, if I was careless, a crescent of my nether region, the hair of which I'd cauterized nearly to my pubic bone. I burned easily and should have been more vigilant about sunlight, but it was 1975. These were the days of cultivating golden skin, of basting oneself with buttery oils and flipping like a fillet so every surface was evenly cooked. Sundrenched limbs meant ripeness and youth, each of which I wanted again, desperately. If I gained nothing more from the next few days, I could at least capture the sun's glow and with it, hopefully, some replenished desire.

In the hot glare, my bare legs looked like rutted roads, shin-pocked by old collisions with balance beams. A slender ribbon of scar tissue seamed the inside of my left leg where a trampoline spring had once zipped my skin open. Matthew had saved me on that fall—early on, before he was my husband, when he was simply Matthew, a graduate student whose stipend as an assistant coach put food in his mouth. I flushed now with the memory. I had relished being coupled, of belonging to another, especially him. He had split me open with laughter and, when we weren't provoking each other, we were crashing and daring ourselves beyond fear. It was everything I had imagined, a thrilling and heightened life—before my body wearied; before injury sent me to doctors and injections, relegating me to a slinged shoulder on the sidelines; before the next crop of freshmen bodies spilled into the gym and captured the attention of my husband. Matthew was fueled by new talent, the possibility of reaching new heights. I had no reason to suspect it was more than this, his staying after hours and working with one of the most promising new young freshmen. But it felt like more. When I dropped by the gym on my way home from the library, bringing him his favorite deli-Cosmo and Coke, I lingered on the bleachers. I watched him urge her back up onto the bars, catch her mid-air and, putting her on her feet, cajole her to try again. I heard his quip and their dual laughter tumble across the gym to where I sat, fully clothed, in jeans and a long-sleeved sweater, sandwich half-eaten on my lap.

I closed my eyes. A wisp of cool air lifted from the pool, skimming my hairline. I had hoped to seal a bond with him, to make a nest of my own. It was too early for me to realize that my desire for joy, for a family of easy informality, of humor and generosity, would draw me again and again into mismatched unions. I didn't know I was a woman whose origins would make coupling a hard climb in life, that my patterns of attraction, to lively and charming partners who thrived on attention, who took all the air in the room, were rooted deeply in my childhood. In my marriage, I mirrored the role I had always played in my family: the independent one who not only took care of herself but persevered, who didn't make demands or ask for affection, who tempered the drama around her with self-control and seeming indifference. Who was fearless and who felt lost if she wasn't perfect, nabbing the blue ribbon, the top prize.

If I was in denial about just how this wasn't working for me, I only had to take note of where I was sleeping (in my parents' den with no privacy) and how I was living (out of a poorly packed bag). The night before, as I had made my way to the bathroom in the dark, feeling with flattened palms in total blackness, I had rammed straight into the door frame, a blow that had watered my eyes and slithered me to my haunches.

I lifted my finger now, lightly touching the aching district above my eyebrow. It felt meaty and overwarm. A blinding shard of light glanced off the chrome of the barbecue cart and some shuddering movement scurried along the edge of the pool. I jumped from my chair, shielding my eyes, and spotted a lizard, over by the ladder, clinging to the edge of the concrete. He flicked his eyes, *tick-tick*, uncertain whether to move into the shade or stay where he was, clinging to the hot stone, burning his pads.

I couldn't bear to look at him. I felt parched and cooked. The single palm tree squatting on the far side of the pool, the thorny grass suffocating in the sun, the six-foot slatted fence wrapping the yard and walling off the neighbors, closed around me. Swiftly, I moved across the concrete. The pool was a small peanut-shaped affair, no more than ten feet deep and ill-suited for even a shallow dive. But I launched from one foot anyway, off the pool's edge, soaring out over the glassy green surface like a low-flying pontoon.

In an instant, my head pierced the shimmering surface. The bright cold took my breath and I scraped the pool's floor with my palms, my legs pumping as I pulled forward, slicing and parting the water with cupped and stinging hands. Within seconds I'd reached the shallow end, where I gulped a quick, hard breath and dove again, heading back to the deep end, dragging along the floor. Rays shot from above, rippling along the walls; chlorine seared my eyes. I squeezed my lids, feeling for the wall, slapping it and flipping, heading back the other way.

I kept on like this, lapping the pool ten, twenty, thirty times, until my lungs groaned and I gulped water. When I surfaced again at the shallow end, sputtering and pushing ropes of hair from my eyes, I flinched. A few feet away, at the pool's edge, sat a blurry figure, watching me.

"Oh, hi, Rod," I said.

"Hi, Mossie!" he shouted.

Pain bloomed in my ear. It had been two years since I had last seen him, long enough for me to have grown sloppy with the nuances of how to pitch and temper my voice. Low and languid was the rule. I paused, then tried again.

"It's nice to see you," I said.

His eyes darkened. He looked down, thinking this through.

"Yaas," he said, at last.

It didn't occur to me, either then or for many years to come, that my brother had missed me. Easing gently forward, I moved through the water slowly, as if traveling through syrup, to where he sat on the pool's edge. He was eighteen years old, dressed in a pale blue, baggy-legged swimsuit, which covered his thighs and framed each of his ivory kneecaps in navy trim. His tank top dipped low enough in front to reveal a chest sprouted with dark hair—a new thing. His feet, rippling underwater, rested on the first step of the pool, pigeon-toed.

I paused at the bottom step, not too close.

"May I sit with you?" I asked.

He held a frosty glass of iced tea, the contents of which he was sipping in miniscule swallows, like a bird pecking at a bird bath. He made a soft sound, part hum, part snort.

"Okay, I'll just dry off first," I said, rising up the steps, dripping, edging to the left so as not to spray him.

I wasn't sure how to be around him now that he was a man. Now that he had turned dark and resentful. His sweet nature had disintegrated with the beginning of puberty, his body whipped around with hormones and urges he couldn't understand. The last time I'd visited, two years ago, I'd been sharing tea with my mother in the kitchen when Rod exploded in the back bedroom, yelling at my father and stomping down the hallway and into the kitchen, opening and slamming drawers, picking up a saucer and throwing it into the sink. I had sprung to my feet, spilling tea and moving behind the counter, away from him.

"Now, Rod," my mother had said, her voice tinged with anxiety, though she was not surprised.

I had not seen him act that way since he was a child, his frustration and anger exploding in hot tantrums. All I'd had to do when he was smaller than me was lean over him and turn his attention to a

Popsicle or a bag of marbles, or take him outside. Now, he was a man, nearly a foot taller than me, and I didn't know what he was capable of. I wasn't sure I knew how to distract or appease him.

Warily, I reached for my towel. Rod cast a furtive glance back to where I stood rubbing my legs and scruffing the cloth through my hair. The towel made me wince. My skin felt tight and raw, my back like a tenderized cutlet, exposed. Aside from thin spaghetti straps, my suit bared the whole of my back, its lines plunging nearly to my tailbone, and, foolishly, I had neglected to rub myself with suntan lotion. Grabbing up the Coppertone, I hastily slathered my limbs, then my face, and finally came to my back.

Despite my years of stretching my limbs, my body held onto a stubborn and uneven flexibility. My left shoulder, with its history of inflammation, had a tightness that would one day pop my rotator cuff and send me into surgery. Right then it meant I couldn't reach my upper spine. I thought suddenly of all the times Matthew had granted me this small favor. Early in our courtship we had spent many a steamy afternoon at the beach in Belchertown, during which he had smeared lotion all over me, taking special care with my back, massaging it between my shoulder blades as I lay half-asleep on my stomach. We had stayed in the hot sun for hours, oblivious. By the time we'd packed up and retreated to our tiny apartment in North Hampton, showering in the sweltering closeness, we knew a stinging and sleepless night lay ahead. But neither of us had minded; we were blurry with desire.

Now, this deep and wounding memory came back to me. Tears pricked my eyes. I snatched up my towel and turned toward my brother, about to say I'd changed my mind, that I'd had enough sun and I'd see him inside. I didn't want to say the truth: that I needed to escape myself, that coming south had failed to comfort me, that I didn't belong here, any more than I belonged back in my old life, my dissolving world.

But as I caught sight of Rod sipping his tea, the fingers of his other hand patting the water, it came to me that I didn't want to flee him just yet. Something about his glances and the way he smiled into his tea glass made me sense he was pleased to have my company.

Years before, when Rod was ten years old, he had come out of our house wearing that same smile, holding my mother's hand, to where I was bouncing on our new backyard trampoline. It was June, and that morning two men had arrived in a truck, hauling out metal frame parts, a box of springs, and a nylon bed. In short order, they'd set up my surprise birthday present. I was fourteen and thrilled with the sensation of flying, spinning in the air, landing on my feet or stomach or back, and spinning again. I couldn't get enough: the thrill of being weightless, of being released from the ground.

As I had flipped and landed on my back, then flipped again, my mother had stood at the end of the trampoline.

"He's been watching you for an hour," she said, at last. "I think he wants to try."

I stopped and stared at her, hesitating, not at all sure my brother belonged on a trampoline. I knew how to control my own body, but not his. My mother lifted him and I reached for his hands, helping him onto the nylon bed, a soft, mischievous floor.

"Okay, Rod," I said, firmly, gripping his arm, a jittery nervousness in my stomach. "You need to learn how to stay in the middle, and then how to stop your bounce. That's all."

I said this more to myself than to him—and to my mother. What could she know of a trampoline's moods and how hard it was to stay on? Cautiously, I showed him how to bounce, how to halt, devising simple steps so he wouldn't be afraid, so he'd try just enough to succeed. He puffed through his nose, listening, not looking at me. And then, he did exactly what I had told him to do. I clapped with surprise and let him do it again. It was all going so well, I lost myself.

"Alright, stand right here in the middle, bounce three times, and when I say three, pick up your feet and sit down. Ready? One, two, three!"

He bounced and lifted his feet up in front of him, full of courage. For all he knew, he might die from this. My heart leapt as he plummeted to the bed, his feet flopping in the air, legs akimbo. His hips hit and he ricocheted sideways, heading for the springs. I lunged and grabbed him before he shot off altogether but not before he landed on his side, half on the bed, half on the springs.

"Are you okay?" I asked, hysterically, lifting him, straightening his T-shirt and brushing invisible dirt off his pants. A deep scratch reddened on his arm, blood beading along the cutline. A furor rose in me.

"Mom! He can't do this; he's going to end up in the hospital. I think he should get down now."

My mother, standing a few feet away on the grass, shielded her eyes from the sun. She didn't answer me. Tiny creases appeared at the corners of her mouth, and a deeper fold in her brow, but her eyes held steady.

"Go again," Roddy said.

I turned to him, astonished. "What? You want to try again?"

"Yaas," he said.

We all stood there, silent. I chewed on my lip. Roddy had so few passions; how could I deny him this, something I so easily and randomly sampled for myself? In a deep place, I knew this wasn't mine to keep from him. His autism had not caused him to ricochet. I had. I'd taught him as if he were me.

"Okay," I said, "but we have to do it another way."

I made him sit still on the bed, his legs out front, and pressed his ankles together with my hands, telling him to squeeze his muscles. I showed him exactly where his hands had to be when he dropped and where his arms needed to reach as he bounced back to his feet. Then, I let him up to try again.

"No bouncing this time, just push off the bed once and pull your feet up," I said. "Go ahead, when you're ready."

In the next instant he dropped to his bottom, legs straight out in front, and bounced back to his feet. I caught him and cried, "There! You did it! You did it!"

I had never taught a seat drop to anyone or any other trick for that matter. I had only been a learner up to that point, a hungry swallower of new things, rather than a giver or a guide.

Mama clapped and laughed, and Roddy smiled his odd smile.

"Again," he said in his flat voice, looking off to the side, as always.

Again and again he jumped. That entire summer we spent in the backyard together, taking turns, me doing flips and twists and Roddy doing ten seat drops in a row, without stopping. I was about to become a champion—eight years of winning lay before me—and I didn't know I could or would want anything else from my life. I didn't know that my brother was seeding in me something that would carry me through, after the winning was over: the sensitivity to be a good teacher, the ability to coax courage and triumph from a child.

Even now I didn't know this as I padded to where Rod sat on the pool's edge and lowered myself beside him. I had no idea what I carried within me or what I had to offer. He shifted an inch away from me, then settled again. We sat together for a few minutes, not saying anything. Finally, I opened my mouth.

"Could you do something for me?" I asked. "Will you rub lotion on my back?"

I had never requested a favor from him, much less something this intimate. The act of smearing lotion on his skin, let alone on mine, was fraught with sensory land mines. This had been true for as long as I could remember, an enduring part of his old self. For a moment, he studied the bottle in my hand, and then he shifted his eyes to his glass of iced tea.

"I can hold your tea, if you'd like," I offered. "I won't drink any, I promise."

He ignored me, choosing instead to set his glass carefully on the edge of the pool. And then, with the tips of his long fingers, he took the Coppertone from my hands.

This alone was a marvel. My brother's response to any request was like a tangled almanac, a set of warnings that might or might not advance to a full-blown tornado. Often, without warning, he bellowed, "No!"—especially when the request meant contact, eye or otherwise. Touch to him was like a thorn.

I had no reason to believe he would behave calmly or do as I'd asked. But I was desperate for distraction and unmoored enough to throw caution aside. Holding my breath, I turned, offering him my shoulder blades.

In the moment that my brother touched me, the broad stretch of flesh between my shoulder blades rippled awake, an ocean of nerves. His touch was like nothing I had felt before. In those first few seconds I thought it couldn't be him. He pressed the pads of his fingers and palms flat to my skin, sweeping and circling around the peaks of my shoulder blades with an inexplicable rhythm. I had expected a tentative touch, a dabbing of sorts, but his strokes were smooth, as if coming from a learned someone who had been soothing skin for years—nuanced, subtle, graceful, tender, kind.

I sat there, stilled, my eyes closed. The wings of my scapula unfolded with a sensation of cool, purling air.

If he and I had grown up embracing, tangled in one puppy knot or another, I might have glazed over this moment, barely marking it in my mind, the familiarity of his touch little more than a rote sensation, like the brush of a terry cloth towel, or the bump of an elbow, rather than what it was: a shocking, breathless sensation.

In those first few seconds I realized he had never touched me of his own volition. I had always been the one reaching for him, closing my fingers around his soft hand when stepping from the car, tapping his knee when I needed his attention, pressing on the back of his flapping hands so they quieted for a moment. All of these were planned touches, without surprise or spontaneity, triggered for safety and designed for protection.

Unlike now. Three minutes passed. Under the temperature of his touch, I fell back to what might have been possible: to the brother he might have been if he'd been born free of autism. I imagined him pestering me to play tag, pulling me outside to escape our parents as we rolled our eyes, his teenage arm flung about my shoulders, goosing my side, or, as now, his young man's hands smoothing lotion on my shoulders. Not a lover's touch, or even a friend's, but a brother's—a touch that echoed the very beginnings of childhood, of sorting out bad dreams and monsters together, of weathering the storms of family.

I wished for more—for his touch to last. I was losing everything, all that I had yearned for: a husband, a nest of my own, a sense of rhythm and purpose to my life, the joy of a young body's strength and fluidity, and the satin assurance of blue ribbons around my neck; a life that added up to something—to triumph. Folding my arm across my chin, I reached around to the back of my shoulder and tapped the scapula with my forefinger, that oh-so-human gesture.

"Can you put a dab more, right there?" I asked.

"Yaas," he said.

I don't remember how long he complied. Perhaps it was the nature of his fingerprints, the whorls and arches, the tiny ridges unique to him, a special signature, a kind of personal map that made me believe, made me realize his touch was showing me a part of him I'd despaired of ever knowing.

I learned years later that touch is the most ancient sense, that feeling doesn't take place in the topmost layer of skin, but in the second layer, the deeper one. This is where I felt my brother's touch. His may not have been a caress to console me, but I felt it as one.

How kind of him, I thought, as I sat there warmed by the sun and his hands, to set himself aside, to deny his aversion to touch for these few moments. For me.

Chapter 24

Sebastian

On a muggy New England afternoon, I knelt in a small windowless gym, surrounded by a forest of equipment: low and high balance beams, two tethered sets of uneven bars, and, pushed up against one wall, a slow-bedded trampoline. A haze of chalk permeated my nose. Sweat filmed my hands and face, staining the thighs of my sweat pants.

"Okay, up up up, on your feet," I said. A gaggle of preschoolers, seven tiny people, unfolded their legs and jostled for a place in front of the line, closest to me.

I was barely twenty-three, fresh out of college with an English and journalism degree and a national gymnastic championship, and, for the first time, I didn't know how to live my life. Having aged out of competition with a creaky set of leftover joints, I longed to follow my other self—my passion for poetry, words, and stories. Still, this physical side had a grip on me, entwined like a vine throughout my veins. I didn't know it had more to teach me and that, in time, it would shape me into a teacher and a mother.

I couldn't see this yet. In my mind I had failed at this sport, failed to reach the heights I had hoped for, and I had failed at my marriage. All I could see was that I was a beginner again, a beginner in my own life. For months I had been going through the motions, hour after hour, teaching preschoolers to lift tiny bottoms in the air, duck chins, and roll without snapping necks, to get up on a four-inch-wide piece of wood and walk across without crying and clutching my hand.

"Don't start yet!" Ellie, my former teammate, and now the gymnastics school director, called from across the gym. Coming toward me, she held a four-year-old boy by the hand. He was slight and gently brown-haired. He didn't look at me. "This is Sebastian," she announced, cheerily.

I bugged my eyes at her. If there was one thing I had learned in these few months of teaching, it was that little ones have a tendency to zoom off in all directions. Eight was a large number to keep safe and under control. "Sorry," she mouthed, sloe-eyed, exaggerating a frown, and then, leaning closer, added, "His mother begged me. She asked for you as his teacher. He has allergies and he's shy."

In the five years we had known one another, Ellie and I had slid back and forth between friendship and vexation. She was theatrical, sensuous, overwrought—the opposite of me. I was observant, wrapped, reserved. Together, we had carried our collegiate team to a national championship—half the time with her in tears. Separately, we elbowed each other for first place in each event. We couldn't have been more different on the gymnastic floor: me, a lover of kinesthesia and technique; her, of power, punch, and cheeky charm.

Now, she trotted away in her monogrammed sweat jacket, knowing exactly who she was and how she was going to make a go of it, this life after competitive death.

"Okay, up you go," I said, grunting and lifting each miniature body onto the trampoline bed, and then hoisting myself up onto the frame. Patiently, I waited as they all settled in a row on the frame pad, like miniature Peeps. In spite of the hour and the sticky heat, I smiled. Little Max, as always, sat with his arms wrapped around his knees waiting for my next word. He was a dreamboat: blond curls and big eyes. Beside him was Zoey, beribboned and adorned in a purple leotard, already possessing flair and fearlessness; she didn't know the talent she carried. Her limbs and torso were supple and strong, graceful and precise in an effortless way. Even at this early stage, before she could balance on one leg or hold a proper headstand, it was unmistakable: she would be a champion.

And then there was Sebastian. He lolled to the side, his muscles and joints like jelly on a warm day, flopping and squirming.

"Don't be on me!" Zoey cried, full of despair, pushing him off.

Suddenly, Sebastian bounded to his feet and leaped off the frame pad onto the trampoline bed, *boing*-ing helter-skelter, arms flailing like spaghetti. In an instant, his body ricocheted to the side, shooting straight for the springs. Lunging, I grabbed him, stumbling, but catching my footing just before we both flew over the side.

Part of my job was discipline, planting the proper percentage of fear in a child's heart. Squatting down on the bed, I held him firmly in front of me so we were face to face.

"Look at me, Sebastian. You must sit and wait until I say you can take your turn. Understand?"

His gaze darted away, even though his nose was a few inches from mine. He twisted his chin to the side.

I hesitated, taking him in: the small slump of his shoulders, the anxiety in how he pulled on his lip. Slowly, a deep and old recognition came to me. His fragility, the dark circles under his eyes the color of smoke, his hollow gaze. *I know this boy*, I said to myself. A wave of protectiveness flushed through me, muddied with dismay. *I have known him all of my life.*

The children sat still and silent. They had squeezed together so there was no room between them, no chance for this odd boy to wriggle his way in.

"Sebastian," I said, exhaling and relaxing my vocal cords, dropping my voice. "Come sit over here, by me. You can help me teach today."

Interest flickered and died on his face. Still, he came with me and, as soon as he was settled, he melted into me, a soft, exhausted puppy. I put my arm around him and called Zoey out onto the trampoline. Like the champion she was, she stood at attention, waiting for my cue.

"All right, Zoey. Three bounces and a seat drop. Ready?"

"One two three!" Sebastian shouted, sitting up for a brief moment, then collapsing against me again. The other children stared at him, wondering and unsure.

Out of the corner of my eye I caught sight of a mother in the doorway, one hand gently holding her throat. As a rule, parents were discouraged from watching class, their presence proving too much for the children. It triggered show-off behavior and a lot of incessant waving in the middle of a trick. Apparently, the rule had been waived for this mother.

She stood just shy of the door frame, young, dark-haired, carefully groomed. Her features were a tangle of uncertainty and misgiving. Her face, the way she held her throat, the longing and the worry in her eyes, told me that she was Sebastian's mother. Around the edges of her mouth hovered a dread that this would turn out like all of the other times—all those activities when, in every instance, Sebastian had been asked to leave class before it was over and not return. Nudging Sebastian to his feet, I took his hand and stepped with him onto the middle of the trampoline bed. Then, I said what I said to every child.

"You can do this. Listen carefully; I'll help you."

He rubbed his eyes, wearily, as if he held all of the confusion of the world. Squatting down, I looked into his face, even though he wouldn't look back. I knew he could hear me.

"Stay with me, Sebastian. I know how it is."

Ever so slightly his chin tipped back toward me. His eyes still did not meet mine, but I could tell he was with me. Softening my grip, I let go and stepped back onto the frame.

Sure enough, he waited for me, his arms by his sides, his little body gently bobbing on the bed.

"Now, just push off, lift your feet up, and sit down. I'll be here to catch you."

He stood there, glancing around the room as if he hadn't heard me. Then he did exactly what I'd told him to do, full of courage, and when he rebounded back up to his feet, he reached for my hand.

I didn't know at the time that this moment was indelible. It would always stay with me, this touch of a small boy's hand in mine, a boy like my brother. It awoke a protectiveness and tenderness in me that I hadn't felt in a long while. I was about to embark on a different life, an independent quest to reach another dream, to be a writer. I had an English degree and not a clue as to where to go from here, but within a few rapid years I'd be in Boston, writing for a women's sports magazine and interning in the newsroom of WBUR. I would go on to win broadcasting and journalism awards, and I would marry again. And also for many years I would coach an elite girls' gymnastics team. All the while, this moment with a child would stay with me, reminding me of the tender spot I had for the heart of every child, a sensitivity I would take with me into motherhood.

Chapter 25

Apparition

I always cherished visiting the farm—craved it, really. In 1986, we arrived halfway through August, later in the summer than usual. The northern Canadian air had already cooled and light drenched the wheat fields in a deeply golden hue, bending toward fall. Ahead of us lay weeks of respite. This trip to Prince Edward Island was the only time all year I felt my husband, Don, and I and our two-year-old son, Dylan, were a true family, away from Boston, away from my in-laws, away from the interdependent bond my husband had with his parents.

Flinging off my seat belt, I freed Dylan and together we scampered together toward the back door. The house was a big Victorian, over a hundred years old, with carved cornices and a dried fountain in the front yard. Don's parents had snapped up the property in the recession of the Seventies, and restored and furnished it to its 1880s glory. Now it was the family's coveted summer compound, a rural hideaway cut off from the frenetic urban pace of our Boston life, where we could replenish ourselves in the farming life without having to do the work.

"Wait a second, Turkey. Daddy needs our help," I said, stopping Dylan from scurrying up the stairs. He was a sweet, sensitive boy, high in emotion and curiosity, and so intuitive and aware that at times he astonished me. Life was not going to be easy for him.

We retreated only to find Don nowhere near the car. In the distance, across the vast front yard, I spotted his bulky frame hurrying for the shore. Not to take in the sunset or inhale the sea air, but to smoke a cigarette, a habit he assumed I hadn't noticed. I let him believe it was undetectable—a mistake on my part. The more I colluded in his secrecy, the more I nurtured mistrust in both of us, though I didn't know this at the time. He had tried to quit twice since we had married, each time turning hot-tempered and bullish. When his snoring worsened, rattling me awake from the depths of my exhausted mother-sleep, I knew he had started again. By day, he slipped away on sudden, urgent errands, refusing to take Dylan along so that he could smoke freely in the car.

"Where is he?" Dylan cried, stricken.

"Daddy's checking on the studio," I lied, in a lilting voice. "Let's get all our stuff inside before he comes back. We'll surprise him."

Dylan nodded his curly head, vigorously. "Yeah!" he said. Grabbing his tattered blanket, bag of toys, and crumpled pillow, he staggered toward the door. The next moment I heard him in the parlor, noisily wrestling miniature bulldozers and race cars out of his backpack.

As for me, I grabbed the banister and steadied myself. I was pregnant again, four months in, with late-afternoon nausea that worsened with fatigue. My stamina this time around was alarmingly thin. This baby had surprised me, coming so close on the heels of Dylan's birth, which had been a forty-eight-hour hard labor, ending in a cesarean. I didn't feel quite ready for another.

A moment of reflection would have reminded me that Dylan, too, had come as a surprise. Part of me knew that surprise pregnancies were the only way I'd ever have babies, given my childhood and my conviction as a young teen that it was better not to have babies at all. Since that long ago afternoon in Bea's Laundromat when I was on the cusp of womanhood, I had tracked my cycles like a scientist, knowing exactly when I ovulated and down to the hour when I would start my blood flow. In my second year of college, the birth control pill burst on the scene and I dashed to the university health clinic along with hundreds of other young women for the slender package of protection. Nevertheless, Mother Nature stepped in and, in my early thirties, tweaked my hormonal cycle enough to ovulate one day earlier. Even more surprising was the reckless thrill I'd felt the moment I learned I was pregnant. Soon afterward, in a kind of romantic whirlwind, Don and I married and within the year we had a healthy baby boy. At last, I had my own family.

Inhaling, I picked up the suitcase and mounted the front stairs, pausing on the landing for a few breaths. Beyond was the alcove, its sun-faded curtains drawn to the side. The view from its window was my favorite. Moving to the pane, I parted the sheers and took a deep breath at the sight: a startling rush of lush golden wheat, stretching to the distant road. On the left, a stroke of iron-red soil slashed down the side of the field, marking the half-mile rutted lane from the highway to this house. And in the far distance, chomping through the wheat was a dollop of dark blue, moving steadily, shrinking toward the horizon, then turning and swelling toward me.

"Currie's combine," I marveled aloud. "We're here."

Another wave of nausea swooned up my throat. I dropped the curtain and backed onto the rocking chair, perching on the edge. I wasn't very good at this—the surging of nature, the upheaval of organs and blood and digestion to prepare the womb. Unlike Barbara Ann, who reveled in pregnancy and glowed through the months, I trudged from conception onward, vomiting all the way.

Tiny feet clomped up the stairs, followed by a rumble, smack, and wail. Swiftly, I rose and reached for the banister. "Okay, honey, I'm coming."

Descending the steps to the landing, I squatted where Dylan sprawled on his belly, sobbing into his blanket. Hefting him up, I settled him on the top step, sat beside him, and checked for damage. None that I could see, save for his pride. As I brushed damp curls back from his forehead, a smoky odor whiffed up the stairs and encircled us.

"What's going on?" Don called from the bottom of the stairs, frowning.

"Dylan took a tumble," I said airily, "He's okay."

"How did that happen? Was he running?"

My husband didn't believe in accidents. If someone got hurt, it was due solely to carelessness and wanton disregard.

"He tripped on his blanket," I said, cheerily, as if Dylan had done something delightful.

I didn't like the person who used this voice. She wasn't me. She had a high-pitched, skittery tone, defensive and off-guard, and she was trying to head off what was going to happen next.

"Your blanket stays at the bottom of the stairs from now on," Don commanded, as if the blanket were a dangerous weapon. "Do you understand me?"

Dylan leaned into me, buried his nose in his blanket, and pushed his tongue forward, massaging his bottom lip. Pressing my arm around his small shoulders I said, "How about if we make a bed for your blanket—we can put a basket at the bottom of the stairs, and your blanket can take naps while you go up and down."

I looked at Don. This was our pattern: he swooped in, punched the dough, and slapped it on the table. I reached in, kneading, softening, shaping it into something palatable. In the years to come, he would hurl these incidents back at me, claiming that I undermined his authority, emasculated him in front of his son. Now, he simply gazed at me, levelly, hatefully, and then turned and disappeared, footsteps pounding out the door.

I exhaled and listened. The car engine turned. He'd show me now: drive off to the shore and his art studio, just as he often stomped off to his studio back home in Massachusetts, and stay there for hours. I had not yet snuffed the cinder of resentment that flared in me every time he did this, but I no longer challenged him. When he was in one of his moods I preferred his absence.

"Come on, sweetie, let's put your clothes away," I said. "Then let's sit on the balcony and have a snack."

At that point in my life, I trusted my mothering instincts, one of which had been to leave my journalism career to cover the home front—running interference with playdates, Gymboree sessions, skinned knees, naps, doctor's appointments, breakfast, lunch, and dinner. I hadn't started out thinking Don and I would work our marriage this way. I'd hoped he and I would share the home front equally—particularly since I had come with an established career and credit cards. But deep down, my husband felt diminished by childcare, unable to manage the tedium and frustration or to ignore his own father's attitude that childcare was unseemly work for a man. This had become a splinter between us, our quarrels prickling with ever-increasing fervor. Bit by bit, partly out of a longing for calm, I had let go—agreeing to more hours of childcare, vacuuming, cooking, and less time at my writing table. I did not want my children growing up as I had, in a fraught and unhappy home, hole-punched by disapproval. I wanted harmony.

To that end, I now set about the house, creating our summer nest: making beds, unpacking toiletries, opening windows. I clipped peonies and larkspur from the garden and set vases throughout the house. When Don returned at dusk to my oven-fried chicken, he came with a handful of wildflowers plucked from the field. I smiled, kissing him on the mouth.

"Better?" I teased, relieved to push my own anger aside. I didn't ask what I would have a year ago, when we were honest with one other: "Why do you resent our life? What is festering inside you?"

A thin sliver of time ago, when art, sex, and Pad Thai were all we needed or wanted from life, Don and I would awake tangled in the sheets of his bed in his small studio. Outside, the garbage truck growled in the alley right behind our heads, and across the stretch of floor, beyond the easels and rolled canvases and spattered cobalt and ocher, through the cuts of factory windows, the city traffic pitched a high white hum. I would slide from the sheets into dance clothes and slip out for a morning class, returning to find him in a spattered painter's apron, palette in one hand, moving toward the canvas, then back, cropping his vision with a flat hand, lunging forward again. I'd set his coffee on the paint-smeared table and sit in whatever chair was not covered with rags and random images ripped from magazines, scissored into new shapes, new ways of seeing. I wrote by hand until the light faded, not looking up until he said my name and gestured for me to come around to the front of the canvas. Standing off to the side, he waited for my reaction, for me to tell him what I saw, what spoke to me in the language of arc and line. I was not a painter, nor he a writer, but inside those moments we breathed the same air and spoke a melded language that was inherent and effortless.

On the farm, we inched our way to these moments—granted, with an altered flavor and a toddler between us, but we settled into a simple and easy rhythm. Rising early, I fed and dressed Dylan, then handed him to Don, who roused a good two hours after I did. The two of them, father and son, snorted and rough-housed among the covers before tromping outside to fix the lawn mower. This arrangement suited our biorhythms, mine being the early bird, Don the all-nighter. It didn't do much for eroticism—but neither did caring for a toddler or vomiting. I trusted that one of these days, when all of this was over, I'd feel my body wake again.

This phase of my life—being out of control, out of body, and largely without adult company—made me desperate for distraction. I missed the grittiness of being out in the city chasing stories and then racing down the radio station's hallway just before I was to go on the air. I had given all of this up when I was eight months pregnant with Dylan, largely because I just couldn't move that fast, not with nearly nine pounds of baby pressing on my bladder. But my desire to be a writer had persisted and no matter where I was, I searched for ways to satiate my thirst for writing and telling stories.

The house and its history provided that for me. It seduced me with its tales, vivid and colorful, retold for miles around Rocky Point. The original owner, Jeb McAlister, had boated his family to these shores in the 1800s and designed a stately home that was romantically impractical, with a high-peaked red roof, a balcony off the bedroom, a sweeping lawn, and, inside, an elegant banister of cherry wood, a parlor, a dining room with a chandelier, and, in every room, finely crafted ceilings with ornate trim. Off the kitchen, a small staircase led up to a spare bedroom reserved for the farm hand, which now served as a mini art studio for Dylan's drawing and clay projects.

In the long afternoons, with Don away in his studio, I packed a snack and took Dylan's hand and we wandered around the property, coming upon rusted and weed-infested plows, discarded tools, hunks of boat hulls half buried in the sand. They stirred the past, whispering moments of closure and abandonment. I sensed the hopes and dashed dreams that had come before us, unrecorded in census figures and deeds. Apparently, Dylan sensed these, too.

"Mama, can I see the puppy place?" he asked one warm afternoon, two weeks into our stay. We were camped out on the balcony, munching on apple slices and animal crackers.

"The what place?" I replied, confused. We had never owned a puppy, much less brought one up here to the island.

"Where the puppy sleeps," he insisted, looking up at me, mouth rimmed in crumbs.

It dawned on me. He meant the grave that lay at the foot of the rotting elm, its marker stone flush with the ground and sinking beneath the grass. A dog's grave. I'd forgotten about it since we were here last.

"All right," I said, "I think it's under the big tree."

Descending the back stairs, we crossed the yard and passed by the hulking chestnut to arrive at the base of the elm. Dylan pulled me around the trunk, serious and intent on the ground.

"It's here!" he cried, squatting down and tearing away the thatch of grass covering the stone. Chiseled into its surface was one name: Blue.

I knew only a small part of this story. Blue had once belonged to Audrey, the middle daughter of the McAlister family. She had fallen in love with a Catholic boy from across the cove, a forbidden love. Her Protestant parents refused to let her marry him. As a parting gift, the boy gave Audrey a puppy to keep her company and to remember him by. In the months of tears that followed she doted on the puppy, feeding it from her plate and keeping it with her inside the house, unheard of on a farm. When Audrey finally married, it was to a Protestant man, a charmer and gadabout who was known to spend plenty of evenings at the bars in Charlottetown. Audrey's puppy never took to him.

"He's a nice puppy," observed Dylan.

"Oh?" I said, surprised and amused. "How do you know?"

"I saw him."

"Aha."

Dylan was a vivid dreamer. I had discovered this not too long ago as I was tidying up breakfast dishes in our little converted barn house in Massachusetts. I had settled down on the rug to read him *The Nose Book*. Suddenly, he pointed to the ceiling and announced, "The couch is all gone, Mama."

"What couch do you mean, sweetie?" I had asked, puzzled.

Lying back on the rug, miniature body dwarfed by the furniture, Dylan pointed up again and said, "The couch up there, with Grandpa in it."

Looking up, I stared at the ceiling and pictured a floating couch with dust balls clinging to the underside and Dylan's grandpa, my father-in-law, peering over the side with his dour moustache. After a few minutes I stretched out next to Dylan and proceeded to explain the idea of dreams; how they were in your head, sometimes resting, other times waking up. They weren't real.

Now, I wondered if Dylan had dreamed another dream—triggered, as mine often were, by this hundred-year-old place.

"Well, that's good to hear," I said. "I'm glad Blue was such a nice dog."

"He *is* a nice dog," Dylan corrected me, insulted.

I paused, realizing I was still new to this mothering thing, with its constant unknowns. How much to reveal, how much to withhold, how much to protect this small boy's heart from disappointment and the hard reality that all beings come to an end?

"Let's go find him," Dylan insisted.

For the most part I believed in imagination, the joy and fun of it, and in those early days of motherhood, I rode it with courage. "Okay, then. Where shall we look?"

"The beach," he said, instantly.

I paused and weighed this idea. "You know, Daddy's studio is down there, on the shore. We can't disturb him."

"Oh," Dylan said, hesitating now, uncertain, a tiny wrinkle in his brow.

This stirred some embers in me, my husband's entitlement to quiet and focus, imperative for creative work and so out of my reach, which I couldn't accept. I yearned for my old rituals—not only the solitude and time, but also the ability to focus for endless hours without thinking of Dylan, without the trickle of guilt that inevitably seeped into my consciousness when I was trying to work on my writing, to descend to the depths I knew were necessary. Those depths had eluded me for three years now, retreating behind some scrim, some netherworld into which I had forgotten how to cross. Instead, I had settled for small snippets of sentences scratched in various notebooks, particles of thought that floated around the house like moths, fluttering awake and then settling again. I had no idea what I was doing, why notebooks were accumulating, what if any purpose they were serving, except to remind me that I had lost the concentration and discipline it took to be a writer, or that I had never possessed it in the first place. Enough of these tiny bloated notebooks had accumulated to fill a large box, which I hauled with me up to the island, ignoring Don's exasperated sigh as I had wedged it into the back seat of our packed car.

"Let's go anyway," I said to Dylan, surprising myself. "We can go the long way around. Then Daddy won't hear us."

"Okay!" said Dylan, popping up and fisting his hands in the air. Then he stopped and crinkled his brow. "What if he barks?"

"Who?" I said, brushing grass off my knees, "Daddy?"

"No, Mommy, Blue!" Dylan rolled his eyes.

"Oh!" I burst out laughing. "It's okay if Blue barks—just you and I have to be quiet." I whispered the word "quiet" and crouched into a furtive tiptoe, waving him to follow me.

"Okay," he whispered back.

I believed wholeheartedly that I was protecting Dylan. By teaching him to accommodate his father's short-wicked temper, I was hoping to avoid it myself, to calm the household. I had been doing this all of my life, mollifying my mother and Roddy and now my husband, a habit so ingrained I kept on doing it. I hadn't yet realized the futility.

We took our time. This was the part of mothering I relished, slowing down, being where Dylan wanted to be, allowing him to be an explorer, loosening the rules and the schedule. That afternoon, he transformed into a sea creature in the tidal zone, dropping to his hands and scuttling from one pile of exoskeletons to another. Gathering sea glass and shells, I meandered alongside him, squatting from time to time to see what wonder he found in the sand. This was as new to me as it was to Dylan. I had never explored like this as a child—on a beach with my mother beside me, digging clams. Mama had rarely, if ever, played with me. Even if she was as curious as I was about the muck of nature, she couldn't have messed about this way, not with Roddy along. I thought of her now, with two more young children and still with Roddy, a thirty-year-old man. As such, my mother had never had a chance to be a grandmother, not to Barbara Ann's children, or to mine, and I knew it was unlikely she ever would. I had already turned to Don's mother for that, and in many ways I had grown closer to her than I'd ever been to my own mother.

When Dylan and I finally came upon the studio, perched high above us on the shore cliff, we climbed the rocks silently, crouched past the studio windows, and ran down the path to the house. Dylan was happily tired and didn't protest a bath and rest time in his room. He fell into a deep sleep halfway through a lullaby, opening a rare free hour for me at that time of the day.

Whenever one of these windows of time came to me unexpectedly, I turned to laundry, partly because it was mindless and kept me from sinking into my writing, at least until I knew Dylan was fully asleep. Most often, he snoozed for twenty minutes and then padded around the house to find me. Far easier to stop mid-towel and swoop him into my lap than to yank myself away from a quest for the exquisite word or synonym.

I mounted the wide staircase with an armful of towels, tiptoeing, pausing, and assessing the noise level from Dylan's room. In truth, I just wanted to lie down. My limbs felt sluggish, as if my blood was slowing and pooling in my ankles. My breath turned shallow and, on the landing, I leaned against the wall, still holding the basket. For a moment I thought I was going to faint, my dizziness veering toward a swoon. Swallowing, I exhaled slowly, turning my head to the alcove, and froze. Something was over there, by the window—a form of some kind.

I shook my head, lowered the basket, and straightened again. Yes, it was still there, poised at the window, unhurried, arrested, waiting. Its form was not fully drawn. More like a gesture, edgeless and suggestive. Without mass. Female.

Nothing moved. Time yawned around me; I stood, breathing, weightless, the light in my eyes striated with dust, a static buzz to my skin. *How silly*, I thought, trembling. *What is wrong with me?*

The figure shifted, or rather, lifted. It was featureless. How did I know she was looking at me?

"Audrey?" I spoke, not sure if I had said this out loud.

A slight metallic cast hung in the air and I tasted iron on my tongue. A spattering of dots blinded the edges of my vision. Suddenly, a wave of sickness surged in my gut. I lunged to the bathroom, diving for the toilet, spitting vomit into the bowl. I was still hanging over the rim, hair dangling and clumped with throw up, when I heard the door whine. Startled, I looked up. Dylan stood in the doorway, peering at me with wide blue eyes, his blanket pressed up on his mouth and nose.

"It's okay, honey," I said, still on my knees. "Mommy's okay."

I was reassuring myself as much as Dylan. My stomach felt raw, my insides too large. Nature was proving too big for me with this baby, too uncontrollable, just like the first time. And now, this haunt of a woman.

Shakily, I rinsed out my mouth with water and mouthwash. Then, I took Dylan's hand and walked steadily out into the hallway, glancing furtively at the now-empty alcove as we went down the stairs, out the back door, into the yard. I felt an urgent need for the mundane, the reality of touched things, of real bugs and flowers and bird feathers.

What had I just seen? Clairvoyance had never been a part of me. I had always relished hearing about ghosts, whether they were conjured by Charles Dickens or a camp counselor, lit by a bonfire. As a Baptist child, I had been taught that souls either flew up to heaven or down to hell. That was that. They didn't stick around. Some years ago, I had jettisoned Baptist dogma and, along with it, the idea of souls dwelling anywhere after death, whether in some burning pit or foamy cloud. If a soul lingered anywhere, it was in our minds. In my mind.

Still, I had sensed this presence before. Not in the dark silences of night, as I padded around from bedroom to kitchen to parlor, searching vainly for sleep, but oddly, in the late afternoon, just like now, when the dense August heat collected on the landing and the slow light teased along the banister.

For the rest of the afternoon I avoided going back inside, searching for bugs and digging up worms with Dylan until daylight dimmed and Don appeared for dinner. I didn't tell Don about the sighting. I prided myself on being the sane one in this extended family, the one who wasn't prone to drama or hysterics. Still, I cajoled him into taking a night off from the studio and driving over to the Aberdeen burger shack for dinner, then staying around as darkness fell. For the first time, I didn't want to be alone in the house.

Over the next few days, I clomped noisily up the stairs and spoke out loud, as if noise were some kind of ghost deterrent. "Heading upstairs," I announced, or "Off to the kitchen."

Dylan copied me, cupping his hands around his mouth like a bullhorn. "Going poddy!" he called. I let him abandon his rest time and, instead, play games with me, putting together puzzles in the parlor or, preferably, outside on the front porch. The more I avoided being alone, the more I seemed incapable of shutting the alcove out of my mind. I couldn't let go of what I'd seen or shake the notion of Audrey. She hadn't felt like a ghost; she'd felt like a person trying to tell me something. What was the connection between her layer of life and mine? Was she an omen?

I thought of my child in the pouch of my body. For the first time in a long while, my mind turned to my brother. In my mother's womb,

Roddy had already harbored his affliction. No matter what nutrition my mother partook, or how diligently she cared for herself, or how obediently tended to her duties as a wife and mother and Christian woman, her fate was coming: she would bear a severely disabled child. This would determine everything in her future and mine. It would root deeply in my gut and, as it was doing now, bloom my fear.

Three years before, when Dylan was in my womb, I had opted for every medical screening. Each procedure soothed me, ruling out spina bifida, Down syndrome, heart anomalies. Each negative result I celebrated with Don over a candlelit dinner. But none of the tests could detect or rule out autism, or aphasia, or developmental delay. The moment Dylan was in my arms I checked him for signs, tracking his eyes, his touch, and later, the sounds rolling off his tongue. Only recently, with the flutter of this new child in my womb, had I allowed myself to believe that Dylan was out of danger and I had been spared my mother's heartbreak. Now, here came another child, and I was even more suspicious with this pregnancy, more vulnerable. Birth defects were a random game of chance and ill fortune, a kind of Russian roulette, where you dodged harm on the first few rounds but, inevitably, your luck ran out. The more you spun the barrel and pointed the muzzle, the more certain a dire outcome.

I had never mentioned this fear to my mother. Partly because I sensed it would stir up memories for her and distress her to know her daughter was nerve-wracked about becoming a mother. But more so, it was my mother's religiosity that kept me at a distance. She still believed these things were determined by God and weren't to be questioned or even to be prevented. I hadn't told her I tested for birth defects during my pregnancy with Dylan or that I was waiting for test results for this new baby.

The next Saturday afternoon I found myself pacing around the backyard while Dylan dug in the dirt. I couldn't rid my thoughts of Audrey and, inexplicably, decided to find out more about her. Putting Dylan in the car, I drove to the McHale place, two farms away. Junior McHale, an eighty-year-old farmer, had known the McAlister family well. He had even helped dig Audrey's grave. He was a yarn-spinner and an ardent believer in ghosts—so vividly that he made sure never to drive down his two-mile lane after dark, in case the headless horseman burst from the trees into his headlights. He had revealed this with a chuckle but also a wary look in his eyes.

Bumping down the rutted lane, I realized why Junior was so skittish: his lane was barely six feet wide, encroached upon by trees on both sides, many of which clasped branches overhead, blocking out the sun and cloaking the road in shadow. I had never driven down this lane without Don and, suddenly, I felt uneasy. *Stop it*, I said to myself. *You're being foolish.*

"What's 'foolish'?" piped Dylan, from the back seat.

"Oh, Mommy's thinking out loud. Foolish means silly."

"Is that bad?"

"No, no, not at all. Silly is fine. It's actually downright appropriate at times."

But was it fine for a thirty-four-year-old woman? When did it mean some sort of slippage on my part?

The lane opened out into the farmyard, and as we pulled up to the ramshackle house, Junior appeared out of nowhere. He stood and greeted me awkwardly, his wizened frame like an old gnarl. He wore pants hitched with a rope, scuffed and manured boots, and a plaid shirt with wash-faded patches at the elbows. He wasn't accustomed to seeing me without Don. I could tell from his expression he wondered what in the world I was doing there.

"Just dropping by," I sang out, hoisting Dylan onto my hip. "Dylan wanted to see the cows. Do you mind?"

"Nope, nope. We got cows," he said, rustling his bent fingers in the air.

We made the rounds, first into the calf barn, then to the fence where we watched the cows watching us, their big jaws grinding. Finally, Junior invited us inside and, sitting down to the kitchen table with tea and freezer-burned Blondies, I cajoled the story out of him, pulling my reporter's pencil and small notebook from my pocket.

What I had suspected was true: Audrey had been unhappy. She took over the farm but didn't own it; laws at the time disallowed married women from owning property. Her husband, Val, swiftly lost his charming ways and was often spotted in town with a woman on his arm, leaving Audrey out at Rocky Point, alone, to manage the everyday farm chores. When she was thirty-three, Audrey gave birth to a daughter at home, and not three days later she was up and about, doing chores. As she strode across the backyard, hauling two heavy buckets of potatoes, she called out to Val to open the gate for her.

"Open it yourself!" Val had yelled from high on the tractor. "I'm busy!"

She stood still, not responding.

"Aw go on, jump over it!" Val yelled again, exasperated.

In the next instant, Audrey dropped, crumpling to the ground.

"Gone, she was," said Junior, snapping his callused fingers. "That quick."

"You mean, she died—right there?" I asked, horrified.

"Yes, ma'am. Blood clot in her brain."

Something clattered to the floor in the next room. I sprang up from the chair and through the door to find Dylan frozen by the couch, shards of a broken candy dish at his feet, a look of terror on his face.

"Oh, honey," I said quickly, alarmed at the dread in his eyes. The instant he saw me, he sighed and crumpled into tears.

"It was an accident, sweetie," I said. "It's okay."

Above Dylan's sobs I apologized to Junior and asked for a broom and dust pan. He waved me away, so I ferried Dylan and his hiccups out to the car. On the way home, I glanced in the mirror. A deep unease entered me. Dylan had looked too mortified for a child at his tender age. His was an old look of shame and failure.

"Mama?" he said now, his blanket muffling his voice.

"What, sweetie?"

"I won't tell Daddy."

"No, sweetie. You won't and I won't."

He puffed and leaned back against the seat, blanket up to his nose. Before we were back in our driveway, he fell dead asleep. I had little choice but to let him nap and pass the next few hours alone. Carrying him upstairs, past the yawning alcove, I slipped him under his bed covers. As soon as I closed his door, I scooted through the servants' quarters and downstairs to the kitchen and outside. I knew exactly where Audrey had fallen in the backyard and in a few quick steps I was there, halting a few feet from what used to be the gate to the barnyard. The gate was gone, now marked only by a slender arched opening in the overgrown hedge: an unassuming place to die.

I stood still, feeling the body of another woman who had only moments left to live, whose womb was still raw from childbirth and whose husband did not cherish her. I cupped my lower abdomen, noting that I hadn't felt movement all day. Instinctively, I stepped away from the death spot, through the hedge, and entered the neglected orchard, quickening my pace past the blueberry bushes and heading on down the lane. When I was far enough away, I turned.

From there, I could see the whole house, including the upstairs windows. The alcove's window was empty, or at least I thought so. This was the angle at which Junior claimed to have seen a ghost in our window, in the wintertime, when he came to check on the house and its groaning pipes. The glare on the glass made it impossible to see beyond it. But then I saw a movement, some stutter of shadow. Instantly, I felt protective, both of Dylan, asleep in his room, and this new child, asleep within me.

Hurrying back toward the house and glancing at the window, I half walked, half trotted along the red lane. I still couldn't tell if the light was playing tricks or if the movement was what it had looked like: human. Bounding through the door, I clipped up the stairs, making no effort to be quiet, and stopped on the landing. The alcove was void of anything save the bureau and rocking chair. Cracking Dylan's door, I saw he was fast asleep, knees tucked under him so he looked like a little snail. Closing the door, gently, I turned and walked straight into the alcove. If this house—or some aspect of this house—was trying to tell me something, I wanted to hear it.

Standing at the window, looking down on the lane, I held utterly still. I didn't know if I was in the present or the past. The edges around me felt porous. I sensed a consciousness, the kind you cannot see but feel when you're outside in the dark, an animal watching you from the shadows, then dissolving, silently, an exhaled breath.

I did not want to live Audrey's life: bound by circumstance and trapped in a depleting love. Was this her message? That my husband did not cherish me and he would someday turn away? This thought was so frightening and repellent I pushed it off. All my life, I had held fast to the idea of a warm and steady home, an indestructible fort against the wallops of life, a home fueled by a fierce love between a man and a woman. We had a healthy boy. Surely this meant we were blessed—we were meant to hold.

A mild breeze puffed through the screen, lifting the sheers. In the distance, squall lines of black rain. Deep inside me, my child moved.

Chapter 26

Implosion

In the earliest hours of morning, Boston's waterfront was a shadowy jumble of buckled pavement and docksides. The stench of low tide and fish guts assured me that I was in the right place, the soiled black water of the harbor lapping inches away from my feet.

My nerves hummed. I was late. As a revived radio reporter, I remembered every nook and cranny of the city—the mouse paths, the seedy streets that cut through dark parts of town and deposited me at the scene before anyone else. But on this morning those paths had been cordoned off, forcing me to backtrack twice, take the tunnel route, screech into an industrial parking lot, jump out, and abandon my car.

Now I was running. I had the thick box of a tape recorder slung on my shoulder, its weight banging against my hip, and a shotgun mic in one hand. The mic was two feet long, oddly slender, with a tiny funnel at one end, designed to clutch and pull sound from far away. It was my job to get this muzzle positioned in the right place at the right time—as close as I could get to the site of the story: in this case, an implosion. The Travelers Insurance Building, an aging post-Depression-era skyscraper, built in 1959, was scheduled to disintegrate this Sunday morning at nine o'clock.

I had no idea where I was supposed to be or where I might plant myself to grab the best sound. All I had was the exact time of the detonation, so I was on a tear, in full reporter mode, strapped in equipment, media badge swinging from my neck.

To anyone glancing my way, I looked the part, but, in fact, I was living a straddled and harried life as the mother of two young sons. Dylan was now four and Zachary, a toddler in diapers. It was the 1980s, not a good decade for childcare, particularly if you lacked the income for a nanny. In truth, I wanted to work. I felt my skills were rusting and I yearned for the gratification of seeking and writing a good story.

I had convinced the radio station to accept me back part-time, meaning I was taking assignments on weekends and at odd hours no other reporter wanted. In the old days, before children, I nimbly took on any story, fully dressed, composed, speeding around the city and outfoxing obstacles, always arriving on time. I jumped onto trolleys and into cabs and wrote my stories on the run, rushing into the station just in time to go live. Now, I was lucky to get my blouse buttoned.

A full mile away from the building, I pushed to the front of a thick crowd and bumped into a row of barricades.

"I'm with the media!" I hollered to the nearest police officer standing beyond the barricade. He was planted with his back to me, arms folded, straddle-legged.

"Orders are orders," he said, shaking his head. "One-mile perimeter around the building—off limits to any and everybody."

The thought that I might return to the station empty-handed made my stomach roil. My fingertips turned icy, my throat and lips suddenly parched, dry and papery, my tongue swollen. I didn't know these were signs of a nervous gene that skipped around in my family and settled in different generations. Anxiety was not widely known or talked about then. I assumed everyone panicked this way and had armored myself with a battery of coping mechanisms: inhale deeply three times, distract the mind, count backward, dig in your pocketbook, walk in circles. It hadn't yet occurred to me this was the one thing Roddy and I might have in common. His rocking, counting, and obsessive-compulsive behaviors were thought to be driven by anxiety. Fortunately for me, a young woman in her thirties who was not only an introvert but also raised to be ladylike, panic was an ally, unleashing adrenaline in a way that pushed me to be aggressive and audacious, hallmark behaviors for getting the story first. Without panic I wouldn't have been able to do the job.

"Can you let me strap my mic to that barricade, the one up there?" I called to the policeman, slipping into a tone that was part pleading, part coy.

He studied me for a moment, looking me up and down. I had a head of blondish hair, which I hadn't managed to clamp back into a clip, so I must have appeared like a she-lion, disheveled and wild, determined to stop at nothing. He swung his gaze to the barricade, a good twenty feet closer to the blast site, and waved me in.

"Make it snappy," he said.

I stepped out into the restricted zone. From here, the sixteen-story Traveler's building appeared comically small, squatting amid a bundle of soaring skyscrapers. I doubted that I'd pick up much of the blast at this distance, even with the shotgun. At best, I might capture a faint popping sound and have to cajole the engineer back at the station to enhance the tone and volume so the blast sounded authentic.

Exasperated, I fastened the mic to the barricade with a straitjacket of duct tape. Then, I backed away as promised, unwinding five yards of cable to where the crowd pressed up against the barricades. I checked the sound levels, fiddling with the volume. The red needles jogged softly from the ambient noise. Ten minutes to spare.

Most of what I knew about sound I'd learned while packed into a college lecture hall along with three hundred other college students. The Physics of Sound, a required course for speech pathologists, my college major at the time, had first filled me with dread, given its shady association with math. But by the end of the first class I was spellbound. I saw sound waves push needles across graph paper and control the flames of candles. I studied the whorls of the human ear and the intricate machinery of tiny bones. I marveled that this ghostly invisible force, a rush of molecules, could move and vibrate beyond what my ear could detect, and in the next instant, wash me in melody, moving me to tears. I fell in love with it: the emotion and sensation of voice and tone traveling through the air.

"Hey, what gives? It's nine o'clock!" someone shouted right behind me. A spattering of laughter rippled through the crowd. The cop shot us all a warning look.

My watch was still sitting on the bathroom sink in a suburb twenty miles away—I'd slipped it off in order to wash Zachary's sticky hands—so there was no telling what time it really was or whether something was delaying the countdown. The people around me shifted, restless and bored. Most of them were regular Joes, up from the fish docks or neighborhoods in Southie. They'd come for a thrill and break in the routine, a big boom. I, on the other hand, had been following this story for days—starting with a press conference two weeks earlier. I'd already interviewed the Loizeaux family, who were in charge of the demolition, a father-son-daughter team. They'd told me how they would wire the building with explosives in six hundred locations, a chorus of time-delay charges, igniting each in a careful order so as to jostle the building at its base and crumple it like a Tinkertoy. No flying shrapnel, no windows blown out of surrounding buildings, no collateral damage.

Now, I imagined the Loizeauxes scrambling through the empty building, troubleshooting something that had gone awry. Some fizzle of ignition or last-minute miscalculation. If they didn't fix it soon, my batteries would conk and so would my shoulder. The recorder was like an oversized baby, one I couldn't put down for fear it would get trampled. I heaved it to my other shoulder and released the pause button.

The hardest part of assignments like this was the stoicism they required, the sangfroid in the face of a clock that ticked mercilessly toward a deadline. Drumming my fingers on the recorder, I ejected the tape and put it in again, checked the decibel levels. *Come on*, I whined to myself. *Where's the countdown?*

I thought of Dylan and imagined him in the backyard with my sister-in-law, examining bugs, taking in wonders. All at once I missed him, missed being with him at a moment of surprise. I had been a mother long enough to know those moments came and went rapidly, without mercy, but I shook this off.

Suddenly, there was a shift in the air, a shudder of energy through the crowd. I spied the policeman holding up his thick hands, all ten fingers splayed. He folded one pinkie and the crowd burst into a chant: "Ten, nine, eight, seven, six"—I dialed up the volume knob— "five, four, three, two . . ."

"Do it!" someone shouted.

A fusillade of flashes erupted from the Traveler's bottom floors and scurried up its sides. A split second later, the sound hit. *Boom- boom-boom.* I gasped, transfixed, cringing and hunching my shoulders, stunned by the ferocity. The ground rumbled. I felt as if I were pushed right up against the building's face, taking its blows. I tore my gaze away from the blasts and frantically checked the decibel level on my machine. In the melee, I'd completely forgotten what I was supposed to be doing. *Boom!* The needles slammed to the right, bouncing with a fury into the hot zone. Fumbling, I cranked the dial down, just in time for the final cascade of blasts unleashed from all floors.

In the next seconds a teetering silence fell over the crowd. The building hesitated, as if unsure of what to do. Suddenly, in one soft, swift move, it folded, crumpling in on itself and melting like a glacier in heat, disintegrating straight down to the ground. In fewer than ten seconds it vanished.

I had no time to record my thoughts or those of people around me. A billowing cloud of white dust and ash rushed toward me and, instantly, it covered my face, hair, clothes, and, horrifically, my tape recorder. Frantically, I wiped off the machine with my bare hand as I stumbled forward, following the cable, dodging bodies fleeing the ash cloud. I arrived at the mic cuffed to the barricade. I couldn't breathe; no one had warned me about ash and dust, the hazards of disintegrat- ing concrete, rebar, sheet rock, insulation. I tore at the duct tape, at the same time reeling in the cable. Then I ran blindly, away from the site, recorder pressed to my chest, heading for the outer edge of the fog. My homing instincts took me in the direction of my car and I jumped in and slammed the door. The cloud enveloped me, whiting out the windows.

For a moment I sat and breathed. I couldn't lie to myself: I knew the sound I'd captured was dirty and far too hot. But I'd gotten it. The story was mine. I could hear it already, and when it aired, it would stop people wherever they happened to be. They'd have the sensation of being right there on the docks, in the crowd, counting down, stunned for a split second as the blast filled their ears, awestruck. For a moment they would marvel at physics, at forces, at how small we are, how ingenious.

Starting the car, I felt a bolt of alarm. I still had the script to write, the sound to pull, the entire concert of production, including my squabble with the engineer as I insisted on using the sound, no matter how hot. All of this meant I would return home late, after the babysitter was gone and Don had interrupted his painting time to take over. Anxiety bloomed up my neck and around my ears.

I was a woman who, like thousands of others, didn't know how to manage both career and family. My generation of Seventies feminists had broken through the wall of sexism only to find there were no structures in place on the other side, no supports and no guidance, only bold assurances that we could have it all. With the birth of Dylan, and then Zachary, I was baffled by my exhaustion but mostly by my husband's impatience. He supported my career in theory but not in reality. Our arguments, some of which turned vicious, had crackled through the phone into the newsroom moments before I had to be on air, Don bellowing through the phone line over my son's cries, "Where are you? Why aren't you here?"

More than once I had faltered on the air. I dreaded my husband's voice, dreaded the disharmony and the rent in my marriage. I could not bear the possibility that my children might be growing up just as I had: in a household fraught with tension and unhappiness.

Turning the key, I backed out and inched the wheels into traffic, heading toward the radio station's flat-roofed building. I knew deep down this broadcast would be one of my last.

Chapter 27

Dave's Diner

Somewhere along the stifling stretch of road between Corbin and Hazard, my father swung the Belvedere into the parking lot of a roadside diner. I unfolded from the back seat and shuffled behind my parents and Rod across the hot pavement toward what I hoped was a blast of arctic air and a decent meal— anything other than the sodden sandwiches and Shasta colas we'd been trading around for six hours in the car.

It was 1989, nearly a decade since I'd spent any significant time with either of my parents, or with Rod. Even longer since I'd last set foot in Kentucky. I was thirty-seven, a wife and mother, and I'd left my sons with my husband back in Boston so I could travel with my parents and brother for a few days. We were heading to Hazard, but not to Combs Furniture or my grandparents' dirt farm. This time, it was to a nursing home. Papaw, at ninety, was spitting mad he'd lost his independence and the idea had arisen between my parents that a surprise visit from me, his little-seen granddaughter, might cheer him and make him forget he was never going back home.

Above the diner's glassed-in door, DAVE's blinkered in the buzzing heat, half-lit and spattered with bugs. My father tugged the handle and held the door wide as we all tromped through into a blissfully frigid room. There were cracked vinyl booths, plastic place mats, and bustling middle-aged waitresses, pink-skirted and girdled, trailing whiffs of deep fry and Folgers. I paused and stood like a child, taking it in. I was both surprised and soothed to find life in this part of the Appalachians hadn't changed.

My mother whispered to the hostess that we'd like a corner spot and we trekked by the other tables nearly all the way to the restrooms. As we reached the last booth, my mother, now in her fifties, stepped aside, petite and fleet-footed, allowing my brother to maneuver in first.

"Scooch in a bit, so I can fit, too," she said, her voice breezy.

Rod's eyes shifted darkly, a quick zip sideways, but he complied, pushing himself along the vinyl bench. At thirty-three, Rod sported hints of a dissolving hairline and a thickening paunch, and from the unbuttoned collar of his shirt sprouted signs of a furry chest. Even now, these features rocked me. He was inked into my heart as a boy, and his manhood always struck me as a fresh surprise. Though he bore my father's full name, he hadn't taken on the sleek, dark-headed spindle of my father's physique, but rather the shorter, barrel-chested, and balding figure of my maternal grandfather.

My mother slid into the booth and my father and I closed ranks on the opposite side of the table, tucking Rod safely against the wall, within the family. In the next instant, Dad ordered coffee all around, meatloaf, corn bread, and baked apples for himself and Rod, and for my mother and me, Cobb salads with ranch dressing on the side.

"Mercy me, this feels good," said my mother, fanning herself with the menu.

The breeze ruffled wisps of her graying hair. Sometime in the last few years she'd grown diminutive, her small frame nearly doll-like now. The menu whooshed side to side, threatening to blow her backward, like an enormous turbine.

I had spent enough years away from my family to miss them and feel remorse—a persistent sense that I'd run off without good cause. Perhaps it was because I was nearing forty and felt time whizzing by, but a deep part of me wanted to reconnect, to feel my way back to my roots. Also, after all of this time away, I was deluded; I had forgotten that disability doesn't get any better or even stabilize. When my parents had called, surprising me with their invitation, I considered it a sign. Settling now in a plastic booth, about to share a meal with my family and the simple pleasures of coffee and conversation, I felt a wash of gratitude.

In short order, the main dishes arrived and for fifteen minutes we ate in peaceful silence, clinking the tines of our forks against scarred, durable dishware. Twice, the waitress sidled up in her apron and perky hat, lifting an eyebrow, her hand gesturing with the coffee pot. The third time, my mother, father, and I chorused a hearty "No, thank you!" and broke into laughter at our shared horror, Dad cupping his hand like an umbrella over his cup. We had the good sense to pass— three cups of caffeine were too much at this dimming hour of the day—and besides, with another hour's drive ahead of us, it was time to push on.

Roddy, however, thought differently. He thrust his cup across the table, aiming for the spout in the waitress's hand, bumping the lip of the pot, and sending hot blots splattering over the bread basket.

My father raised his hand to keep the waitress from pouring.

"Now, Rod," he said, "you've had enough."

"Oh!" my brother barked, banging his cup down on the tabletop. Little pings rang out from the silverware. He hunched his shoulders, tilting his head, pulling his eyes to the side.

Left to his own devices, my brother would swallow all the Folgers in the world, loading every cup with mounds of sugar and dollops of cream. For all of his thirty-three years, he hadn't acquired restraints of any sort—no matter how diligently my parents had tried to teach him. If allowed, he'd take in third and fourth helpings of coffee, not to mention Coke, burgers and fries, milk shakes, and pie a la mode, until his chemistry jittered and his symptoms of flinching and twitching rose to a feverish pitch. Recently, the doctor had warned my parents that Rod now had high cholesterol and elevated blood pressure, and he'd urged then to redouble their efforts with his diet.

"I'll just check back with you in a little minute," the waitress said, eyes flitting to each of us. Tucking the pot to her ribs, she hurried away, her nylons *zizz-zizzing* to a faraway booth.

To anyone glancing from across the room, my brother would have appeared in that moment as a stricken boy, subdued and hushed, his dark-circled eyes receding beneath the ledge of his brow. But I knew differently. My breath quickened and I pushed my shoulders back against the seat, bracing for what I knew would come next. Rod dropped his head forward and shouted straight down to the table top.

"Dad! Have some more coffee!"

My mother flinched, her hands hopping in the air; then quickly, she straightened the napkin in her lap. A memory flashed in my mind, not of a moment, but of a time when she didn't have this kind of composure; when her frustration and sorrow at what had befallen my brother billowed out from her like smoke. We'd never spoken of those early years when I was five and six years old, when life was a blur of doctors and thickening horror that my baby brother was broken and nothing was going to fix him. Even now, sitting in this booth, slipping into middle age, it didn't occur to me there was any reason to retrieve those years, to sort out their confusion and undo their hold on me.

My father paused, leveling his gaze.

"Lower your voice, please," he said.

"Oh, no!" Rod shouted. "More coffee!"

Now, we had an audience. Without lifting my eyes from the mug pressed between my palms, I knew most people in the room were fixating on our commotion. Chatter diminished in widening rings, until the only noise other than my brother's was a spattering of muted kitchen sounds.

"Let me have your cup, please," my father said.

My brother's eyes cut hard to the side, a startled shot from beneath his brow.

"No!" he barked. "Have my coffee!"

His body trembled in the seat and his fingers fluttered about his mouth. A thick pulp moved through my chest. I stared at the black surface in my coffee cup as it shuddered from his outrage.

How was I here again? A mere week ago I was in my own life, navigating normal chaos, knowing which way to move and what was expected of me. If there were tantrums thrown, they belonged to my two- and four-year-old sons, tiny rages I calmed with hot baths and story books and soothed with early bedtimes. I had forgotten what it was to face a tantrum larger than me, and hopeless.

"Have some, Dad, now!"

Gripped with a sudden weariness I leaned my head back against the booth. Across the table, my brother's features hung over his plate; the delicate moon of his scalp shone through his thinning hair. In that small moment, I wondered where he'd gone; so little was left of the boy I remembered. I thought of his flat-footed steps chasing after me in Grandpa's store; the shy dip of his chin when he said "Hi" for the first time. A quick stab shot through me. I wished now for that boy, and all of his childhood passions: for his mechanical lady bug toy with its blipping eyeballs, for color-in-the-dots and worn-out Crayolas, for Elvis's syrupy songs spinning round and round the turntable. I also longed for that moment by the swimming pool when he put himself aside long enough to lotion and soothe me—anything but this fierce and furious braying in a booth.

In the next instant, Rod lifted his cup and moved it in a jittery path toward my father's open palm. Then he released it, jamming both hands between his knees, plunging his nose to his plate, and expelling shallow puffs of air. Leftover bread crumbs blew around in circles and out to the far edges of his dish.

When we were children, long ago, I knew how to be with him, how to sound out hard-to-say words, like "six" and "Jell-O," how to teach him again to knot his shoestrings and take my hand when we stepped from a curb. I knew how to keep him from harm, leaping to his side and planting myself between him and the bully world. But now, I couldn't fathom what to do. I didn't know how to help him, to be his sister in this situation, save for lunging toward the pot and plying him with more coffee.

Seconds passed—I could hear the ticking—and somewhere off to the side I sensed the waitress glancing over, checking if she might safely approach with our bill.

Don't, I warned her silently, catching her eye. *Stay there. This isn't over yet.*

Proving how out of practice I was, how thin-skinned I'd become in my years away, I jolted hard as Rod exploded once more, his "Coffee, Dad!" splaying my hands. I rocked my own cup, knocking over my water glass, spraying a volley of ice cubes and sending a flood of sugar and salt packets across the table and splattering to the floor. The couple at the next table, a balding man and his wiry, wispy-haired wife, stared, unabashed, mouths agape. The man's chin pressed back into his collar as he sat alert and incredulous, his mouth dropped at the corners, as if he were about to get up, cross the few feet to our booth, and fix this bad business once and for all. His wife swiveled her chin, as if to say, *Really, how could you?*

My father took no notice.

"You're going to have to lower your voice," he said in a steady tone.

In the midst of my fluster, I couldn't help marveling. My father was tightly wrapped and reserved, a man of few words and little laughter. Not an affectionate man. But he was exactly the type of person to have with you when your brother was losing it in a restaurant.

"Okay! Yes!" Rod's chin whapped the table. "Have my coffee!"

"You're not lowering your voice."

Turning his head, Rod touched his ear to his plate and grimaced, pulling his lips back into a toothy grin, like a horse.

"Okay! Okay, Dad, I be nieeeeece."

"You're still speaking too loudly."

"Ray . . . he can't," my mother said, her voice a whiff of sound.

"Okay, Dad!" Rod bellowed. His ear-splitting volume was enough to get us thrown out onto the street. "Have my coffee now!"

Inside that moment, I felt a deep, unspeakable shame that I hadn't somehow spared my brother or my parents from this, fixed it so they could find some peace. For all of my blue ribbons and straight A's and diligent patience teaching Rod numbers and words growing up, and for all of the healthy boy children and grandchildren I went on to bear, I couldn't thwart the relentlessness of my brother's struggle. A great lumbering guilt stirred in me, shifting awake the memory of my departure all those years ago, its moments catching up to me: my open suitcase on the bed, my breathy bustling about the room, my mother bending to the floor, layering a steamer trunk with linens and extra towels, the two of us sitting and bouncing on the lid, defied by its bulge as we pounded at the latches, choking with laughter.

Consumed with packing for college, I hadn't thought of my brother for several hours, perhaps even days. As I had lifted the trunk lid and packed down the layers of bulk, I didn't notice him in the shadows. Not until his voice ventured softly into the room, saying my name the way he always did, without the *r* and *g*.

"Mossie, I'm not going to college," he said.

I looked up. He stood in my bedroom doorway, sorrowful, dazed with comprehension. Unable to manage the *l*s, he pronounced it "cawedge."

His voice had uttered an unspoken truth. That he would not follow me out into the world, but rather, stay in a life where one day he had a sister, and the next, she was gone.

"Okay, Dad! Have my coffee, now!"

This volley pierced my ear. I lifted my hand, cupping it over the whorl of my earlobe, and closed my eyes. Tiny tears clawed their way around in my eye sockets. I still hadn't grown numb to this scene, hadn't grown calluses along with my parents. How had I been born so ill-equipped? I fought a desire to hurl my voice into the mayhem, to cry out to my parents, "What is your secret? How do you breathe through ruined moments, over and over? Tell me."

I knew then why I'd run from my family: to escape the undertow of my brother's tantrums, but even more so, to flee my failure to make him my whole life. I couldn't have known I wasn't alone. It would be years before I learned how many siblings of disabled children flee into marriages or faraway careers.

In the next instant, my father lunged over the table, reaching for Rod with both hands before he clamped his fingers together, mid-flight, yanking both palms back to his chest and dropping once again to his seat. Jamming his clapped hands between his knees, he bent over, head bowed, breathing hard. He so rarely showed emotion that, when he did, it felt dire. I shot a look over to my mother but her gaze beaded toward her lap.

Dad lifted his eyes, releasing his words in a careful row.

"You must lower your voice, Rod."

"Okay, yes!" Rod thundered. "I will, Dad!"

In the distance, I could see the restaurant manager emerge from behind the cash register and look our way. In another minute he was going to march over and ask us to leave. Some diners were getting up from their tables and leaving without dessert.

Then, without warning, my brother found the off switch somewhere deep inside himself. His next words, softly spoken, eased from his lips, contrite and subdued.

"I be nice, yes, have my coffee back," he said. His tone was calm and, astonishingly, laced with a touch of kindness.

We sat in silence, not moving, uncertain whether this squall had blown through. I sensed for a surprised moment that my parents, despite of their steadfast wills and years of practice, were addled and shaken.

"Well, all right then," my mother said, softly, raising her bowed head.

Clearing his throat, my father lifted Rod's half-filled cup and handed it back across the table. Quietly, with a long-fingered and delicate gesture, my brother took it back again.

The next few minutes passed in near silence. Rod took tiny bird sips from the edge of his cup, eyes flitting around and back to the table. Each of us was careful not to look his way, avoiding, at all cost, the dreaded eye contact, which could send him off again.

My father paid the bill, pressing the money onto the table and, as always, counting the change twice. Then, on his cue, we stood to go.

My eyes found the couple in the next booth. Their faces were wary and they wouldn't meet my gaze. Their eyes, like so many others in the room, followed my father, mother, and brother, as they trundled, single file, to the door.

For the smallest of moments, I paused, fingertips touching the table, with its mess of coffee stains, strewn packets, and empty cups. This was the very moment when, as a child, I would slip the other way, making for the restroom and its few moments of hidden respite. Where I'd wait my turn and then stall at the sink, carefully rinsing my hands, re-banding my hair and pretending, at least to myself, that I was separate from my family. And from where, a few minutes later, I'd emerge, heading for the front door by myself, hoping the crowded tables had forgotten what had happened and to whom I belonged.

Now, I brushed flecks of sugar from my fingertips. And then, inexplicably, I slid out of the booth, rounded the coffee stand and, in a few steps, caught up to my brother's funny loping walk. Thick air from the faraway exit billowed toward me and, with it, the smell of hot rain. I felt the ember of an old instinct. I did not put my arms out to hide him, but nevertheless stayed close behind and, with the angle of my torso, shielded him from the roomful of gawking eyes.

Chapter 28

Losing It

After the debacle of Dave's Diner, we spent the rest of the car trip resorting to fast food drive-throughs. McDonald's, Wendy's, Wimpy's—any place where we could get a meal and stay inside the sanctuary of the car. These were the days before crisp salads and grilled chicken were added to fast-food menus, before fat and sugar were associated with ill health, so our choices amounted to Big Macs, Fish Filets, and various volumes of French fries, topped off with synthetic milk shakes.

Part of me was relieved not to get out of the car, but each time I unwrapped another oily Fish Filet in the back seat, trapped in my seatbelt, thighs sticky with the heat, I swallowed little shards of resentment. I was an adult now, and I wanted to be able to get out of the car if I so chose, to select from a variety of food groups, to have a tension-free lunch in a comfortable, roomy booth with my mother, order a glass of iced tea, split a piece of coconut cream pie without my brother spoiling it, making us stuff food down our throats and high-tail-it for the door.

At the next hotel stop, the final one on the trip, I tried proposing this idea, catching my mother in a rare moment by herself. She was tidying up the hotel room as Rod and my father took a drive to go fill up the car with gas.

"Mom, let's seize the day and walk to the café. Maybe split a piece of pie together?" I suggested lightly, as if this were not a big deal and we would not be doing something behind the back of my father, or admitting that we'd like a moment away from my brother.

"Oh?" she answered. Her voice rose as if she were questioning the air. She finished folding Rod's shorts and added them to the prim tower of T-shirts on the bed.

My mother rarely stopped tasking, picking up, wiping the counter, putting away dishes. Years later she would admit this was her way of relieving anxiety and the boredom of housewifery. Aside from bending over the crossword puzzle on Sunday afternoons, she never sat down.

"I don't know," she said vaguely, "I suppose . . ." Her eyes, hazel-gray like mine, drifted toward the window, then down to her watch while she frowned, and then back up to the window.

In the next moment, tires crunched outside, and I knew the moment had passed.

"Never mind," I said, exasperated. "I'm going to run to the store down the street. I need a few things."

This was not true. What I needed was the same thing I had yearned for most of my life: a moment alone with her. Not for any profound reason, just to be mother and daughter over a piece of lemon meringue pie. This simple wish was wildly unattainable. When I was a child, I had merited her attention when I was competing, but I didn't have gymnastics now.

I couldn't tell whether she registered my frustration. She bent over the laundry basket and picked up another shirt.

It didn't occur to me that my mother's incessant housekeeping was a coping tool, a way to allay boredom and stave off depression. She was a woman with a gifted mind who had never had the chance to use it, a musician whose only outlet was an occasional solo at church, a former beauty queen who now faced an aging, ordinary woman in the mirror. She did not want to sit down and take time to be present, or reflect, or think about the future; it was too hard.

"Well, as long as you're going, can you pick up some crayons?" she asked, checking the shirt for ring-around-the-collar. "Rod's upset about the black, it broke the other day. I'll give you some money."

"Mom, really, I can spring for crayons." My voice was flat and petulant—teen-like. *Small.*

I gestured for the keys as Dad came into the room, and then, turning quickly, whacked shoulders with Rod as he came through the doorway. The two of us ricocheted in opposite directions, whamming into the door frame.

"Sorry, Rod. Are you okay?" I said, gaining my balance and rubbing the lump already bulging over my ear. I touched his arm and he flinched.

"Oh, yaas, Mossie!" he shouted in my ear.

Cocking both wrists, palms in the air, I moved backward through the doorway and onto the porch, keys dangling from my fingers.

"Just go on," my mother said, hastily closing the door.

In the next moment, I was in the car and driving out, clipping the hotel hedge as I went by. The moment I reached the straightaway I gripped the wheel and vigorously yanked myself back and forth, back and forth, teeth clenched. Swiping at my eyes, the view more and more blurred, I slid through two stop lights and my collarbone burned from the seat belt as the car slithered under my haunches, the loose belly of the embankment giving under my swerving, scudding tires.

Somehow, I made it to the A&P parking lot without running off the road, swinging into a parking space between a Valiant and a pickup truck and snapping off the engine. *What on earth is wrong with me?* My throat throbbed and snot ran into my mouth. Rummaging into the glove box I found Kleenex and blew hard, the smell of heated rubber wafting through the open window as I pushed my spine back against the seat and sat there, breathing, appalled.

I had forgotten this part of myself—having been away from my family long enough to believe that I had recovered from such viral, thwarted frustration. It had taken only a few days of traveling with them in the confines of a car to bring it roiling back. If Barbara Ann were here she would laugh me out of this—show me the ridiculousness of the situation, how silly it was to want a few uninterrupted moments with our mother and a piece of pie. But she was not here with me, and this was a rooted anger—the same one I had felt all those years ago, when I drew the picture of my family and ripped it to shreds. The only way I had found to manage this feeling was to distance myself from my family. Thank the Lord I only had another day on the road and soon would fly away, back to my own life. This thought and a few more minutes of breathing calmed me enough to get out of the car. Despite the heat, I stood there for several minutes, composing myself and blowing my nose. Then I slipped my sunglasses on to camouflage my eyes and crossed the parking lot, heading for Excedrin and crayons.

An hour later, when I brought the box of crayons in from the car, I handed it to Rod, wordlessly, keeping my gaze averted. My eyes were dry and swollen in their sockets, and I could think of nothing I wanted more than a hot shower and the closed door of a bathroom.

Something, though, made me glance his way, and I noticed on his mouth a certain kind of tilted smile. I detected a bit of remorse in the cocked angle of his head. His face dipped, nose down, and he muttered something.

In our old way, I understood what he was saying. He was asking me to color with him. As always, I felt a softening in my heart, but with it, a new kind of despair: I didn't have the right to be angry. I couldn't have a good sibling row with my brother; he was no match for me, and any form of fury I hurled at him was shameful. He was not to blame.

I did not yet realize that Rod was not the one fueling my frustration. Flipping open the latch of my parents' suitcase, I dug out his Batman coloring book, handed it to him, walked into the bathroom, and shut the door.

That night, lying awake, I listened from the other side of the hotel room through the darkness. Sometime in the last ten years Rod had started snoring; not surprisingly, I reasoned as I stared at the ceiling, since he took after my grandfather. But also not in the expected way, no rambling inhale, whistling exhale, but odd random bunches of arrhythmic snorts and snuffles. I could hardly stand the sound, the randomness and lack of rhythm startling me anew each time he paused and started up again. There was something disconcerting, disturbing, crazy-driven about the sound, something hopelessly entrenched. I got up, rustled quietly in my suitcase and slipped on some jeans, then stepped outside the motel door and sat in one of the flamingo-pink metal chairs to wait out the long night.

The next day, on the final few miles of the trip, I awoke from an exhausted, drooling nap in the back seat. The car tires slowed and bumped over a curb. Lifting my head, I saw we had pulled into a Denny's parking lot.

"What's wrong? Why are we stopping?" I slurred, dropping my matted hair back to the bunched-up pillow.

"Well, I don't know about you, but I'm hungry," my father announced robustly, unhitching his seatbelt and unlatching the door. "Anybody else hungry?"

"Yaas," Rod said.

What on earth is my father thinking? Is he mad? I didn't say this out loud. I closed my eyes and felt a distinct slump beneath me, a loss of altitude. *I'm the one who's crazy*, I thought, *or I will be, soon.*

Slam, slam-slam, the car doors banged around me as I sat up. The three of them, my parents and Rod, walked away from the car, heading toward the glaring mouth of the place. My father's tall frame ambling in that gangly long-muscled way; my brother's soft, shapeless, mildly paunchy figure gimping a few steps behind; and my mother's petite, once-trim, now-rounded figure clipping along in clean white slacks and sneakers.

For a moment I pondered whether to call after them and feign a headache-need-to-nap excuse, but, already, I knew I wouldn't go through with it. I was too desperate for something—anything—to eat other than fried food, and for any reason to get out of the car, even if it meant walking into a family restaurant and sitting down in a booth with my brother.

Groggily, I got out and trotted across the parking lot, where my father was waiting with the door held open. He herded us in, detouring himself and Rod off to the bathroom to wash up, and then came back, settling into the strategic booth, across from my mother. Here we were again.

"Well now," he announced, clapping his hands together and rubbing briskly as if he were about to embark on a healthy and pleasurable hike up a mountain. "I'm going to have Rod order tonight."

God in heaven, I thought. My lids flattened and I looked over at my mother. Studiously, she kept her eyes down on the menu. Just when I thought we'd been through it all. After days of Rod-incidents all along the route, acting out in the lobby, in the public bathrooms, on the sidewalk, shouting and stubbornly refusing to pipe down, my father decides to cattle-prod the bull inside my brother one more time.

If I had been younger, this was the moment my mother would have looked up from her menu, frowned across the table, and said, "Wipe that bad attitude off your face, young lady."

But I wasn't younger, and suddenly I realized where my seething frustration came from. Not from my brother, who every day struggled with the world of others, following their rules, working harder than any of us just to say hello, keep eye contact, respond, and ask for more coffee. As maddening as his behavior could be at times, I knew deep down I was seeing him box with life, his valiant attempt to do as he was asked, to fight back when he could, to come out swinging at a fate that he did not chose, and that he knew none of the rest of us had to endure.

My frustration came from the fact that I was buckled by it—the relentlessness of his struggle and the impossibility of peace. I wanted a harmonious family and knew this was secondary to my brother's struggle—that when it came down to my need for peace or my brother's struggle, my parents would choose his struggle. My father would not only bring Rod into a restaurant and risk another debacle, but he would do it with me here, and furthermore, he would add a twist, a new challenge: he would have my brother order the meal.

The moment came, the waitress stopping at our booth, her pencil poised, and I jumped in to order first, the full sum of my rebellion. Next, my father ordered for himself and my mother, as always, and then he said, "Rod, it's your turn. Say what you'd like to eat for dinner."

"Yaas," Rod said, looking sideways and mumbling.

"Speak a little louder so she can hear you," said my mother, touching his arm.

"Okay!" he said, and then, as if he were practiced at this, he ordered a hamburger, Coca Cola, French fries, and apple pie, seamlessly, without having to repeat a word.

I exhaled and slumped, like a slow-leaking balloon. I should have been elated but I'd been at this too long. My brother's unpredictability defeated me.

"That was a very nice job, Rod sweetie," said my mother, pleased, releasing her napkin ring and shaking the cloth onto her lap. "How about that."

Chapter 29

Lift Off

Florida was a deadly place to be in May. Heat and humidity cloaked me like a wet towel as I trekked toward my father's Plymouth Belvedere with Don and our adolescent boys, each of us hauling an inordinate number of suitcases. Moisture sprouted up and down my vertebrae as if my spine were a soaker hose. I didn't have to guess how my husband was faring. He loathed heat and perspiration.

"Whoooee, is it hot!" sang out my younger son, Zachary, cheerily.

Just shy of puberty, Zachary was a perpetual delight. Light and wiry and always in motion, he tended to shimmy up trees and leap off stairs and rooftops, resulting most recently in several stitches to his forehead. He found joy in the ridiculous and adventure in any scenario, including this one, a weeklong visit to my family. Dylan, on the other hand, was appropriately self-absorbed at fifteen, dressed in black jeans, cool Vans, and a Scream T-shirt. In the last year he had burned off his layer of baby fat and was now a slenderized version of Don. As the lead singer in his rock band, he worried that he was away from his high school friends and missing rehearsals for Battle of the Bands, and, if given the choice (which we did not give him), he'd plug into his Walkman.

"Yes, sir, a tad warm," my father agreed, amused, sauntering before us like a giraffe on the Savannah, unperturbed by the cotton-like air.

The boys and I squeezed into the back of my father's Belvedere, Don up front, and we set off for my younger sister Camela's house. She had married a British engineer and birthed a daughter, the first female grandchild in the family. Don took out a handkerchief and wiped his forehead. He was more agitated than usual and I wondered if he had started smoking again. If so, he'd be desperate for a cigarette right about now.

I had an uneasy feeling about this trip. We so rarely visited my family, caught up as we were with our speeding lives in Boston: Don's blossoming art exhibits, his father's retrospective shows, his mother's portrait commissions of Supreme Court justices. His younger sister's wedding to a fellow musician, the subsequent launch of their band, and release of their first album. My life was subsumed by theirs. I was the scaffolding, the backstage crew, the non-performer, the one who dressed the boys properly and drove them to the art openings and performances and ferried them home before the party was over, and the one who took the paying job with benefits so Don could remain free to paint.

Recently, it had dawned on me that my husband and his family did not know me. Somewhere along the way I had become the one who did not have a dream—who was not aspiring to anything bigger than daily tasks. This truth had arisen harshly some months before when a longtime friend of Don's family, a patron of sorts, offered to build a writer's studio for me right in our backyard.

"You need a retreat," she had announced cheerily over the phone, startling me. I had not expected to receive such a gift. She was a childless divorcee who had inherited a fortune and had already given Don the money to build a magnificent art studio, with soaring ceilings, walls of storage bays for finished paintings, and drawers for artistic supplies. Tucked behind a knoll a few hundred feet from our house, his studio was a sacred place, the kind few can ever afford, insulated from the raucousness of growing boys and dogs and pet gerbils.

Breathless and pleased, I had shared the news of my potential writer's hideaway with Don, and he, in turn, responded tepidly. The next I knew, he had spoken with his father and the two of them had counseled the family friend that her money would be better spent on a family car for us, a solid station wagon that would replace the aging sedan I had been hauling the boys around in.

"The car's not safe; we need a new one," Don had stated, taken aback by my silence at this news. His exasperated tone, laced with disapproval, implied I was selfish and sufficiently ungrateful. "You already have an office upstairs."

"*We* have an office," I corrected.

"You mean you'd rather keep that car and put the boys' lives at risk?" Don said.

I suddenly felt sick. I was outgunned and my husband had ceased to be my ally. Don went on to inform me he had promised the patron that he would clear out of the family office upstairs and let me turn that into my exclusive space. I knew this was an impossible promise: the one computer we owned was in that office and, out of necessity, he would have to enter, settle into the chair whenever he needed to tend to his art business, and leave his papers scattered over the desk. I had gathered those papers several times now, stacked them, and moved them to the kitchen table.

I couldn't fully blame my husband or my in-laws. My deep need for a close family, for a life of art and music, for a sense that I was centered among people who felt like my tribe had made me willing to acquiesce, to be patient. Add in my tendency to behave, to keep the peace as the child of a traditional family, especially one with a disabled child.

I agreed to the car—we needed one, after all—and to the inevitable intrusion into my office space upstairs and all that this implied: I had not yet earned the right to a studio of my own. I did not deserve it.

Now, riding in the sticky coolness of my father's car, past miles of housing developments and dwindling orange groves, I felt more out of body and disoriented than I had ever been. We arrived at a security booth, showed our licenses, and were buzzed through the gate into a walled community, one of thousands in Orlando. My younger sister's ample house appeared and I hastily leaped out of the car and made for the front door, diving into the air-conditioning and swooning from the chilling gusts of central air.

"I'll be darned, they're here!" trilled my mother, coming from the kitchen and reaching to hug me. She was turning gray and her aging spine had begun to shrink so that she stood barely five feet tall. Cami, on the other hand, was taller than both my mother and me.

"Well, it's about time," Cami said, coming forward with another hug. Dressed impeccably, she wore a crisp collared blouse and white slacks, her feet strapped into elegant sandals that highlighted her slender feet and pale pink toenails. Having grown up in this tropical climate, she knew how to dress in airy fabrics and string shoes. As we all chatted about minutiae, Cami slipped away to the next room and then suddenly reappeared, this time with my brother. There he was, forty-three years old, heavy-browed and frowning, his eyes on the floor.

"Hi, Rod," I said, softly.

"Hi, Moss."

I had seen my brother only a few times since the debacle at Dave's Diner ten years before. I gave him a light hug and a kiss on the cheek, which he didn't like, and then I turned and gestured to my sons. "Do you remember Dylan and Zachary?"

"Yaas," Rod said, sharply. I wasn't sure if he was mad at me for speaking, or mad at the boys for not visiting more often, or simply mad at everything.

Uncertainly, Dylan and Zachary said hello, but neither stepped toward Rod or attempted a handshake. They had been young children when they saw him last. For all they knew, their uncle would shout and slap them if they stepped closer; he looked dark enough to do so.

"And you remember Don?" I went on, turning to my husband. Don's features were oddly arranged, a mixture of pity and distaste.

Silence.

"He's my husband," I prompted, anxiety leaking into my voice as perspiration dampened the collar of my blouse.

"Hi, Rod," Don said, his bulky frame all but hidden behind the boys.

"Hi!" Rod barked.

Long ago, I had noticed that Rod was easier around women. He had grown up surrounded by sisters and the lighter voices and gentle touches of females soothed him, more so than the hearty deep voices of males. Dogs and children similarly unnerved him, though for different reasons: as bundles of raw, open emotions and sudden, unpredictable movements, they set him on edge.

Awkwardly, we stood bunched in the foyer, not knowing what to do next. An overwhelming sense of chagrin flooded through me. Why hadn't I come here more often to visit my family and my brother? Deep down, I knew why. It had been easier not to come. My husband didn't like it here, and neither did I, though for different reasons. Don had grown up in an erudite, liberal Jewish family, not a rifle-packing coal mining Baptist fundamentalist one. It had been easier for me to adapt to his side of the fence than for him to adapt to mine.

As a consequence, my children did not know my brother or my parents or my younger siblings, something I had never intended even as I allowed and perpetuated it.

"Have a seat at the table, Rod," Cami said, finally, diffusing the moment. "I'll get you some iced tea." She was thirty-three years old, fifteen years my junior, and had grown up underneath Rod, without me or Barbara Ann nearby. She was the daughter who had stayed near my parents, living at home as she went to college and then settling in the next town over. She had become the on-site sister, the one who looked after Rod when my parents traveled, who sometimes picked him up from his group home on the other side of Orlando and brought him to my parents' house for Sunday dinner, and who a few years into the future would, along with her husband, assume Rod's guardianship, taking on the morass of state and legal accountabilities for his welfare.

"Okay!" Rod shouted, darting from the doorway and yanking out the chair.

The room tensed and drew back. This was not going well.

"Now, Rod," my mother said, reaching out her hand to pat his back.

Something new about this moment disturbed me. I felt a dimensional shift in my perception as if I were peering through binoculars. I had first gotten to know my brother as a sweet, cuddly baby, a normal little boy. For all of his encroaching handicaps I had not forgotten who he was underneath his cloak of disability. I held the sound of his delightful laugh when I tickled him as a small boy, the quietness of his voice as he handed me his ladybug and said, "Fix it." The touch of his gentle grownup hands lotioning my back. That's who I saw when I thought of him.

Now, I was seeing him from a distance, as a neighbor might view him, as my sons and my husband saw him: imperfect, hard to look at, unpredictable, impossible to accommodate. *Hang onto your hats*, I thought, sardonically. *Just wait until you see him eat.* I winced at the cut of these words. I didn't like myself. I was not good at this, straddling two completely different worlds, two cleaved and conflicting lives. I didn't know how to ride both at the same time and keep myself from falling off. This was why I had stayed away and why I wanted to get away again.

True to form, we sat down to a trying and awkward dinner. Both of my boys reached for their milk glasses instantly, but hastily withdrew as Cami said, "Mom, will you say grace, please?"

We bowed our heads and my mother sang out, "Dear Heavenly Father, we thank you for this bountiful table and especially for bringing our family safely here today . . ."

Out of the corner of my eye, I saw Zachary crack his eyelids and cast a perplexed look around the table. Dylan did the same thing, and I made a silent sign to them both to bow and be still. From the moment we finished grace, Rod turned frantic, shouting "Yaas!" to everyone, spooning extra helpings of sweet potatoes, blurting "Okay, Dad!" each time my father said "That's enough." Blessedly, Rod never shouted when he was actually chewing food, so at last, he fell silent, hunkering down to eat what was piled on his plate. By then, we had all withdrawn into ourselves. In those minutes of quiet, I struggled to find conversation. How to make up for years of disconnect at one meal? How to help my sons get to know their grandparents, when all we wanted in that moment was to wolf down this meal and scatter from the table?

"Are we in for any rain this week?" I asked.

I couldn't help but think of our gatherings back home in Boston, on Sundays and holidays, with just Don, the boys, and me, or with Don's parents and sisters. The conversation was full of art, politics, music, story-telling, joking, laughter.

Rod hung his head over his plate, agitated, mincing his mashed potatoes into miniscule bites. From what I could tell, nothing had changed since Dave's Diner. My brother was utterly miserable, a seething and frustrated young man, either catatonic or bellicose.

My parents were convinced there was a conspiracy afoot. Several, actually. Aside from the communist plot to fluoridate drinking water and government lies about the ozone layer, now there was a widespread mission to drug handicapped children.

"They just want to shut 'em up," my mother often said, nodding in agreement with Dad.

They were adamant Rod not be treated with any medications whatsoever, whether or not he was suffering from depression or anxiety. If he needed to shout, let him shout. They did not believe a carefully monitored dose might actually bring him some relief.

"You know, he might need some help, Mom," I had ventured on a recent phone call. I had dialed my parents in April to wish Rod a happy birthday, and he had bellowed answers into the receiver until I grew weary and asked him to give the phone back to Mom. "His symptoms seem worse."

"Well, maybe so," my mother responded. I knew she wouldn't act on this idea, even if she thought it had merit. For one thing, she would not counter my father's opinion that doctors and especially therapists were not to be trusted. And for another, her treatment of choice was prayer. When she felt helpless, or her children were suffering, prayer was her action item; it made her feel empowered, as if she were doing something.

Getting up to clear the dishes for dessert, I asked if anyone wanted coffee; I couldn't wait until this meal was over and we'd all said goodnight. But no one else rose with me and I realized I was supposed to stay seated until Rod had cleaned his plate, even if it meant another thirty minutes. He was not to be rushed; the fallout wasn't worth it. Sinking back into the chair, I poured myself more water and waited. Once again I was a petulant teenager, impatient to leave the table, to leave my family. I looked at my sons, Zachary fidgeting, Dylan glancing around the table. No one spoke. The week ahead yawned like an enormous open maw.

If Barbara Ann were here, she would apply practicality to the situation. She had the uncanny firstborn ability to take charge and treat predicaments like renovation projects. Unlike myself. As the second-born, I detached and sank into a familiar torpor of resignation. Over the next few days, sweaty and overdressed, at odds with the elements, I ventured with the boys and Don out among thousands of other tourists braving the lines at Universal Studios and Epcot and dropping stressful amounts of cash. By mid-week we had transposed into native Orlandoans, staying indoors from nine in the morning to well after dusk. Even after the sun went down we sought canned air and walled-in spaces. The oppressive heat and humidity turned us into sloths, slow to rise and even slower to chew. We had no appetites and were generally out of sorts. I wondered how long it would take us to simply cease moving. The only exception was my father, who rose to play tennis every morning, unfazed by the heat. He had grown up in the steam bath of the Appalachian Mountains and, like his Pappy, he had little use for air-conditioning.

The day before we were to leave Florida, I plunged into laundry and packing, flitting from the dryer to the bedroom, fussing at the boys to organize their clothes. In the late afternoon, my mother and father arrived without Rod. He had already returned to the group home he lived in from Monday through Friday, and his penchant for routine made it better not to disrupt him again. I would say goodbye to him over the phone.

My father had barely come into the door before he opened the newspaper in his hands and announced that the Space Shuttle Discovery was scheduled to launch Thursday morning.

"Think your boys would like to see that?" he asked, looking over the paper at me, glasses perched on his nose.

"We're supposed to leave tomorrow, Dad," I said, put out and edgy, cramming socks into the pockets of my suitcase. Instantly, I was sorry.

It occurred to me that my father wanted company. For the most part, his passion for aeronautics had gone without companionship. I had been the only child of five to accompany him to model airplane contests as a fellow flier. My mother traveled with him now, going for days to Pensacola and other towns for model airplane meets, and had even learned to track and retrieve the planes, but she was there for my father, not for the planes, not for the love of flight.

I looked at Don, who was pointedly silent. He expression told me there was no way he would stay here another day. Then, I called to the boys to come out to the kitchen.

"Cool!" Zachary chirped. "Let's go see it blast off!"

Relief flooded through me. I wanted to see it, too, partly for my dad, partly to feel awestruck again, a feeling I hadn't had in a long time. In moments, it was decided: Don and Dylan would fly back as planned; Zachary and I would change our tickets and stay for another day. My father would cover the difference in price.

The day of the launch, I awoke in the dark to an empty bed. It was 3:00 a.m. and we'd have to leave soon to make it to Kennedy Space Center by launch time. I groaned and rubbed my face. An odd feeling seeped through me—a premonition, rousing the memory of an argument. I had wanted Dylan to stay, arguing that seeing a space launch was rare and this was a time for grandsons to be with their grandfather.

"Don't be insensitive," Don had snapped as he clipped the latches of his suitcase. "Dylan shouldn't have to stay if he doesn't want to."

Don had been doing this a lot lately, insinuating that I was insensitive. I knew Dylan might balk at first, but after he took in the launch, I knew the experience would be the first thing he shared with his friends. I suspected this wasn't really about Dylan, but more about Don simply wanting to get away. He could not abide my family even for a few extra hours. Somewhere, deep down, I felt Don pinching his nose: *your born-again parents, your hillbilly ancestors, your dad's guns, your exasperating brother who ruins every family gathering and every meal.*

Gently, I shook Zachary's shoulder and prodded him awake. He was so groggy he turned down cereal and even chocolate milk, but soon rallied as we got on the road, peppering my dad with questions about the launch. How heavy is the Space Shuttle? Why is it going up there? Where is it going?

"Two hundred sixty-two thousand and thirty-five pounds," my father answered instantly, as if this were an everyday answer to have at the tip of your tongue. "This'll be the first shuttle flight to dock with the International Space Station. It's filled with cargo for station outfitting."

My father had done this enough times to know how to get close enough to see the launch without security clearance. With our last-minute seat-of-the-pants arrival, we'd get nowhere near Kennedy Space Center, but my father was unperturbed. He headed the car down an open-sided road that had a clear flat view for what seemed a hundred miles straight out to the ocean. As we got out and crossed the road, we joined a bunch of other people, jostling and making room so we could all see. Then, we waited, propped against the guardrails, tearing into granola bars. With all eyes tilted skyward, we watched as color smeared across the sky and morning dawned on our side of the earth.

Far away, the hatch closed and was locked for flight at 5:36 a.m. The countdown began. At the T-minus-9 mark they paused the clock and we all turned restless, the temperature of the day upon us. I peeled off my sweater.

"It's a sailboat holding up the countdown!" called out a man, sitting with his ear to a radio and laughing. "It wandered into the area!"

Fifteen minutes later the same man called out, "There we go; clear to launch!"

A magnificent plume of white light flashed and smoke billowed beneath the cone, rumbling out on all sides. I tensed and held my breath.

"Look, Mom," said Zachary. "Look!"

"Yes, sweetie, I see it."

The sleek rocket lifted, detached, hung for a split second as if to fill its lungs, and then rose smoothly, liquidly, as if weightless, its tail fiercely burning fuel, flaming with a dragon's fury.

Inexplicably, tears sprang into my eyes. I felt a flood of desire and regret that I would never sit inside that capsule and feel that kind of otherworldly power. And I felt something else: a sorrow that my husband was not with me, nor my oldest son, and we were not sharing this together as a whole family. Just as the ground shook from the blast off, I felt some deep sensation that the ground was cracking beneath me, and the rushing realization that, in my effort to escape, to break from the gravity of my family, and to create and keep a buoyant home of my own, I had rushed into my first marriage too soon and was staying in this marriage too long. I had broken off something essential in myself—some spiritual tie to my roots and to who I was, where I came from, most of which I had denied to my sons.

As the plume fought its way upward from the earth, through the bubble of air, I pulled Zachary close. He hugged back.

"Did I ever tell you your grandpa built rockets like that?" I said.

"Like what?" Zachary asked, his wiry monkey-body flinching with surprise.

"Like that one, right there," I said, smiling, pointing at the fiery speck burning toward the membrane of our atmosphere. In another minute it would pierce through to another realm, beyond ours. I kept pointing until it was smaller than the tip of my finger and, lastly, the pinpoint of a star.

Chapter 30

Batman

The year Rod turned fifty he abandoned his coloring books. Batman, Birds of Paradise, Tom and Jerry suddenly untouched on his desktop, and his box of sixty-four Crayola crayons, worn down to the nubs, forsaken in his top desk drawer.

"He just quit?" I asked, dismayed, holding the cup of Lipton tea and spitting crumbs of a Ritz cracker. "Since when?"

Four of us siblings, spanning seventeen of our mother's child-bearing years, were perched around the Formica breakfast bar in the fluorescent light of my parents' Florida kitchen. Mom and Dad had left a few moments before to pick Rod up from his group home in the Lake Margaret neighborhood on the other side of Orlando, and, in the meantime, Barbara Ann, Cami, James, and I were sharing hot cups of tea: an unusual sight. We didn't know each other very well, in part because we lived on opposite coasts, and in part because we had grown up decades apart, in two different eras: Baby Boomers of the Sixties and Gen X-ers of the Eighties. Barb had been seventeen and I fifteen when Cami was born, and by the time James arrived, Barb had married and birthed a child, and I had flown off to college.

"We don't really know when or why Rod quit. Dad says he's just done with it," said Cami, holding the tag of her tea bag with slender, manicured fingers.

"Oh dear," said Barbara Ann. "Now what are we going to give him for his birthday?"

We all chuckled, the sound rattling quickly and then quelling into silence. We had convened from our different corners of the continent to celebrate this Easter holiday, the most sacred day of the year for our mother. She was moved more by Christ's suffering and resurrection than by his birth. For her sake, we would all attend service at the Lakeside Baptist Church in the morning, and then sit down to ham, deviled eggs, and strawberry shortcake. I had long since given up celebrating the tortured death of a prophet and, instead, devoted my hallelujahs to the arrival of spring and sprouts and splashes of yellow and purple crocus—the sweet and brave persistence of new life.

Roddy's day of birth, April 15, fell close to Easter, as did my father's, April 11. This coincidence had, for a slender moment long ago, delighted my mother—before, as she often said now, "everything changed."

"Shoot," I said, biting into another cracker. "I already bought him *Batman Returns.*"

We all coveted the chance to gift Rod a new coloring book for his birthday. Coloring was one of the few tangible hobbies he still seemed to enjoy, at least up until now. This year, I had shopped early, spending a good hour in Toys "R" Us, leafing through coloring books and scanning Batman story lines. I doubted the plots meant anything to my brother. I suspected his coloring obsession had more to do with filling in empty spaces, his wish to complete the uncompleted. It soothed him in some way. And now he had forsaken it.

"Do you suppose something is upsetting him, something at his group home?" I asked, slipping into my investigative reporter mode, wanting to know the reasons behind anything and everything. But in fact, I was not in the position to note anything wrong with my brother's living situation, or with his health, or with his emotional state. I was not in the vicinity of his daily life.

"A lot of things upset Rod over there—mostly his roommates," said Cami. She would know; she often carted Rod to and from Lake Margaret.

The one time I had visited Lake Margaret a few years ago, one of Rod's roommates, Jerry, had hovered around me like a giant fly, introducing himself over and over and asking me if I was married. The fifth time he stood directly in front of me, blocking my path, and put his face a few inches from mine, forcing me to say again, "No, I'm not married, not anymore." I knew Jerry pestered Rod to no end, often charging into his bedroom, opening drawers and looking in his closet, stealing the odd pair of socks and, once, a set of brand new pajamas. Or at least that was one theory. The other was that a staff member had lifted the pajamas, which was why my parents now kept Rod's good clothes at home.

"Maybe he's just having a midlife crisis," observed James, dryly, surprising us that he was still in the room. James tended to disintegrate from our family circle, noiselessly vanishing to his bedroom hovel where he kept the curtains closed and played video games until all hours. Since quitting his power-up job at Charles Schwab and moving back home at thirty-one, James rarely emerged from the back of the house, and when he did, he drifted about like a specter from kitchen to garage to patio for a smoke. Most often, when we looked up from our dinner plates, he was simply not there.

At the sound of James's voice, I looked up. His stool was vacant and the only thing that indicated he had been there a moment ago was his half-empty tea cup. I caught the back of his gray T-shirt and faded jeans diminishing down the hall, leaving us to ponder whether he could be right. Could Rod be going through a midlife crisis, just like the rest of us?

An old familiar grudge bubbled up in me. The notion that Rod would have to endure this part of life, that he could be bummed out and unsheltered from the dark phases and stages of aging, rankled me. Typical, I thought, glancing upward at the acoustic ceiling tiles and beyond, where God supposedly dwelled. Naturally, He wouldn't see fit to spare my brother this struggle.

In my mind, Rod remained youthful, a perpetual eight-year-old boy, his development arrested at the third grade. As firmly as I knew this was not the case, he always came to my mind at that age, partly because that was when he had been happiest and full of passions. One by one, he had given up his toys as he grew older, as we all did, but he had always kept his coloring books. Lately, he'd swapped to velvet color-by-number, and among all of us siblings, we had cleaned out several craft and art stores in our respective neighborhoods, buying multiple velvet kits in case they went out of stock. I ached as I imagined my little brother now suffering through the angst of a midlife crisis, tired of coloring and despondent that nothing new lay ahead.

Thirty years ago, I had aged out of competition, feeling old and beached, done with the best part of my life. I had come to know this was not an ending, but was blind to that at the time. Now, I was crossing another midlife threshold. My sons, healthy young men, were making a go of their lives: independent, industrious, talented, flying solo—exactly where they should be. I wasn't sure how to be the mother of men. I knew this was my time as a parent to watch them from afar, but how was I to do this without their father? Single again, I had little desire to run out and find another mate. Was this a good thing? I sensed so, but did not yet understand why. It would be another five years before I understood that I was finally giving myself a quiet, steady space to write.

The sound of the front door opened, making us all set our tea cups down and turn. I slipped off the stool as my father, graying at the temples and beginning to stoop, came into the kitchen, followed by my mother, whose once-supple movements had slowed with the ache of her joints.

"Where's Rod?" I asked.

"He's here," my mother said, cheerily, setting her pocketbook on the counter and nodding her head back toward the vestibule.

Following her gesture, I stepped into the vestibule and there he was, standing just inside the door. He wore a bright blue Izod shirt tucked into khaki pants and brown Hush Puppy shoes. As always, he stood with a slight twist to his torso, his right shoulder pulling right as his pelvis pulled left. His eyes were down and he held a wooden pencil to his nose, spinning it as if in deep contemplation, drawing comfort from the tangy wooden scent. I felt a sigh of relief; at least he had not discarded this pleasure.

"Hi, Rod," I said.

"Hi, Moss."

Tiptoeing toward him, I circled my arms around his shoulders and hugged him, lightly. His hand gently patted my back. It struck me that he was the one who knew all of his siblings best. We had come of age in two separate families: Barbara Ann and I in front of him, Cami and James after him. Rod was the only one to have lived his entire life in both families; he was our glue.

After supper, as everyone lingered over coffee, my mother chirped on about the Easter service we would attend in the morning. The choir had been working hard on the music and my mother, though no longer able to sing the major solos, was going to perform a small part. Her face was full of pleasure; she was always her most animated and passionate around her faith.

I thought of Rod and his forsaken crayons. Coloring had seemed to be a meditation for him, a kind of prayer, and I couldn't imagine him giving this up any more than I could imagine my mother giving up her faith. Both were forms of sustenance, manna from heaven.

I thought back to when I let go of my religious faith. It had not been a sudden desertion, but rather a steady kind of flaking since I was a young child, a shedding of skin. I had come of age looking down on Catholics and Jews, yet I had fallen in love with, and married, two of the latter. By blood, both of my sons were Jewish, and had I borne them at the time of the pogroms or the Spanish Inquisition, they would have been slaughtered. Adding insult to injury, my sons were not going to heaven—at least according to my mother and the tenets of the Baptist church. Indeed, they were going to burn in hell.

In my deepest soul as a mother, I could not abide these assumptions and had discarded religion for this very reason. If there is a realm that awaits us after death I will know it soon enough. I had no need to guess at what it might be, or to deny entry to anyone or any beast.

Still, I missed certain elements of worship—the coming together, the song, the Bible's poetry, the laying aside of tasks for an hour of reflection. I had spent most of my adulthood searching for these elements elsewhere, and, one by one, had brought them into my life. Meditation had become my prayer, writing my reflection, nature my sanctuary.

Now, I worried for Rod's sanctuary. As children, we had colored together, staking out a spot at the kitchen table, or on the floor of the den, side by side, sharing the crowded box of colors. At first, when he was five or six, Roddy attacked the image, scribbling with one color over every part of the page, fiercely icing it with thick layers of royal purple and pine green, blotting out any semblance of dog or cat or flower. I didn't mind. I didn't try to teach him otherwise. Young as I was, I sensed his pleasure in sharing this ritual; it was not about coloring inside the lines, it was about companionship—about being brother and sister. About simply sitting with each other, bent over the same question, like "What color is Batman's hair, anyway?"

Now, at fifty-four, I slipped away from the table and fetched the coloring book I had so carefully chosen in the toy store and carried it back to the table. Then, sitting beside Rod, I opened the book and asked out loud, "What color is Batman's hair, anyway?" I didn't expect an answer.

"Lello," Rod said, instantly.

"Oh," I said, taken aback. "Yellow it is, then."

Plucking out the deepest gold, the color of Grandpa's poplar honey, I put the tip to Batman's forehead, marking him with bangs and curls sprouting out from under his skin-tight hood. Out of the corner of my eye, Rod reached for the box with its chorus of crayons. Pulling out the richest, most sumptuous purple, he bowed his head and bent over the paper. For the next hour we colored side by side, brother and sister, like the old days. Together, we resurrected Batman.

Chapter 31

Valentine

In my fifty-sixth year, I moved to an island in the Salish Sea, where I found a small studio nestled down in a hollow, surrounded by towering cedar and madrone trees. Three thousand miles from Orlando, in the opposite corner of the continent, I couldn't have been farther away from my family without falling into the ocean. I had moved to Washington to be near Barbara Ann, and also nearer to my sons, both of whom were living in Los Angeles. Among its many virtues, my new home had a back porch entwined with honeysuckle and a view of wild daisies scattered across a small field—a place of reverie. Finally, after all of these years, I had my studio, my quiet place to write.

For all of its blessings, my island hovel had no cell phone reception, which was why, on a chilly afternoon in February 2012, I found myself parked at the Winslow grocery, sitting in the one spot where I could get a connection. I wanted to confirm that Rod had gotten my small box of Lindt milk chocolates and a big heart-shaped valentine.

"Oh yes," my mother spoke with her familiar high trill, "he took your card to bed with him."

Pleasure slipped under my ribs. I was still raw from divorce, and hearing that my brother cherished my valentine comforted me. I envisioned him during his weekend visit to my parents' home, in his plaid pajamas, my mother pulling up the covers to his chin and kissing him goodnight. He was fifty-two years old, older than my parents had ever expected him to be. What was he thinking as my mother left the door ajar, the hall light spilling over the covers like starlight, the heart of my valentine in his hands? My brother so rarely showed joy. When he did, it was never as I'd expected. I knew this, and still managed to forget, over and over.

If I were to believe the experts, I'd have to assume my brother did not have empathy. That he was incapable of recognizing someone in distress and knowing how to respond. Yet he has defied this assumption all of his life. Once, when he was a teenager, Rod was sitting on the couch, watching my mother feed my baby brother, James. She laid James down for a moment and turned away to fetch a cloth from the diaper bag. Only a few months old, James had not yet flipped from his back to his belly—until that very moment. In one fell swoop, he arched his back and flipped with such vigor his baby body kept rolling—belly to back to belly—heading for the cliff edge of the cushion and, mere inches away, the rock hard rim of the coffee table. As he pitched over the side, my mother turned and cried out, and at the exact same moment, Rod dove forward and caught James in his arms.

"How about that," my mother said every time she repeated this story to me.

As I sat in my car so many years later, I listened, phone to my ear, as my mother described Rod. *Here he is again*, I thought, *showing a glimpse of his hidden heart.*

"How about that," I said, perched in the front seat of my car, both ears plugged into the phone.

"He misses his sisters," my mother said, her voice feather-light, a tender soft down of words. "He remembers."

A sting of regret ran through me, piercing rapidly and inserting a swollen ache that would stay with me for the rest of the day. *What does he remember?* I wondered. Does he remember when we were together as a family? When his two older sisters were with him at the breakfast table every morning, and again at dinner, and on weekends, a flurry of activity that sometimes riled him, but mostly assured him all was well? Sitting in the midst of it all, he contributed his own level of noise, the rattle and clack of marbles thundering down a marble chute, his own unique sound, the noise of my brother. At home, in the swirl of his family, he was part of the gang, part of the bustle of life.

Now, he was living with roommates he didn't particularly like, and if given the chance he would move back home with my parents and sleep there, all of the time. His two older sisters were mostly voices over the phone, words and questions he had to listen to, decipher, and respond to, no matter what his mood; the precise thing he hated most in life, aside from looking someone in the eye, was talking.

I had spent so much of my adult life away that I could not get a purchase on what or how he thought of me. In what way did I come into his mind and how long did I linger? I liked to think we talked to one other and, sometimes, I saved him from bullies. I hoped this was true. Or was I a source of loss? Was his internal life a string of losses as I imagined it to be, or did he have some moments of satiation and contentment? When Rod came to my mind it was never as a flapping boy or an angry one. But as the grown brother who once, when I was visiting, stood across the kitchen counter from me, and when I looked up, met my eyes with a frank, open gaze. He didn't blink or look away, and for a sliver of time we held each other's gaze across that vast neurological gulf. When I finally smiled with my eyes, he turned away, but I had that moment. I had it still.

"Thanks, Mom, for sending his photo," I said into the miniscule microphone, freeing the photo from my wallet and holding it in front of me. There was Rod, caught in a rare moment on my parents' back patio, stretched out on a lounge chair. He held a fresh glass of iced tea and for some unknown reason he was looking straight at the camera, making eye contact, and smiling his funny crooked smile. The expression on his face was one of pure pleasure and left no doubt that he trusted the person behind the camera, my mother.

Mom giggled into my earphones.

"He's in hog heaven!" she said airily. The tone of her voice was from the far past, before I turned five, before my brother's diagnosis fell on her ears. It was full of mirth.

I laughed. Her voice stirred a memory of my long-ago road trip to Kentucky with my parents and Rod, the stop at Denny's restaurant where Rod up and ordered his meal like a perfect gentleman. Coming back from the restroom, I had paused, caught by the sight of my mother. Leaning across the table, she was holding both of Rod's hands, teasing him gently, with a look of sheer delight on her face, sheer adoration—a mother's love.

One day, she was going to be gone, and I didn't know how we were going to tell my brother. How to make sense of it for him; how he would survive that tear in his heart. The only thing that could be worse was for our mother to feel his loss, or the loss any of her children, but especially her first boy.

"So honey, when are you coming to visit us?" she said to me now. "We've got sunshine here, you know."

"Yes"—I laughed again—"more than I could ever want."

"We need to talk about some things," she said, her voice turning serious, "about Rod."

"Oh," I said, alarmed, "Is he all right?"

"Oh yes, he's fine," she said hastily. "But your dad and I aren't going to be here forever."

This was a truth I continually ignored—that my parents would someday cease being anywhere on this earth, where I could reach them, visit them, if not this year, then next. We had longevity in my family, meaning we were somewhat spoiled, inured to death. My psyche assumed they would be here as long as I was here and their deaths would be timed with mine.

"I know, Mom," I said, reluctantly, feeling the child rise up in me.

Ahead lay an unknown phase of life with my brother. Like me, he was aging, and from all indications, he would be around for a while. Here he was in his fifties, going strong. My parents had never dreamed he would outlive them. When he was born, the life expectancy of a disabled child like him was thirty years, and because of this, my parents hadn't planned for his extended life.

The truth about disability is that it lasts. And it doesn't get better; it grows worse and more complicated with age. I wasn't certain I had enough stamina to manage my own aging, much less my brother's. Recently, I had learned from Cami that Rod was refusing to wipe himself after using the toilet. This was a brand-new development. He didn't like the feeling of reaching back there with a tangle of toilet paper and risking the chance he might come away with feces on his hands. Now that he was a cranky old man, he was refusing to cooperate. I didn't blame him; feces on my hands did not appeal to me either, which is why I didn't want to clean up his. I had no idea how this was playing out during the week at his group home, but my father was running Rod baths when he came home on the weekends, making him soak after every bowel movement.

Did I have enough love? My worry was no different than any sibling of a disabled adult. After my parents were gone, caring for my brother would be a full-time, nonstop job, without respite. Like a true second-born, I had always seen myself as the backup—the one who could step in and assist, but never the one on the front lines, like Barbara Ann. And in a way, my younger sister was also a firstborn—she had come of age without the presence of her older sisters, and with her older brother needing the same attention as the younger brother.

As if reading my mind, my mother said, "Say, your dad's about to drive Rod back to Lake Margaret. Want to say hi?"

"Sure," I said, straightening my spine and shifting taller in the seat. I never knew which Rod was coming to the phone: the sweet little brother or the sparring boy. Like all of my siblings, I had learned to brace myself, and then, if a sweet brother just happened to show up, it was that much more sublime.

A few seconds of rustling and mumbling told me Rod was on the line.

"Hi, Rod."

"Hi, Moss."

"I just wanted to wish you a happy Valentine's Day."

"Yaas."

"Did you have any of my chocolates?"

"No!" he shouted.

"No?" I asked, flustered, realizing too late that I should have asked my mother to brief me before handing the phone to him. I suddenly remembered she had toned down on his sweets.

"No! Pie!"

"Oh, I see, you had pie for dinner? Well . . . that sounds good. What kind of pie?"

"Rhubarb!"

No matter how many times we did this, I couldn't seem to get from hello to goodbye without making Rod blow his stack. Taking in a deep breath, I exhaled, slowly. He mumbled something I couldn't understand—the static and his grouchiness garbling the words. I wasn't about to ask him to repeat it; that would send him into a paroxysm. Sighing, I tried another route.

"Mom sure makes a good rhubarb pie, doesn't she?"

"Yaas."

His voice softened. He didn't have to struggle with this answer. My mother's pies are an indisputable pleasure, her savory fillings just the right measure of tartness and sweet zing. If my siblings and I were there, we'd be jostling for seconds and feebly putting dibs on the last piece, even though we all knew it would be shared by my father and Rod after the rest of us had gone to bed. To stretch out the contentment in my brother's voice, I dispensed with questions.

"I hope you liked the card I sent."

"Yaas. Valentine," he said.

For a miniscule moment I paused. I could come up with something more to talk about but I sensed we had reached a threshold—both his and mine. Better to quit while we were ahead.

"It's nice talking with you, Rod. Happy Valentine's Day."

"Yaas. Okay."

"I love you."

"Okay."

"Can you give the phone back to Mom?"

"Yaas, I will!"

A loud bang hit my ear, followed by a rattling that told me he had dropped the receiver, leaving it to dangle on its cord. In the next instant, I heard the distant noise of voices, which I realized were coming from the television set. Fox News was turned up high so my father could hear without putting in his hearing aid.

"Hello, Mom?" I called out, absurdly. "I'm still here."

From somewhere in the kitchen a cupboard closed, or maybe the garage door.

"Mom, are you there?"

I pictured the receiver, dangling near the floor, calling out with its tiny twangy voice. After a minute more of dead air, I let go.

Chapter 32

Little Wing

Recently, a deep truth came to me, unexpected and unbidden, on a bright winter day in the year 2015. Happily mussed and dirty, I was in the kitchen of my new home on the island doing an ordinary thing—sorting through a stack of books on the kitchen table when I spotted an oddly made box tucked back in the closet. I'd forgotten it was there.

Slender and upright, the box itself was a marvel of craftsmanship and engineering, its custom cut panels fit together in a seamless concert of cardboard and packing tape. It must have taken my father an entire evening to fashion it for me.

Curling my fingers around the handle, an arching twist of duct tape, I lifted. The box floated to the table top, feather-light, as if bearing thin air. Laying it gently on its side, I reached for the Xacto knife and carefully razored away the packing seal, the cardboard lid, and six stitches of scotch tape binding the bulges of bubble wrap inside.

Part by part, Little Wing emerged. First, her stabilizer with its shredded edge; her fuselage, its dark wound soldered beneath a knob of aging glue; and finally her wings, each adorned with red paint, the left with black lettering, wobbly and brave, marching down the center surface.

Magically and improbably, here she was in my hands, light as breath. All these years after I abandoned her and then fled to the east coast and my adult life, my father had kept her like an heirloom. Through the Seventies and Eighties, she survived the unraveling of the missile defense program, the massive layoffs of engineers, job hopping with my father from Colorado to Florida to Virginia and back to Florida. Each time he found a new job and, along with Roddy and my mother, set up a new home, my father chose a corner for his workbench and mounted, on the wall, his finest models. There, among his beauties, he always hung my scruffy little plane.

Now, I lifted her to the gray light of the window, turning her like delicate and ancient wonderment. She twirled like a dancer, an acrobat, as if winged with ailerons.

Far away, in warmer skies, my father's planes were still winning trophies. He and my mother made the long drive to Pensacola each year and stayed the weekend, officiating and competing for the trophy, my father maneuvering his plane in the sky, my mother chasing after it, tracking its path. When I imagine my mother running through a field smothered in reeds, eyes skyward, beaded on the diminishing speck of plane against a pale hot sky, keeping it in her sights, I see her as an adventurer, as the child she once was, before fever took her down. This brings up a wild admiration in me and a floating feeling of comfort. It has taken me the whole of my life to see my mother—to see that she broke over and over for her boy and yet at the same time prayed with the fervent passion of a disciple for his well-being and for her other children, and yes, for me, her second child, the daughter who was the hardest one to keep close. She was in those stands cheering me on as sure as she was chasing doctors and tutors and struggling to help my brother.

The air in my kitchen stirred, and the late summer light of my childhood, the heat of the garage, the pinging of moth wings off the garage window entered the room. Around me breathed the warm perfume of oil and tires, the ticking of the Volkswagen engine. I touched the plane's wingtip to my nose and inhaled the soft citrusy fragrance. Balsa. My father's scent. His essence.

Once every year, my father turns away from his planes and leaves them hanging idly on the walls of his workshop. Rather than fly, he travels with Rod to the Florida Everglades on a camping trip sponsored by the Baptist church. He and my brother have been going on this adventure for as long as I can remember. Whenever I ask what in the world he and Rod do there, my father chuckles, "He likes to watch the alligators."

I imagined them, father and son, standing together on the bank of a swamp, taking in the slide of reptiles through the water, thrilled by a sudden scaly thrashing. An epiphany rose in me, an uncanny revelation that my father never needed me to be his stand-in son. He already had a son. Since his retirement, my father had doted on my brother, driving faithfully to and from Rod's group home so he could come home for Sunday dinner, fetching Rod a second piece of pie and sitting with him at the table long after everyone had drifted off, allowing him all the time he needed to excavate through a mountain of pumpkin and ice cream and chastising my mother for not bringing Rod a second cup of coffee.

My father was no longer the stern man of my childhood. Life slapped him hard and he was a different man now. Fragile. Vulnerable. At least two times in his life he had cried hard—once when he was laid off from his job, and once when he learned about my brother. I didn't see his tears—he never cried in front of me or any of his children; I learned this from my mother.

It came to me then, what Little Wing meant to my life. What drew me to my father's work bench all of those evenings was not ambition, or guilt, or a duty to be a surrogate son. I simply needed to be with him. To feel his steadiness in a home rocked by affliction. As my mother fell apart, and my brother cried and bit his hands, and my sister withdrew to her fantasies of wild horses, I sought the gentle and precise way my father brought a plane to life, the comfort of minute sounds, and the sanctuary of being inside a moment, shaping something beautiful with my hands.

What I couldn't understand as a child, I felt now. In the stillness of that long-ago garage, I was piecing together more than an airplane. I was assembling what would carry me through the rest of my life: an inner strength born from my childhood and my family. I was learning to trust beauty, to turn to it when life dealt a hard blow, and to know that if I searched hard enough, it would be there.

Now, as I held Little Wing up to the light, this companion, this piece of myself, I felt something truly marvelous. Joy.

Epilogue

On a crisp sunlit morning in November 2015, I pull my car off Miller Road and park at the Grand Forest trailhead on Bainbridge Island. My aging Honda is the sole car in sight, evidence that I'm the only one foolish enough to venture outside. A raucous windstorm overnight has slapped around the island's hemlocks and cedars, and now, branches lie shredded and flayed across every inch of wet soil. I crawl over a massive felled trunk and step into the forest. Fingers of light rake down around me.

Something about the aftermath of a storm has always calmed me: a washing away of the old, a cleansing. A gratefulness that I am here and want to be; I want to see what another day brings. And a renewed sense that what governs life and death is not so much in my hands.

The main trail is clogged with debris, forcing me to stray left and descend a small embankment, then high-knee it across a creek. I'm happy to be dressed as I am, in a frayed cotton sweatshirt and disintegrating black jeans, red fleece vest sprigged with cat hair, and fingerless yarned gloves that I should have tossed months ago. My feet are clad in square-toed, black leather shoes, which I don't want to be caught dead in. Grudgingly, I've brought along a cell phone on this hike of mine—a safety measure and sign that I've let go of my younger habits of disappearing, unplugged, into the wilderness. As a sixtyish mother whose two sons live several hundred miles away, I've grown more cautious. Should nature shake loose a branch somewhere high in the trees and spear me, pinning me to the ground, I'll want to make a call.

Still, the phone weighs like a stone and I would have left it behind if not for the worried face of my sister in my mind. As I hoof it up a soft bank and rejoin the trail, the phone hums against my thigh.

"Hi there," Barbara Ann's voice sputters and skips across spotty island reception.

She is in her Saturday mode: taking care of business, likely armed with a neatly handwritten checklist and riding in the passenger seat of the Explorer, her husband driving, zooming from Safeway to Home Depot to Ace Hardware for PVC pipe, chicken feed, and organic fertilizer. Before I can answer, she barrels on.

"Did you get your key copied yet? I can do that for you. We can swing by now and pick it up."

The key she speaks of is the one I have managed to lose again: my front door key. Actually, my entire key ring, gone into the ether somewhere, which means that, once again, I'm down to my last spare key, the one Barb usually keeps on her key ring for emergencies. I've borrowed it back to get through the week, and she's agitated not to have it with her. She no longer wings life the way I do; she's had enough of life's surprises and now spends contented hours in her garden, nurturing pole beans and tending to her three chickens. As for me, I'm still taking chances and then throwing fits when it all goes awry.

"I have it with me. I'll get it copied," I say breathily, rounding a bend in the trail and heading uphill. For a moment all I hear is my own puffing and the drum of my high-pressured heartbeat, and wonder if I've lost reception. But no, she's still there, perturbed.

"Well, I want you to drive straight to me afterward and give me one of those copies," she says.

This is my sister's firstborn bossiness, aroused by my faulty track record, my feisty life where I misplace keys and spouses at a similar rate. Her insistence that I march directly from Ace Hardware to her front door on the opposite side of the island with a new spare key, no matter what my schedule, chafes against me. Partly because her worry is warranted: I'm liable to misplace this last key at any moment, and then where would I be? Nevertheless, if I were a cat I'd be arching my back against a tree right now and flattening my ears. This is the

Combs in me, a peppery independence and urge to say back off, I have a life of my own, a right to order my day in the way my life has never allowed me. And to lose keys, if it comes to that. I've earned it, my right to screw up, to drive anywhere, and in any order, on a Saturday.

But everything stops me. The yawn of our childhood years, the ache of our divorces, our worry as mothers of sons, our melancholy as siblings of a disabled boy, and our shared desire to heal our family, and our families, has rendered us as fragile as we are resilient. What I say to her now in this small standoff is, for my sake, non-compliant, and for both of our sakes, kind.

Without hesitating, I call forth my brother.

"Yaas! Okay, Bob!" I bark in into the phone, in Roddy's voice.

Laughter bursts from both of us, a bright bubbling sound. It makes me stop and throw my head back on the trail, my laugh echoing through the hemlocks and alders.

"Okay, Mossie!" Barb shouts back, into my ear. "Have some coffee!"

I sit down on a freshly ripped stump and laugh all the harder. Inside this moment I don't care where I am or who happens by or if I lose momentum in life. A mountain biker pops into view, *zizzing* right for me, but I don't flinch—I'm laughing too hard. He barely misses my ugly shoes, his knees flexing as he lofts over a massive tree root and lands, niftily, glancing over his shoulder.

If he, a stranger, knew what I was laughing about he might take offense, seeing my behavior as mocking and making fun of a disabled boy—but my sister and I are not strangers to each other or to our brother, and we share a tie deeper than disability, the bond of siblings twined by familiarity, exasperation, and affection. Our mirth holds all the tenderness of family, of deeply internal moments between the three of us. It's as if Rod is here, telling both of his big sisters to get over themselves. He has that ability to humble us and to soften our edges. He often steps in this way, albeit unbeknownst to him, helping me to see how silly and irrelevant is my current complaint.

"Okay, Bob!" I bellow, holding the cell in front of my mouth like a microphone.

We keep this up for several minutes, laughing and coughing. Nothing more about the key needs to be said; she knows I'll bring it to her, if not today, then tomorrow. And if I lose the key again, she'll help me, even if it means holding the ladder so I can crawl through my kitchen window. And if my brother needs us, when he needs us, after my parents are gone, she and I will be there, as our younger sister is now. We will have to be. Some things are not chosen.

I hang up, still laughing, having accomplished nothing. As I strip off my sweatshirt and tie it around my waist, I strike off toward the trailhead and take the Upper Loop. Steep and winding, it pulls me higher, like a giant, thick vine. Dollops of rain splatter on my head. Destruction is everywhere: hulking branches flung across the trail, whole root systems ripped from the soil.

There was a time when I believed, fervently, that to bring an afflicted child into the world was unconscionable, and I would have done everything to keep that from happening. Seated across from my parents in a booth somewhere in 1972, in the wake of *Roe v. Wade*, when I was a junior in college and newly married, I shouted, "Yes, of course I believe in legalized abortion!"

My mother had gasped, "But why?" Her delicate features crumpled, her eyes reared back into her head, horrified and deeply pained.

I felt no mercy; I looked right at her. "If you don't really want the child, don't bring it into the world. The chances are too high that something will be wrong, that it will ruin your life."

I was speaking from a hardened fear. That I could conceive a child like my brother and that it would break me. Growing up with a disabled boy in a time of ignorance had wracked my family, crippling our rhythms and feeding our sense of shame. It's hard even now, in this age of genomes and awareness. No matter how informed a new mother or father might be, the word "autism" hits like a blast wave, concussing the family and altering every sibling's life. The memory of my mother collapsing, of my father lifting her from the floor, of my brother crying in my mother's arms for a Sherry-friend, still pierces my lungs, making it hard to breathe.

And yet. And yet. In the calming company of trees that wear the scars of a hundred storms, I miss my brother. He carries all these complexities, which will not go away, no matter how far away I am from him. I think of him a continent away, slipping under the covers, clutching my valentine, my papered love. I feel the comfort of his smooth hands lotioning my back. I hear him barking for coffee, standing up to my father, his courage breaking through. I see him lunging, arms outstretched, catching our youngest baby brother rolling off the couch. I see his gaze, steady, penetrating from across the kitchen counter, at me, an intensity that takes my breath away.

As a woman, I still adamantly believe in the right to choose. I have come to know another truth. If my mother happened to be beside me now—a young woman of twenty-four and pregnant with her third child, a boy with brain damage—I could not say, "Abort, Mother. Do it for yourself, for your baby boy, for all of us." Knowing my brother, I would not say it. There again, a surprise. A fortuity.

This is what I know. Every cell in my brother's body wants to wake up and try it again, to give life a whirl. Just as I do, with my imperfections, struggling every day to figure it out, to know why I'm here. Why life is the way it is. Why I'm fortunate enough to be alive inside this moment. Barbara Ann, me, Roddy: we get to wake up and go at it again. Just as we've always done. Just as our elders, our parents, and our lives together have taught us to do.

I'm no longer trying to make up for the one thing that pulled my family sideways. I have arrived at the place where I see not just one thing—the worst thing—but the ten thousand things that make up a life. I don't have all the answers, and in some distant place, my urgency for answers, for restitution, releases. Not all at once, but gently, fortuitously, one breath at a time. Perhaps this is why I've lived this long—long enough to accept surprise. To give in to what cannot be undone. Genes happen; they happened to my brother, and they happened to my family, and to me.

I round the last corner and, through the blackened trunks, spot the green hood of my car. I feel a kind of surrender, a deep relief that my parents did not send my brother away. A surprise and a solace.

As fraught and arduous as the journey has been, and will be, they let me know him. My story does not include a brother who was sent away, a ghost who was lost to me. My desire to run from home was not because of my brother. I didn't flee him as much as I fled my parents' anguish and sorrow.

My brother's gentle voice, *Yaas, Mossie*, stays with me as I slip into my car, and for whatever reason, I suddenly recall the pleasure on his face when I visited his group home in Florida a few months before. There I was, with Barbara Ann and Cami, following Rod through the front door and down the hallway. Wearing his tilted smile, he showed us his bedroom and where his clean clothes belonged, every shirt and every sock, every pair of underwear. He opened and closed his bureau drawers, smiling shyly and whispering to himself. It took forever. Then, we toured around his room, and one by one, looked at his photos, picking up the frames and saying the names aloud— Mom, Dad, Barbara Ann, Margie, Cami, James—our family. Other families had other special moments. But this was ours.

Inside that sliver of time, that small ritual, he felt cherished. And so did I.

Acknowledgments

I want to thank my family—especially my parents, Ray and Bertha Ann Combs— for their indelible strength and enduring love. I am deeply grateful to my older sister, Barbara Ann, who has been there from the beginning and generously helped me navigate through life, love, calamity, and the making of this book.

Many thanks to my astute and perceptive editor, Olga Greco, and to everyone at Skyhorse Publishing. I am indebted to my agent, Sarah Jane Freymann, for her deep knowledge and guiding hand.

A warm thank you to my generous and talented teacher, Brenda Peterson, for her sage wisdom and guidance in this journey. An enormous thank-you to my fellow writers in the Salish Sea Writers collective, who generously and honestly steered me through numerous revisions.

I want to thank my friends, many of whom read and reread my work or simply sat still long enough to listen: Laura Foreman, Amanda Mander, Elisa Rhodes, Cestjon McFarland, Judy Tingley, Suzanne Brassel, Amy Hughes, Amy Weber, Laurie Sugarman-Whittier, Anne Murphy, and Patti Murphy.

Many thanks to the librarians of the Bainbridge Island Library who put up with my continuous presence and patiently plied me with answers to my questions.

Finally, a special thank-you to the staff at the Marketplace Café at Pleasant Beach for providing me with a coveted corner in which to write, and likewise, to the trees of the Grand Forest, for offering me the sanctuary to ponder and the serenity to see.

Portions of this memoir have appeared previously: "Aileron" in *Lost Magazine*, Summer 2010, Issue 38; "Aileron" in the *North American Review*, Spring 2011, Vol. 296; "Cracker Jacks" in *Secret Histories: Stories of Courage, Risk, and Revelation* (2013).

With the exception of my siblings and parents, all names have been changed to protect the privacy of those mentioned in this book.